CW00345922

THE
COUNTRY
HOUSE
SERVANT

PAMELA A. SAMBROOK

SUTTON PUBLISHING
IN ASSOCIATION WITH
THE NATIONAL TRUST

First published in the United Kingdom in 1999 by
Sutton Publishing Limited · Phoenix Mill
Thrupp · Stroud · Gloucestershire · GL5 2BU

This new paperback edition first published in 2002 by
Sutton Publishing Limited

British Library Cataloguing in Publication Data
A catalogue record for this book is available from the British Library

ISBN 0 7509 2988 X

Typeset in 11/15 pt Ehrhardt.
Typesetting and origination by
Sutton Publishing Limited
Printed in Great Britain by
J.H. Haynes & Co. Ltd, Sparkford.

Contents

Acknowledgements

My thanks are due firstly to the Scouladi Foundation, London University who contributed financially towards the cost of the initial research for this book; also to the numerous administrators and officers of the National Trust properties who answered my original enquiries and patiently searched for photographs and documents – especially from Berrington, Beningbrough, Cragside, Dunham Massey, Kingston Lacy, Petworth, Polesden Lacey, Shugborough and Wimpole. I am particularly grateful to Mr and Mrs Angell-James for giving me access to their wonderful laundry at Berwick Hall.

I am grateful also to the following for permission to use archival material: Peter Lead; Miss A.M. Amies; Trustees of Kelmarsh Hall; Harborough Museum and Leicestershire Museums, Arts and Records Service; Staffordshire Record Office; Dorset Record Office; John Rylands Library, University of Manchester; Rural History Centre, Reading University; Museum of Welsh Life, St Fagans; and the National Trust Tape Library. For encouragement and many suggestions I am grateful to Ruth Taylor, Faith Hines and Margaret Willes.

My greatest debt, of course, is not to the living but the dead. Many years ago, my interest in affairs domestic was first aroused by conversations with a number of laundresses and housemaids and more have followed. To them and to those who, years ago, painstakingly wrote down or otherwise recorded their memories, this book is dedicated. I have no doubt they would take me briskly to task for its inadequacies.

CHAPTER 1

Introduction

In recent years there has been a tremendous growth of interest in the domestic organisation of our country houses. A whole world is opening up before us, as both private and National Trust houses rediscover their kitchens, laundries and housekeepers' rooms – interiors which in an earlier decade with different values were destined to be converted into cafés, bookshops and public lavatories. The story of household management is now a major part of many historic houses, an economic reality of modern times. To accompany the interiors there is no shortage of books about country house servants or their physical environment.

So why yet another? Modern publications about domestic servants in the country house are of several types: some are plainly reminiscent, full of anecdotes of eccentric owners and snobbish servants;[1] some describe the material culture of the house, and are redolent with gleaming copper, scrubbed wood and sparkling tiles;[2] others are based on documentary extracts from country house archives,[3] or focus on individual households;[4] finally, academic papers and books explore the social and economic structures of domestic service.[5] Despite this variety only a few describe the actual work done by servants in the country house, and even fewer touch upon systems of skill or work management or what they might mean.[6] This is strange, for work defined domestic servants and their place in the hierarchy of the community of the country house. It dictated the objects with which they were surrounded, the food they ate and the place they slept. Very largely it governed whether they were happy or wretched. So this is the heart of the book – viewing the country house as a place of work for the domestic servant rather than a home for the élite family, it explores the nature of the work done, how it was organised and what was its meaning.

Since this is such a large subject area I have limited my scope, focusing on those servants who were involved in cleaning the country house. In particular, I have chosen three functional types: housemaids, footmen and laundrymaids. These were the people whose task was to keep the house comfortable for its occupants and to look after its treasures for future generations. This choice inevitably ignores others who were involved with cleaning – the kitchen staff, scullery maids and grooms – who constituted separate groups of servants deserving their own study.

Given this focus, a number of themes – of status, skill and gender – form a thread running through the book and herein lies another reason for writing it.[7] Although the nuts and bolts of objects or processes are interesting in themselves, what is truly fascinating is the insight they bring into the social context of working lives. If the interpretation of country house domesticity is to move into the exciting future which I believe it deserves, the heritage world needs to learn more about the material goods, skills and technologies of domestic service, but also it must address questions of management, motivations and meanings. To do this we need to borrow from some of the ideas debated by academics.

Any individual may be trapped by a material culture which requires laborious upkeep; but societies have choices about the value-systems which drive them, dictating the nature of the goods they strive to own. As one historian of material goods has written: 'Buildings and interiors were constructed to convey social meanings as well as for practical purposes. . . . Material goods, such as furnishings, made physical and visible statements about accepted values and expected behaviour'.[8] Another explains: 'every object bears a meaning and tells a story: belongings are good to think with'.[9] It is just these 'social meanings' which this book hopes to explore through the minutiae of interiors, material goods and behaviour patterns in the backstairs world of the country house. It does not aim to be an encyclopedia of household objects; the only piece of equipment which is dealt with in some detail is the box mangle, which relates in a unique way to the context of the country house.[10]

Hierarchy and status are essential components of a society based on deference. Status systems ran from top to bottom of the country house through all its structures – physical, economic and social. Sometimes the boundary-defining features are obvious, sometimes extremely subtle, sometimes cruel. We can see them not only in hierarchical wage structures, but also in the clothes servants wore, the food they ate, the particular work they did, the tools they used and the way they behaved towards each other. Yet there was also a common-sense rationality mixed up with this. That upper servants were waited on by lower servants reinforced the hierarchical nature of the household, yet served also as a useful training system for inexperienced youngsters.[11]

Within the domestic household, work helped delineate the boundaries of status systems. In a study of lower- and middle-class homes in the seventeenth and

Staff at Noseley Hall, Leicestershire, in the 1930s, photographed during the August seasonal cleaning while the family were away in Scotland. From left to right are Frances, the school-room maid; Peggy Herbert, third housemaid; Charlie, the footman; Mary Postle, head housemaid; and Olive Newell, second housemaid. On the bay window behind stand the 'odd man' and the estate carpenter. (Leicestershire Record Office)

eighteenth centuries, Lorna Weatherill recognised that the material culture of the domestic scene was subject to complex considerations of status, some work acquiring 'front of house' status while lower-status jobs were hidden at the back.[12] In a way, the household was a stage on which goods were presented to show different levels of status, and where individuals played different roles in different parts of the house. A complex set of variables influenced the pattern of accumulation of goods and the roles of servants.

The playing out of roles within the household was further explored by Amanda Vickery in relation to a single household in Lancashire.[13] Servants were 'monitors' of consumption, the housewife the 'inspector'. But the meaning and roles of goods were complicated and in many circumstances could be related not to status but 'character' and what Vickery called 'sentimental materialism'. For example, in a domestic environment, possessions had meaning and value because of who previously owned them, not the status they gave. Yet this sentiment in itself was an indicator of wealth; the poor could not afford it.

Applying such issues to the country house context, can we see patterns of 'front' and 'back' working practices in the cleaning routines of the élite country house, and did these reflect the different roles of housemaid and footman? How did objects and behaviour express status in the closed world of country house service?

Conscious or unconscious archaism also had connotations of status. People can value possessions because they are new or because they carry the patina of age.[14] The defining features of the country house household were of course wealth, size and quality – quality of goods and quality of services. But the English country house style is something more subtle – a highly characteristic fusion of professional quality of service with an apparent effortlessness. A meticulous attention to detail behind the scenes supported a superficially relaxed atmosphere, even a sophisticated shabbiness – acceptable, even desirable, as characterising a family which had occupied its 'country' for a long time. The household was thus pulled in at least three different directions: towards a status-seeking consumption of goods which developed almost to the point of fetishism; an ambience which we can represent by words like relaxed, homely, family, country, domestic; and a professional, 'businesslike' management which aimed to curb waste and excess. There is plenty of evidence to show that these tensions actually existed on the ground and caused a fair degree of disruption.[15] Did the country house servant fall victim to such tensions?

Status is one element in an equation of work, skill and the use of technology. The élite domestic house has always been in two minds about the last of these.

The indoor and outdoor servant household at Cresswell Hall, Staffordshire, photographed outside the summer house in the 1900s. (Staffordshire Arts and Museum Service)

Given the financial resources available, one would expect the aristocratic household to be in the vanguard of innovation; and certainly there are examples where this was so, at least in relationship to specific areas. By and large these areas were those which carried a degree of status acquisition. In the nineteenth century, for example, the fame of kitchen designers such as Count Rumford, the chef Alexis Soyer or the highly fashionable architect Sir Charles Barry made kitchen planning a respectable activity for the upper classes – witness the aristocratic visitors who trooped around the kitchens of the Reform Club, accompanied by a ladle-waving Soyer, attired in white apron and red velvet cap, expatiating on the unrivalled sophistication of his domain.[16]

This does not seem to have been so true of laundry design. Not much status was attached to the management of large quantities of dirty washing. It was not until the electric-powered washing machine was adopted in the twentieth century that laborious hand-washing was made redundant. Until then, laundry techniques within the country house were labour-intensive, dependent on a high level of manual skill and fastidiousness. So if we wish to characterise changes in the work processes of the country house laundress we have to engage with detailed methods of handwork and systems of work management developing over centuries, rather than with technological expertise. This is true also of the two other servant-types dealt with in this book.

It may be that when we come to study progress in working systems we will find that what resulted was more work for the servant rather than less. Studying the field of technical innovation in housework, Ruth Schwartz Cowan propounded the startling idea that the introduction of labour-saving devices into housework did not result in a real saving of either time or labour.[17] New technologies brought higher expectations of cleanliness, new jobs expanded to fill time saved, and new patterns of ownership of goods needed more complex methods of servicing. This theory has been explored by many researchers since, within different contexts and

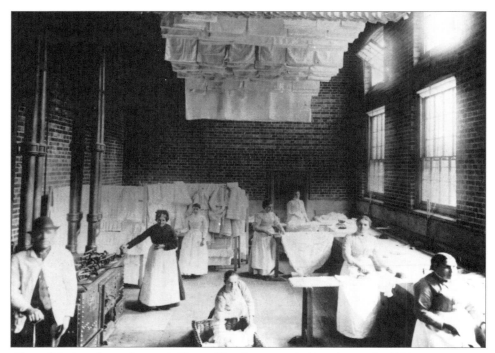

View of the laundry at Petworth House, West Sussex, probably taken in the 1870s. Notice the ranks of identical towels and the number of irons on the massive stove, which is tended by a laundryman or odd man. Among the flat irons is perhaps a heater from the Italian iron which stands at the back of the ironing table. The third ironer from the front is goffering frills on the bottom of a petticoat with a pair of tongs. (West Sussex County Council)

time-frames. In the country house of the eighteenth and nineteenth centuries, did changes in work practices reduce time spent on housework or cut down on labour input or drudgery?

A reliance on manual dexterity rather than expertise with technology is common to many areas of work traditionally associated with women, and this highlights a third theme, the gender-related barriers erected between different aspects of work. These might be particularly meaningful in relation to cleaning, a process which has strong connotations of purity or impurity.[18] Within the country house, there seem to have been clear-cut divisions between men's work and women's, but since the work environment of servants was also their home, the gender implications were complex. This was especially so given that the country house had historic traditions stretching back over centuries and many of its definitions of women's as opposed to men's work related to a context developed in the medieval household.[19]

Historical studies of women's work by Judy Wajcman and others have shown how widespread were traditional mindsets in relation to the confrontation between women's work and technology.[20] Inherent in these were a number of convictions which still strike sparks today within gender discussions. They include, for example, the belief that all men were naturally strong; that all work which was typically feminine was also typically unskilled; that women could not understand machines even when they could operate them; and that the techniques used in women's work (requiring qualities which women were good at such as dexterity and patience) came 'naturally' to them, did not have to be learnt and were therefore of low value. Leonore Davidoff has explored such issues in relationship to the élite household in a collection of writings which includes discussions on the boundaries between hierarchies and genders, the way in which the change from productive household to consumer household affected attitudes to housework, the tendency of a household to become ever more specialist and structured, the relationship of women's work in the household to notions of uncleanliness, defilement and impurity and the definition of separate spheres of life for men and women.[21] How do such issues relate to the detail of work in the country house?

It has been argued that 'an in-depth study of the trivia of domestic life' is essential if we are to understand the dynamics and motivations behind the ownership and organisation of goods, be they necessities, decencies or luxuries.[22] Such studies in the context of middle- and lower-class households have earned a respectability denied to the élite household. With few exceptions, academics have

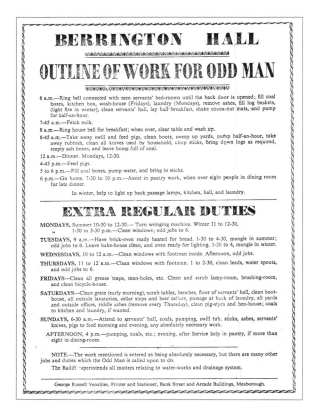

Job specification for the 'odd man' at Berrington Hall, near Leominster, undated but probably late nineteenth century. This illustrates the wide variety of jobs given to the odd man. Note that he had to pump water into the main cistern for half-an-hour three times a day; on Mondays he helped in the wash-house by turning the wringing machine and on Tuesdays he operated the mangle. (National Trust, Berrington Hall)

been reluctant to enter into the minutiae of day-to-day work in this context, partly because of a conviction that such employment was divorced from the 'common reality' facing the more numerous general servant employed in middle- and upper-working-class households.[23] This is a pity, for although it is true that country house service represented only a fraction of the whole context of domestic service, this minority was hardly negligible and might well have performed a useful function in providing an exemplar for the rest, perhaps a target for both employers and employees to aim for and a model for the working-out of difficult relationships.

The working household of the élite country house was after all a highly intricate social union. The complex hierarchies of stewards, butlers, footmen, housekeepers and laundresses who inhabited the stewards' rooms and the servants' halls were themselves serviced by younger, older, less skilled or less intelligent servants. The aristocratic household threw up its fair share of filthy or tiresome jobs, and the honourable tradition of such households was to put these out to its weakest members – old men, old women or young girls.[24] Where would the country house have been without the 'odd man', who carried logs and coal, humped trunks, pumped water and did any job which no one else would? Or the army of female day labourers – charwomen, washerwomen and seamstresses – who brought to the household both flexibility and consistency of family service, sometimes over centuries, which was pegged to a stable local rural population for whom the 'big house' was a vital and long-term source of employment. Or the young girls who even early in the present century went into service on the great estates at the bottom of the house, laundry or kitchen hierarchy, aged a mere thirteen years, working for little or even no wages, serving unofficial apprenticeships.[25] In some respects the situation of these unfortunates who propped up the bottom of the wealthy household was little removed from that of servants working for masters who hailed from a lower level of society.

A few recent studies have tried to address the complexity of country house domestic life, emphasising, for example, the different kinds of people going into service and the important role played by casual day labour.[26] As yet the enormous numbers of specialist contract craftsmen and craftswomen, tradesmen and professionals who also serviced the élite household await research.[27] Some of these contractors worked in the house and lived with the servants for months on end, others were casual visitors. Many were associated with the supply of goods from local or regional centres and in particular many were involved in the transport of supplies and the movement of horses. Others serviced equipment: the tortuous chimneys which needed sweeping twice a year; the smoke jacks which ground to a halt unless greased once a month; the bell-pull systems which required regular overhaul. The balance of advantage between the employment of permanent live-in servants and the putting-out of work to contract has always been delicate and subject to considerations other than the functional. Thus the picture of any one household is extremely intricate, with different people employed on different conditions, town-based households mixing with country households, individuals moving up and down the employment ladder and the whole sometimes changing wildly with the fortunes of families or developing slowly with increasing commercialisation and growing technical sophistication.

PRIMARY SOURCES

Given that we are searching for details of experience rather than statistics, the choice of sources is limited. Manuscript evidence exists within collections of landed estate family archives, yet the three types of servants selected all give

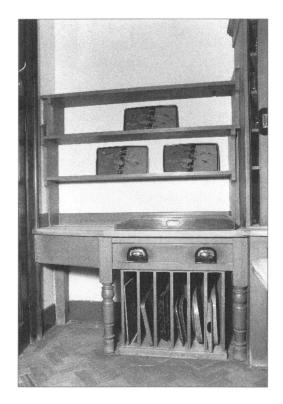

A detail of the corner by the door in the Dunham Massey butler's pantry, showing the tray slots. Trays for various purposes were made of papier mâché, metal and wood. In this pantry the sinks were fitted at the other end under the windows. (John Bethell, National Trust, 1984)

problems. None of them left a substantial body of records. Two of them – footmen and housemaids – had only limited complex specialist interiors connected with their work such as can be seen in inventories or plans; their workplace was the house itself. We can gain access to individual names through wage lists but these are intermittent over time and can be supplemented in the nineteenth century by census data only once a decade. Other household documents such as servant tax returns, malt composition returns, meal books and beer consumption records are useful but highly variable in their survival; and the nature of servant work is barely indicated in household disbursement books recording the purchase of raw materials for cleaning.

One large family collection of manuscript records in particular figures in this text – the Sutherland archives of the Leveson-Gower family.[28] The Sutherlands' main country house at Trentham in Staffordshire survives now only as a ruin and the laundry has been converted into mews houses. In other families and other houses – Beningbrough in North Yorkshire and Berrington Hall in Herefordshire, for example – the material culture has survived better than the documentary evidence. Only in a few instances – Kingston Lacy in Dorset, Shugborough in Staffordshire and Erddig in Clwyd – have households left both objects and documents associated with laundering; and even here the documentary evidence is disjointed. Nevertheless, such records provide a platform to start from and a means of illuminating specific areas.

Discussions of servant work and life draw heavily on diaries and memoirs. These are first-hand sources, yet how representative are they? Very few footmen and even fewer maids were able or willing to commit themselves to paper and those who did must have had particular reasons which affect the nature of the record.[29] The footman Thomas, whose diary dating from 1838 forms the introduction and substructure to the chapters on footmen, was obviously fairly well educated and keen to improve himself. It is possible to see his daily record as an intellectual discipline imposed on himself.[30] Yet most of what Thomas recorded concerned not the details of his day-to-day chores, but people and places he saw. The fact that he bought a *Court Gazette* to send to his father indicates that his parents were interested in the élite world with which their son came into contact and this may have motivated him originally. If so, it would colour the whole journal. The writer of another important footman's diary which dates from 1837, the year previous to Thomas's, was William Tayler. He wrote for his own education, 'because I am a wretched bad writer' and keeping a short daily journal would 'induce me to make use of my pen every day'. Each entry needed to be short, 'as my book is very small and my time not very large'. After keeping to this resolution for a whole year, Tayler wrote: 'I have at last finished the task which I have been heartily sick of long agoe and I think it will be a long time before I begin another of the kind.'[31] Despite their shortcomings, both these two diaries are invaluable sources for personal detail of the social life of servants in the 1830s, the sort of detail which is simply not available elsewhere until we reach a period accessible to modern oral history.

Many of the reminiscences used in this book come not from diarists but from writers of retrospective autobiographies and inevitably these differ in character from the immediate record provided by diaries. Most of the writers were publishing their memoirs in the early or mid-twentieth century after a lifetime in service. They were looking back either to the tail end of the Victorian period or to the early decades of the twentieth century, some to as late as the 1940s. Eric Horne, whose autobiography was published in 1923, wanted to record a world which had long since gone, for readers who would be strangers to that more leisurely age.[32] Less realistically, William Lanceley's book which appeared two years later in 1925, was written for the benefit of future servants and employers.[33] These and other writers such as John James, Ernest King, Peter Russell and Albert Thomas provide qualitative information about the experiences of servants during the crucial period of the decline of domestic service in the first half of the twentieth century, but for the historian they share an irritating problem: in many cases and for obvious reasons they are deliberately vague about names, places and dates, so it is impossible to fix exactly the context of quotations.[34] Yet they still repay study, for the stories they have to tell are special and when looked at as a whole they reveal clear emerging patterns. Neither can we ignore valuable books of the type written by Frank Victor Dawes or compiled by local museums or records services, which are in effect narrative compendia of servant reminiscences.[35]

Autobiography is the written-down version of oral reminiscence, which has formed another source especially useful in relation to house cleaning and laundering. Female servants continued to find employment within the great houses right up until the Second World War, long after the disappearance of servant-employing households lower down the social scale and long after the era when large numbers of men were employed in service. Reminiscence has the same problems of accuracy and romanticisation as autobiography, but suffers the additional problem of inadequate interviewing techniques. Because we are interested in details of work, the interviewer needs to know something about the techniques under discussion; unfortunately many recordings are made useless by the inability to ask appropriate follow-up questions. Interviews with retired servants in Staffordshire have proved useful, as also have a number of tapes from the National Trust and other oral history projects. Flawed as these all are as historical sources, they do present a world which is otherwise closed to us and it is frustrating that so many opportunities to question first-hand witnesses have been missed.

Manuals of instruction written for servants have also been used but in a limited way. Not only are specialist housekeeping manuals scarce, but we need to judge whether such prescriptive literature presents anything other than a theoretical model.[36] If we accept them as a basis for the reconstruction of the actuality of servant employment we will fall into the trap articulated by Edward Higgs: 'To fall back on the evidence of manuals of domestic economy . . . is equivalent to using *Vogue* to reconstruct the life-style of the "typical" modern family.'[37] The area between 'concept' and 'reality' here is a difficult one. Manuals can be seen not simply as useful means of disseminating advice to servants but as a conceptual whole, representing a philosophy of service which is of its nature coloured with the mores of the time. As such they are a legitimate area of interest, especially if we are concerned with images of servants as well as the actuality; and even as a theoretical model manuals present a useful gauge by which to measure individual households.[38] Occasionally, too, retrospective accounts in manuals can help to make sense of otherwise disparate references in specific fields; one example is the account of 'buckwashing' featured in chapter 6, which increases considerably our understanding of early laundry techniques.

Whereas the research for this book has made a conscious effort to find and listen to the voice of the servant, reminiscences of the employer have not been ignored. A number of memoirs have been written about the domestic life of the country house by owners, usually recalling long-gone days of childhood or youth. Lesley Lewis, writing about Pilgrims' Hall in Essex between 1912 and 1939, and Lilian Bond recalling her childhood early in the twentieth century at Tyneham in Dorset, were particularly successful at retrieving the memory of domestic trivia.[39]

The servant corridor at Dunham Massey, illustrating the importance of internal systems of communications. At the end of the corridor we can see a small part of the old bell-pull system. This was replaced by an internal telephone system which operated on a coded number of rings for different people; two receivers can be seen on opposite sides of the corridor. The single bell was probably a calling bell for mealtimes. (Royal Commission on the Historical Monuments of England)

Other contemporary writings about servants have rarely been helpful. The only exception to this is the case of footmen, who seem to have been the subject of much debate at various times. By comparison, little has been written about laundrymaids and housemaids in contemporary literature; and even modern academic works pay them scant attention.

The time-frame covered by this book is fairly wide. Inevitably in a work which relies heavily on autobiography and oral history, most sources relate to the nineteenth and twentieth centuries, though some ideas are pursued briefly backwards in time in order to clarify the developing context. It is hoped that neither this nor the occasional lack of specificity about dates from the autobiographical sources will cause confusion.

In the course of exploring material from all these sources, it became clear that each of the three subjects under investigation suffered with a particular problem of stereotyping. This is true in both contemporary literature and modern writing, which has tended to accept the stereotype with little debate. The most obvious case of this was the footman, characterised over a long period of time as being a lazy, affected, vicious 'flunkey'. The laundrymaid's reputation has been more ambivalent; she is portrayed as being a hard worker physically, but not particularly skilled and with doubtful morals in relation to both drink and sex. In the case of the housemaid, her problem was one of total invisibility in the contemporary life of the country house, where literally no one wanted to see her.

While the theme of the book is provided by the relationship between work, technology, gender and status, the main structure is built around these stereotypes; each of the three main sections in the book examines these depictions through the detail of work as evidenced by manuscript records, memoirs, diaries and transcripts of interviews with servants, as well as the occasional illumination from prescriptive literature. The final chapter draws together some of the meanings we can ascribe to them, and explores some of the ways in which work reflected contemporary value systems.

CHAPTER 2

'A Lazy and Magnificent Fellow': the Footman's Work

In both modern and contemporary accounts footmen have had a bad press. Even the words used – 'lackey' and 'flunkey' – have pejorative overtones. Described by modern writers as 'the peacocks among domestics' and 'ornamental parasites' and viewed as an icon of conspicuous consumption, their role within the élite household has been summarised as being 'one of the most vital parts of his master's equipment of display'.[1] A nineteenth-century author such as Mrs Beeton felt compelled to defend the role of the footman as being 'no sinecure'[2] and both Thackeray and Dickens disliked them, the latter describing them memorably as 'long and languid men, flabby in texture . . . their terrible equanimity and monotonous whiteness appal'.[3]

The footman was an easy target for the cartoonist, but perhaps the cruellest word picture comes from an article written by Lady Violet Greville which appeared in the *National Review* in 1892:

a functionary conventionally arrayed in plush breeches and silk stockings, with well developed calves and a supercilious expression. Several times a day he partakes freely of nourishing food, including a surprising quantity of beer. He has a wholesome contempt for poor people, small families, and genteel poverty; and talks of *us* and *me* in connection with his master. His meals and his pipe appear to be the be-all and end-all of existence. After, there comes the washing of his head. This has to be done daily (so he avers) in order to prevent the powder he wears from injuring his luxuriant hair. . . . He may be seen lounging superciliously on the door-steps of a summer afternoon, his coat thrown back, his thumbs in his waistcoat armholes, regarding the passing carriages and their well-dressed occupants with approval, or glaring contemptuously at the small boy with a parcel. . . . He rises as late as possible; he exerts himself as little as he need; he declines to take up the governess's supper or to clean her boots. . . . A jolly, lazy, magnificent fellow is the flunkey.[4]

Horace Roome, a footman at Shugborough, the Staffordshire house belonging to the Earls of Lichfield. Taken in the 1920s, the photograph shows the footman in dress livery. (Staffordshire Arts and Museum Service)

No doubt Lady Greville had ample opportunity to study footmen, but the tone of the whole article is hardly well balanced. It was one of many publications which were part of a wider discussion of the 'servant question' which came to a head in the late nineteenth century. This focused on the increasing difficulty experienced by employers in recruiting and keeping good quality domestic staff. The growth of alternative sources of employment – industry, hospitals, business – meant that domestic service was no longer attractive to working men and women, who expected more independence, status and freedom in their leisure time than a position as a living-in servant could give.

That there were real problems with demoralisation of menservants at that time is further evidenced by the employment survey conducted in London by Charles Booth, published in 1896, which concluded that 'men-servants are not overworked'. When combined with poor accommodation and a rich diet, this inevitably resulted in addiction to alcohol and betting. Booth summed up: 'As failures, male servants are, perhaps, the most hopeless of all failures. . . . '[5]

Complaints about footmen, however, were common even before the 1890s. Among the manuscript archives of the Ansons of Shugborough in Staffordshire is an account of the day-to-day grievances experienced by the family at the hands of footmen. The account is undated but probably written by the first Viscount Anson, who died in 1818.[6] He obviously felt that discipline in his household had become lax, especially when compared with that of his neighbours in the county, the Chetwynds of Ingestre. In a surprisingly modern way, he drew two columns down the page and itemised each point, describing how the two households compared with each other. The preparation of breakfast was a particular problem, especially when an early start was required by sportsmen in the house. Instead of being served in the Bust Parlour by the duty footman, it was 'prepared any how and anywhere and sometimes by Miss Anson's footman or the steward's room boy'. A few other extracts give the flavour of his complaints:

Servants won't bring up a message and always dispute who shall carry one. . . . Whenever the carriage is ordered to go anywhere or to fetch or set down any person (be they who they may) it is Lord Anson's strict orders that it shall always be attended by one of the footmen – they left the Miss Bledworth the other night after the White's fête to go home without a footman or attendant. . . . No footman appeared at coffee or tea yesterday evening or to make up the fire . . . and he did not see any one footman in the whole course of yesterday evening.

The writer ended with exasperated sarcasm and a final promise:

The Evil has now got to such a height that Lord Anson expects soon to be left to wait upon himself. . . . The more servants any gentleman keeps the more plague he has with them, which is the more provoking as he never refuses them any proper request. If any objections to doing what is ordered occurs again, Lord Anson will suppose the servant so refusing does not like his place and means to quit it – and he shall therefore give directions to have him discharged forthwith.

Again, there is plenty of evidence of dissatisfaction with servants even before this, in the eighteenth century. Throughout the 1720s and 1760s newspapers and pamphlets were full of letters of complaint. Two famous contributions to the

PROBLEM STAFF

'Resolved to change a footman, recently sent to me with a glowing character, of which, it appears to me he is totally unworthy, being pre-eminently thick-headed. People acquire and get rid of servants just as they do Horses – merits greatly exaggerated – defects studiously concealed – ages falsified by the Servants themselves. No one wants to keep them, if bad or unsafe – and will tell any lie to put them on other people.'

Extract from the *Journal of Sir Edward Littleton*, 2 July 1850
(SRO, D 260/M/F/26/51)

debate were Daniel Defoe's *Behaviour of Servants* published in 1724, and Swift's lampoon of servants in his *Directions to Servants*, published in 1745;[7] and the problem of footmen in the eighteenth century was analysed in an article written in 1929 by Dorothy Marshall:

It was the gentlemen, whose footmen were getting out of hand, who wrote to the papers about the insubordination of servants. The maid may have been a domestic trouble, but she was never the public nuisance which the footmen became. She did not swagger through the streets, pushing people off the pavements . . . It was this power, which their numbers gave them, of making themselves objectionable, that focused public opinion on them.[8]

In the 1760s, the London-based footmen even had the temerity to form a society, with the aim of regulating a minimum wage, setting the maximum weights of items to be carried and organising relief for footmen turned out of a place.[9] On the other side of the argument, employers thought footmen were overpaid both in their salaries and their board wages, and intransigent in pressing for vails, tips traditionally distributed by guests at the end of a visit: 'The obligation to scatter vails wherever one went, was so heavy as almost to amount to blackmail.'[10] It was rumoured that a footman working in London society could double his wages by vails;[11] and word went round that Christmas boxes given to house porters could amount to as much as £80. In the 1760s, a campaign by employers against vail-giving was met with serious riots among the footmen:

Great riots at Ranelagh among those *beings* the footmen. It began Friday, when three were taken into custody; but upon asking pardon they were discharged. Last night it was more serious; there was fighting with drawn swords for several hours. . . . [Two nights later.] One gentleman has his arm broke, another his head, some footmen hurt, and 'tis said one killed. . . .[12]

After the riots, pressure to pay vails became more subtle; but diaries and autobiographies show that tipping went on as long as there were footmen. Maybe the trouble was caused by more fundamental problems with the functions of footmen. By the eighteenth century this was a peculiar mixture of ceremonial attendant and domestic skivvy, a combination which originated in a sort of pseudo-military bodyguard role – hence the private family uniform or 'livery'. This was exemplified by the early version of the footman called the 'running footman' – employed to run alongside his master's carriage carrying a pole to test the holes in the roadway and armed with a weapon to ward off thieves.[13] Dressed in a highly distinctive livery which included a skirt, running footmen had all but disappeared by the early nineteenth century.[14]

One potential flashpoint was the demarcation of the footman's work in relation to other menservants. For part of his work he was responsible to the butler, or in grander households to the groom of the chambers; for carriage work he answered to the coachman or the gentleman of the horse. Split supervision was combined with a potentially endless variety of jobs; the manual written by the Adamses described them as 'multifarious and incessant' and autobiographies bear this out.[15] For example, unlike the butler, the footman was expected to help out with valeting – that is, personal chamber service for male guests or family members. Unlike the valet, however, he was also expected to serve food and lay tables. His job therefore overlapped others' work to a degree which varied with the numbers of footmen and butlers employed. He needed to develop a wide range of skills, many of which involved intricate rules of etiquette, and it is easy to see how his role could degenerate into a sort of general dogsbody.

Footmen encompassed both front-of-house ceremonial and backstairs domesticity and because of the former, they were often chosen for looks and presence and their lives were touched by the glamour of their masters' involvement in society – circumstances which might well give rise to petty jealousies within the household. Because this was the most obvious part of their work, it is for this they are remembered. Yet footmen were also heavily involved in menial aspects of large-scale domestic management: cleaning, lighting, security and endless travelling.[16]

The footman's work was thus an amalgam of the gorgeous and the mundane, an expression of an élite society's concern both with pleasure and consumption and with the practical necessities of a highly structured society.

For the employers, keeping footmen was undoubtedly a mark of status – an essential prerequisite of any gentleman's establishment. As Dorothy Marshall pointed out, footmen were particularly important in eighteenth-century élite society. Security escort and communications duties continued to be an essential part of the footmen's work, but domestic responsibilities were also significant. Male fashion was so elaborate that no gentleman could dress himself; furniture was so finely wrought that it needed skilled cleaners; and even in the nineteenth century, being waited on at dinner by a manservant carried higher status than a mere parlourmaid.

In 1777, the minimum requirement of a country squire was reckoned to be five servants, one of them a 'combination footman-gardener'.[17] The Adams's manual, published in 1825, set the threshold for the employment of a liveried footman-cum-groom at around £500 to £600 per annum, whereas the employment of a second footman required a household income of over £3,000.[18] It was not only the extensive establishments of the nobility which employed liveried footmen; even successful tradesmen aspired to do so.[19] A footman was valued not simply because of his usefulness, but also because of his expense. He received higher wages than a woman servant doing the same work, he needed costly livery and his employment was liable to servant tax.[20] Outdoor menservants such as gardeners were not taxable, so pretentious but impoverished households employed a gardener or a groom who occasionally could double as a footman.[21]

Looking back, footmen are difficult to characterise historically. Part of the problem is the footman's inaccessibility within the country house record. The jobs assigned to footmen were highly variable and left little trace among family archives and virtually nothing in the way of material culture, no fashionable kitchen packed with state-of-the-art technology. There is the further problem of change over time. The description 'ornamental parasite' quoted at the beginning of this chapter was given by Burnett, who at the same time admitted that 'the footman was the mainstay of the household'.[22] This apparent contradiction is explained by the contrast between what Burnett saw as the hard-working footman of the eighteenth century and what the footman became later, when much of his manual work had been taken over by women servants.

While it is clear that footmen were a conspicuous status symbol, it is legitimate to question whether this was their only function, or even their main one. If we search a little deeper into the footman's own testament, rather than that of his master, do we arrive at a different verdict of his role? The discussion here begins with an introduction to the incomplete and unpublished diary kept during 1838 by a footman called Thomas who served in the household of the Leveson-Gowers, the hugely wealthy Dukes of Sutherland. In this we will look firstly at the seasonal variation of work. The context will then widen to include reference to another diary from 1837 by William Tayler, as well as a number of autobiographies relating to a later period, the last years of the nineteenth century and the first three or four decades of the twentieth, giving a total study span of just over a hundred years. This pattern is repeated through a narrative which moves from the different jobs which the footman had to master to the wider social context of his life and the degree to which he shared in the luxurious lifestyle of his master.

SEASONAL VARIATION OF WORK

Thomas's employer, George Granville Leveson-Gower, the 2nd Duke of Sutherland, was one of the richest men in England.[23] The diary covers the period from July 1838 to June the following year, when Thomas was twenty-three years old, a country-bred boy from a family of small farmers near Whitchurch in Cheshire. He was employed by the Sutherlands as third or fourth footman, having worked for at least two families before. The Sutherlands were a highly mobile family and during the period covered by the journal Thomas worked in a number of their houses: Stafford House which was their main London residence; their house across the river at Wandsworth, called Westhill; and two of their country houses at Lilleshall in Shropshire and Trentham in Staffordshire. Thomas's life was structured into three phases which changed with the demands of the social season and the occupation of these various houses.

When the diary begins in the summer of 1838, the Leveson-Gower family was at Stafford House and the whole household was subject to a routine of almost frantic social activity. Life was exciting, the entertainment lavish, for the Duchess of Sutherland was Mistress of the Robes to the young Queen Victoria and was famous for her receptions at Stafford House. One such occasion, on 14 July, was described by Thomas: 'The house is all in an uproar with work people as we are going to have a party tonight.' At 6 o'clock in the evening, after a busy day of preparation, Thomas dressed in his best livery, laid the dinner table and helped serve dinner for twenty-four; two or three waiters were engaged to help, as well as a couple of extra footmen accompanying the dinner guests. The meal finished at 9.30 p.m. An hour later the 'company started to arrive' – the after-dinner guests who numbered around 600. The Strauss Band[24] played from the famous grand staircase and the reception rooms were arranged with tables where the footmen served tea and coffee, ices and confectionery. Thomas's job was a daunting one – to stand at the door of the inner hall which housed the grand staircase, showing in the company and announcing their names. He was impressed by the scene: 'All the rooms were brilliantly lighted up, it was supposed there were about 2,000

One side of the great double staircase at Stafford House, mentioned in the diary of Thomas the footman. The second Marquess of Stafford bought the lease of the house (now Lancaster House) in 1827. Thereafter, the staircase became the focal point of brilliant musical entertainments hosted by the Leveson-Gowers and attended by celebrities from home and abroad. In a letter to his family, Chopin described 'the Queen, standing on the stairs in the most dazzling light, covered with all her diamonds and orders – and the noblemen wearing the Garter, descending the stairs with the greatest elegance, conversing in groups, halting on the various landings, from every point of which there is something fresh to be admired'. (From Sykes, Private Palaces, *pp. 266–7) (Royal Commission on the Historical Monuments of England)*

candles lighted and about 600 lamp burners at least.' He recorded with some satisfaction that he did not get to bed till 3 o'clock.

The pace of life at Stafford House can be judged from the diary entries for the days prior to this event. Four days before, on 10 July, there had been a dinner party with over sixty guests. On the 12th, the household had entertained to tea no less a guest than the Duchess of Kent, the Queen's mother. On this occasion, the liveried servants were turned out to meet her in the hall, and after her departure the household had hosted yet another dinner party in the evening. The next day, the Duke dined out at the Guildhall; the two senior footmen and Thomas went with him to help serve dinner, but the queue of over a hundred servants waiting to be called into the servants' entrance was so long that it was an hour after the coachman had set the Duke down from the carriage before Thomas got to his post in the dining-room. By this time he noted that the Duke had eaten his fish course and had started on the beef.

In August, this busy round of the London season was replaced by a more measured pace in the country. Travelling to Lilleshall in Shropshire required forethought and planning; a couple of days before the journey Thomas sent his carpet bag by canal carrier with the rest of the household's heavy luggage, first making a list of everything he had put in it. He then set off with a couple of other servants on a complex journey involving the new railway to Birmingham, and onwards by stagecoach and public omnibus, arriving in Shropshire at 10 o'clock at night.[25]

After a few days at Lilleshall the household was again on the move: 'They are all very busy packing up to go to Trentham' – a house which was then in a state of upheaval, undergoing substantial rebuilding at the hands of Sir Charles Barry. The purpose of this visit seems to have been for the Duke and Duchess to hold a quick meeting with Barry, for whom Thomas acted as valet. After three days in Staffordshire the family returned to Lilleshall but Thomas was given a short holiday to see his own family who lived near Acton in Cheshire. A few days later, Thomas returned to Trentham, only to be off again, firstly back to join the household at Lilleshall, then to Glasgow with the Duke, who combined a visit to two friends, the Duke of Hamilton and Lord Belhaven, with a committee meeting and show of a cattle society. From Glasgow the party returned direct to London and Stafford House, for a short stay which involved a memorable trip to Windsor Castle, where Thomas accompanied the family to wait on the young children and their nursemaids. During this visit he described being shown around the dining- and drawing-rooms at Windsor, which greatly impressed him as being 'very grand, much finer than Stafford house'. A highlight of his visit was being asked by one of the royal pantrymen to help with the washing of the gold plate in the 'Gold pantry'.

Returned to London, the Duke and Duchess prepared for a long trip to the continent with their older children. Thomas was left behind at Westhill to wait upon the governess, the wonderfully named Miss Jelly, and the two youngest children and their servants. There followed yet another different phase of life – long winter days with little work to do. Rarely rising before 8 o'clock, with all domestic chores completed by 11 each morning, Thomas developed his own routine – everyday setting off to visit Stafford House, a couple of miles distant and occupied, in the absence of the Duke and Duchess, by the Duke's mother, known as the Duchess Countess. Here he exchanged messages or parcels between the two households, cemented working relationships with the other servants, exchanged gossip and helped out with portering or waiting when necessary. From Stafford House he then set off on his personal errands – visiting friends, usually

Pencil and chalk sketch of the west front and main entrance of Trentham Hall, the Staffordshire home of the Leveson-Gowers, dated 1840–5, from an unnamed album in the William Salt Library, Stafford. (Staffordshire Record Office)

other servants, and enrolling with a language tutor in Regent Street whom he paid two and a half guineas for three months' lessons in French. He became most assiduous in this, perhaps in the hope that he would be asked to go with the family on their next trip abroad.

The quiet tenor of life at Westhill was punctuated by servants' dances and the occasional visitor, and also by the death of the Duchess Countess, for whose funeral Thomas was provided with mourning livery. In June, one of the children at Westhill, the baby Victoria, started to ail; the household was distressed and after an absence of eight months the Duke and Duchess returned from the continent. The young ladies, Thomas recorded, came home 'as brown as bricks'. The very next day the Duchess took up her courtly duties and Thomas was back into the social whirl, acting as escort to the Duchess on a visit to the Queen; that day he attended the Duke and Duchess to the Queen's ball at Buckingham Palace. On the 19th, baby Victoria died. Thomas and the other footmen closed the shutters of the windows and the household went deathly quiet. Shortly after this, the surviving diary ends abruptly.

The seasonal phasing of Thomas's year described here was accompanied by daily variability of work. This can be categorised into several distinct groups: waiting; carriage duty; household cleaning and valeting.

WAITING

The job which was most closely associated with footmen was 'waiting'. This required the footman to stand on duty at a specific station waiting for his services to be required, perhaps to mend the fire, take a message to someone, or receive and announce guests. There was a distinction between ordinary 'waiting', when the footman remained somewhere convenient to answer the drawing-room bell, and 'close waiting', in which he had to stand in the hall to open doors.[26] During those periods when the Sutherland household was 'at housekeeping' (when the Duke and Duchess were at home) the footmen took it in turns to 'wait' (one day on and one day off). The same system of alternating duties was used for carriage duty and seemed to have been pretty well universal in households which employed two or three footmen. More elaborate households employing more footmen, such as Welbeck Abbey, the Duke of Portland's house in Nottinghamshire, operated a four-day rota.[27]

Message-taking was an important part of 'waiting'. Communication between family and servants was vital and in the absence of telephones the country house

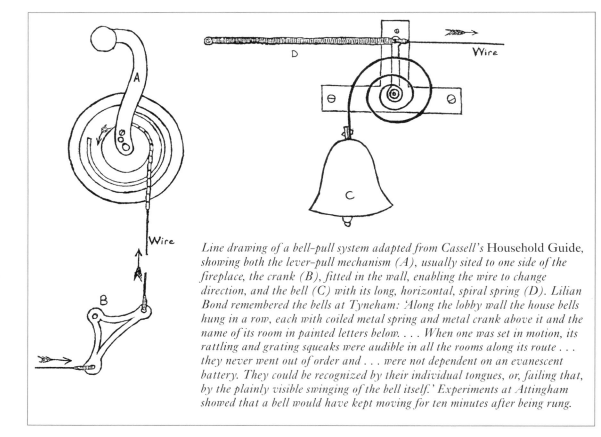

Line drawing of a bell-pull system adapted from Cassell's Household Guide, *showing both the lever-pull mechanism (A), usually sited to one side of the fireplace, the crank (B), fitted in the wall, enabling the wire to change direction, and the bell (C) with its long, horizontal, spiral spring (D). Lilian Bond remembered the bells at Tyneham: 'Along the lobby wall the house bells hung in a row, each with coiled metal spring and metal crank above it and the name of its room in painted letters below. . . . When one was set in motion, its rattling and grating squeaks were audible in all the rooms along its route . . . they never went out of order and . . . were not dependent on an evanescent battery. They could be recognized by their individual tongues, or, failing that, by the plainly visible swinging of the bell itself.' Experiments at Attingham showed that a bell would have kept moving for ten minutes after being rung.*

functioned on a system of bells and message-taking which relied largely on the footman. Besides internal messages, the footman was often sent to deliver messages outside the house.[28] As an extension to this function, a footman or porter dealt with the incoming and outgoing mail.

Even when a footman was 'out of waiting' he still served meals – anything from a highly sophisticated dinner with many courses, to afternoon tea or coffee from a tray in the drawing-room. As we have seen, for Thomas this was not restricted to waiting on the Duke or Duchess of Sutherland; during the trip to Windsor he took meals to the nurseries and during the Westhill period he served and cleared up all the things for breakfast, lunch, dinner, tea and supper for Miss Jelly and the young Lord Frederick, as well as regular visitors such as Lady Dover. It also involved waiting in other houses which could be lucrative – working at the Guildhall dinner earned the footmen an extra 4*s* each.

One task often mentioned by Thomas was laying the tablecloth. Footmen laid the cloth for all meals; this involved first dusting the table, then placing on it a green baize cloth, then the linen cloth, taking care to place the centre fold of the cloth exactly down the middle of the table and any design in the damask facing the correct way. A favourite device in the eighteenth century was to have the tablecloth designed to mirror the plasterwork on the ceiling and of course this had to be placed exactly. Once the main cloth was smoothed in position, the slips were laid on top – these were smaller cloths which went down the sides of the table and which were removed by the footman before serving the dessert course.

It was the footman's job to carry up all the equipment needed for the table from the pantry. If there were two footmen, the first carried the silver, the second the china.[29] In some households the footman set each place, laying out the plates, cutlery, glasses and napkins folded as needed, and arranging the chairs. In larger households there was a strict demarcation between footman and butler – the latter placed the silver and glasses and the footman did the china.

It was usually the footman's job to ring a bell or sound a gong ten or fifteen minutes before dinner, and again when the dinner 'was going up'.[30] In earlier days this would have been the house bell, mounted somewhere on the roof, and from the 1920s Lesley Lewis remembered just such a bell which was still sounded at Pilgrims' Hall in Essex by the footman who pulled vigorously on the 'red and blue woolly sausage' which hung in the servants' passage.[31] In some houses the gong was carried round the house; Diana Cooper described how at Belvoir Castle in Leicestershire in 1905 this was done by the 'gong man' who was very old and wore a long white beard to his waist:

> He would walk down the interminable passages, his livery hanging a little loosely on his bent old bones, clutching his gong with one hand and with the other feebly brandishing the padded-knobbed stick with which he struck it. Every corridor had to be warned and the towers too, so I suppose he banged on and off for ten minutes, thrice daily.[32]

It was also the footman's job to bring up the various courses of the meal from the kitchen. The etiquette associated with serving a formal dinner was complex and changed over the years.[33] In outline, the butler began each service by presenting the first dishes, removing the covers and passing them to the footmen who served, handed out condiments, kept the tablecloth tidied as the meal progressed and changed plates and cutlery when necessary. When not actually serving, the footmen's station was behind his master's or mistress's chair, the butler's at the sideboard. In all of this there were elaborate rules for the footman to follow.

After the meal, the footman removed the cloths. For everyday use, most households would use a tablecloth two or three times before sending it to be washed. Between meals the footman would fold it into its creases, sprinkling it with a little water before placing it into the linen press ready for the next day. His final job in the dining-room was to make up the fire, trim the candles and tidy the table. He then went to serve coffee to the ladies.

Food and dishes were carried by the footman on large wooden or japanned trays, the food kept warm by tin reflectors or hollow plates containing hot water. In households which entertained frequently, the carrying of food trays was a tremendous chore. Ernest King recalled his time in the American household of the de Wichfelds, who leased Blair Castle in Perthshire from the Duke of Atholl after the First World War, and who rarely had less than thirty-six house guests: 'Thirty-six guests . . . meant thirty-six trays to be taken upstairs every morning for breakfast, laden with orange juice, porridge, cream, a hot dish, tea or coffee, toast, croissants, brioche, marmalade (also, being an American household, iced water).'[34] Since it was the footmen's job to carry trays, it was they who were most prone to breakages of valuable pieces. William Lanceley recalled: 'The worst breakages that I remember were thirty-seven engraved and festooned wine-glasses. The footman foolishly tried to open the pantry door still holding the tray . . . '.[35]

There were less obvious hazards for the well-dressed footman, as recalled by William Lanceley:

A sad accident happened at a dinner-party when a footman was handing out two soups (a green pea and a clear soup); he was wearing an aiguillette [a shoulder-knot] . . . and the dining-room chairs had a ball on either side of the top bar. The aiguillette cord caught the ball of the chair next to the lady he was serving and pulled him up sharp, the result was both soups were emptied into her lap. It was a pitiable position for both . . . [36]

Of course a wealthy employer could afford to indulge his whims even if they disrupted the servant routine. Ernest King recalled his amiable first master, Mr Charles Chichester, who occasionally liked to be left alone in his dining-room all night: 'Every now and then after his wife had left the dinner-table he'd lock the door behind her. All knew what that meant. He didn't wish to be disturbed and the table would be left, uncleared, till the following morning. And he'd sleep there the whole night. I remember the grass outside the dining-room window was all brown and dead.'[37] This gentleman's favourite celebration was an annual dinner which he gave for the forty-eight cabbies of Barnstaple, who were constantly bringing guests up to the house from the station. Once a year he liked to thank them with an elaborate dinner; on these occasions all forty-nine diners slept in the dining-room.

CARRIAGE DUTY

Carriage duty was another defining function of footmen. Long after the demise of running footmen, the tradition remained for aristocratic men and women venturing outside the house to be escorted by one or two footmen, who stood on the back step of the carriage, or walked a few paces in front of a sedan chair, or a few paces behind if out for a stroll; if necesssary they carried a flambeau to light the way. The most public and showy part of their duties, this has been seen as primarily an opportunity to demonstrate social status, yet there was also a very real requirement for a personal security guard.[38] This was not needed so much in the country; at both Lilleshall and Trentham, the Duke and Duchess of Sutherland often paid visits to friends in their carriage without a footman, or with a groom or even a stable boy, much to the chagrin of the footmen.

When we read accounts of how a pair of footmen were expected to behave when accompanying a lady on a social visit in the late nineteenth century, it is not surprising they were ridiculed: 'Two matched footmen would get down, march up to the door, and if a double knocker, both would knock (which they had practised beforehand) then march back to the carriage in a stately fashion, let down the steps, and hand out the ladies.'[39] Such style and flourish was obviously designed to show the importance of the caller.

One of the problems associated with carriage duty was the time footmen spent waiting around for their passengers. For example, one night Thomas recorded that he was ordered to go with the carriage to Buckingham Palace to collect the Duke of Sutherland from a ball; as ordered he arrived there at midnight, but the Duke wasn't ready to leave till 3 a.m. This sort of aimless waiting was a daily occurrence. In this case Thomas stayed with the carriage, but many other times he must have spent hours gossiping in servants' halls or sauntering round town, and many footmen and coachmen took to drinking in public houses to while away time.

Carriage duty might entail long journeys as well as short ones. In a highly mobile household such as the Sutherlands' the footmen and lady's maids spent a great deal

One end of the butler's pantry at Dunham Massey, the house near Manchester which until 1976 was the home of the 10th Earl of Stamford. The picture illustrates two of the functions of the pantry – communications and storage. By the door is the internal telephone system and electric bell board which replaced the wire bell-pull system and on the right is a typical butler's cupboard, which was often fitted with sliding doors to save space. (John Bethell, National Trust, 1984)

of time unpacking and packing clothes and carriages – both for other people and themselves. On the journey to Glasgow in September 1838, the travellers were the Duke, his secretary Mr Brown, the coachman and Thomas; the latter worked hard, cleaning and loading the carriage (this involved packing and securing the various fitted trunks or 'imperials') as well as valeting for his master, waiting upon him and Mr Brown, paying tolls, going to the post office to pick up mail en route and helping to negotiate terms for the hire of horses at the post houses. On this journey he sat up on the box beside the coachman, in contrast to the formal journeys with the Duke around London, when he stood on the backstep. Each day they travelled up to ninety miles and each night they arrived at their posting inn between 8 and 10 o'clock; Thomas then had tea and a glass of brandy and water and went to bed about 11 o'clock, to be up again at 6 a.m. Putting the carriage to rights, valeting for the Duke and having his own breakfast took two hours and they were off again at 8 o'clock. Stopping overnight at Lord Belhaven's house meant more work not less for Thomas, who helped to serve dinner, but only in the pantry since he did not have his formal livery with him. The trip lasted a week and when they finally arrived back in London it was to find Stafford House very busy packing trunks for a much longer journey to the continent.

On this trip, the size of the entourage which eventually set out to catch the cross-Channel steam packet gives some idea of the complexity of organisation needed. Three carriages set off on the first day – the young ladies travelled in the family coach with the confectioner; a lady's maid and the French governess followed in a phaeton; and the governess's maid, a courier and a footman brought up the rear in a phogang.[40] The next day three more carriages set out – the Duke and Duchess in the chariot; Mr Jackson with a footman and the family doctor in the briska; and three maids in the barouche with the cook in the dicky seat. Thomas was left in London, sounding a little forlorn. The next morning he cleaned his formal livery and carefully put it away.

When the railways came to the aid of the peripatetic household, footmen still had their place in carriage service, albeit in a reduced form. In the early 1900s, Frederick Gorst used to accompany Lady Howard to the family's country seat in Warwickshire. She had a first-class reservation and he a second-class. He carried several robes and steamer rugs to put over her knees as well as a hot-water container to put under her feet. He wore her jewel case attached to his wrist by a heavy steel chain and bracelet, for Lady Howard was in the habit of travelling with pearls and diamonds worth £100,000. He also served tea to Her Ladyship from a hamper. Whenever the train stopped at a station he ran forward, alongside the train, to ask whether there was anything she wished.[41]

Even in the 1920s some wealthy women travelled with an enormous amount of luggage. In the 1930s Mrs de Wichfeld, Ernest King's employer, had 170 trunks 'many big enough to hold a man':

She usually took seven or eight with her and twenty-nine pieces of hand luggage. All these trunks were specially built, with or without drawers. One contained nothing but her stationery, several contained underclothes only. There were special shoe trunks, fitted with trays, each tray subdivided into baize-lined compartments. First the shoes were put into matching bags, black in black, brown in brown, whatever the colour of shoes it had a corresponding bag made of moiré silk and lined with fine chamois leather. . . .[42]

The footman's carriage etiquette included a number of other duties such as mounting a lady onto horseback. According to John James this consisted of 'clasping the hands low enough for the rider to place her foot thereon, lifting her to the side-saddle and then feeling under the riding habit for the broad elastic loop for her foot. It was at this point that my blushes used to cause Miss Harvey a certain amount of amusement. . . .'[43]

Carriage duty also required the footman to escort his employer to sporting events such as shoots, where it was his job to stand beside his master, loading his shotguns. William Lanceley recalled getting into a fight with a gang of poachers while accompanying his master on a salmon-fishing trip to Scotland. He was hit with a piece of wood pulled from a fence, knocked into the river and hit on the head with a stone as he clambered out – suffering a general drubbing and a broken tooth.[44]

HOUSEHOLD CLEANING

It is difficult to judge how much domestic cleaning was done by the Sutherlands' footman Thomas since his diary only occasionally mentions cleaning up the lunch things, or that 'I had to do my valeting before breakfast because I have to clean the silver afterwards'. The fact that he mentioned silver perhaps indicates that cleaning it was unusual for him, which might well have been the case as the Sutherland household around this time employed a full-time living-in platemaid. Generally, footmen were responsible for washing up after light meals, cleaning all the glass, cutlery and silver, and cleaning and priming the lamps. Footmen were also responsible for polishing the looking-glasses and mahogany furniture on the main living floor, but not on the bedroom floors.[45] They also checked that blinds were drawn correctly so that the furniture was not damaged by the sun.[46]

It was said that English footmen did less than their French counterparts. Unlike English footmen who cleaned floors only occasionally, at the British Embassy in Paris footmen regularly scrubbed the marble floor of the great entrance hall, the grand staircase, the large dining-room, the ballroom and the three state drawing-rooms. They used 'long-handled deck scrubbers and polish[ed] with their feet, never on any account going to work on their knees'.[47] Even English footmen were expected to help generally with spring-cleaning, as when Mrs Galleazie, the housekeeper at Stafford House, required Thomas to dust the books in the library.

Most footmen polished boots and brushed and sponged muddy outdoor garments as part of their morning routine. The footman's main workplace was his pantry, in some houses called the butler's pantry even though it was used by both

TO CLEAN KNIVES WITH A KNIFE BOARD

'Melt mutton suet and put it hot upon the leather [which covers the board] with a piece of flannel; then take two pieces of soft Bath brick and rub them one against the other over the leather till it is covered with the powder, which rub in, until no grease comes through when a knife is passed over the leather. . . . Let your board be neither too high nor too low, but of a proper height, so that you may move your hands and arms backward and forward with ease to yourself; it should also be set so that you may be a little on the stoop. . . . Take a knife in each hand, holding them back to back; stand opposite the middle of the board, lay your knives flat upon it, and do not bear too hard upon them while you expand your arms, only just enough so to feel the board; bear rather harder in drawing your hands together, taking care, however, to keep the knives flat on the board; by this means you will find it easier to clean two knives at a time than only one, and you will be less liable to break them. . . .

   When one side has been done, change the knives over. Then dust the blades with a dry cloth and wipe the handles with a damp one. This process will both polish and sharpen knives.'

(Anon., *The Footman's Directory*, p. 19)

CLEANING KNIVES AT PILGRIMS' HALL

'A series of houseboys, for a year or so on first leaving school, did various odd jobs . . . in a little outside room in the stable range. Clamped to a bench was a circular appliance into which emery powder was poured out of a tin with the Duke of Wellington's head on it. A few knives at a time were inserted into leather-lined sockets and got polished when the handle was turned. The best quality dining-room knives were, however, cleaned individually on a board. None were made of stainless steel and the system of cleaning, while defeating rust, wore them to an extreme sharpness, thinness and indeed shortness . . . and cut fingers, tied up with the clean old rags which were always available, were to be expected in children and the younger maids.'

(Lewis, *Private Life*, p. 137)

footmen and butlers. Clothes could be cleaned here, but it was better if there was a special room nearby for brushing as this could be dusty; all that was needed was a large table, a fireplace, and later on perhaps, an iron. Early morning jobs followed in their proper order: firstly brush clothes; then clean lamps, knives, plate; then get the breakfast things ready. This last was usually done after the footman had changed from his 'dirty' clothes into his morning livery.

   The footman usually cleaned, scoured and polished his own pantry, thus avoiding contention with housemaids. As with the examples at Uppark in West

Sussex and Dunham Massey in Cheshire, the ideal pantry was equipped with work table and dresser, plenty of drawer and cupboard space, a fireplace with cooking equipment sufficient to make toast, a sink and two wooden tubs (or two lead or wooden sinks) – one for washing the breakfast things and another, kept free from grease, for washing glasses. There might also be a shallow lead or zinc sink for draining glasses on and a number of trays and plate carriers as well as a napkin press. The pantry at Pilgrims' Hall in Essex was recalled from the 1910s and '20s by Lesley Lewis:

> The pantry door was normally kept shut to confine the smell of tobacco, the considerable consumption of which was the basis for our collection of cigarette cards. . . . At the window end of the pantry was a sink in which stood a wooden bowl so that silver could be washed without getting scratched. The early morning and afternoon tea-sets, glasses and dessert plates were washed here. . . . There was a fire in one corner with a good accurate clock on the mantelshelf, and solid cupboards, chests and brushing surfaces surrounded the room. These were continued into the small bedroom where the footman slept.[48]

In the pantry, the breakfast, lunch and tea things, dessert glasses, china and silver were washed, using a dishcloth in hot, almost boiling water; drinking glasses ideally were rinsed in cold water or hot water followed by cold. Several brands of soft soap for washing-up purposes were marketed in the 1890s but they were expensive and were reserved for dealing with greasy pots and pans, serving dishes and dinner plates which were washed in the kitchen scullery. Footmen used only hot water with perhaps a few crystals of soda to add sparkle. Therefore, the order of washing was important: teaspoons were washed first, then tea cups and saucers, then plates, then forks; knives were not cleaned with the other things because of their delicate handles, but the blades plunged in a jug of hot water.

In the wealthy household of the early decades of the twentieth century, the amount of washing-up was prodigious. Albert Thomas reckoned that a modest dinner for ten people required 324 items of silver, glass and china, not counting the saucepans and dishes in the kitchen.[49] Ernest King's first job in service early in the twentieth century was as a trainee footman: 'In the butler's pantry I spent most of my time at the washing-up tub. My hands and arms in winter were chapped up to the elbow.'[50] The staff hierarchy impinged even on the washing-up. From the 1940s Peter Russell remembered that in Princess Marina's household at Kensington Palace the butler and under-butler washed the best china and the odd

---

WASHING UP

'Pots and Pans, if greasy, ought to be washed inside and out with warm water in which is a little soda. Once a week the sauce-pans ought to be well scoured inside. Rub the inside of tinned sauce-pans well over with soap and a little fine sand or bath-brick till they become quite bright, then wash them with warm water, and dry well.'

✳ ✳ ✳

Tin food covers and brass pans were washed in warm soapy water and then polished with whitening moistened with cold water, then rubbed with a dry cloth until bright.
Spoons were washed and then rubbed with a little moist whitening.
Wooden implements were scrubbed in cold water unless they were very greasy, in which case they should be washed with warm water, a little soda and rubbed with sand.

(Mrs Black, *Household Cookery and Laundry Work*, Collins and Son, *c.* 1882, pp. 138–9)

---

man did the ordinary china (the household did not have any footmen). This mentality went right the way to the top, for in this household Princess Marina herself washed her collection of ornamental china, twice a year.[51]

The disposal of waste could present problems in a footman's pantry, especially before the days when plumbed slop sinks were fitted upstairs. *The Footman's Directory*, published in 1825, warned: 'If you have a sink and a pipe to take off the dirty water, let it be scoured and kept clean and sweet. Never throw the chamber-ley down the sink, as it is a filthy trick, and makes the place not fit to be in; neither empty the tea-leaves into the sink. . . . I have often seen such things done, but it is a slovenly practice.'[52]

Pantries had secure silver cupboards or safes nearby, with fitted shelves lined with green baize.[53] *The Footman's Directory* warned about exposing the plate to public gaze: 'Be very careful not to expose your plate in the pantry or kitchen window, particularly if fronting the street; many servants . . . have lost their plate and their place also.' Most households kept inventories of plate, but these were often out of date and incomplete; other valuables besides plate were kept in the safes, perhaps with inadequate security. The house steward William Lanceley recalled one house where 'Her Ladyship's tiara was kept in a plate closet in a box not even locked, and on going through the contents I found twenty-nine loose diamonds wrapped in tissue-paper. There were three men who had daily access to this plate closet.'[54] Nevertheless, Lanceley thought that dishonesty in servants was rare, considering the temptations which were open to them. In all his years, he could only remember one case of theft by a servant, a footman who was suspected of stealing a silver tankard. A good butler kept close watch on the silver vault; at Cragside in Northumberland, Andrew Crozier, footman and butler to four Lord Armstrongs from 1891, allowed no one, not even Lady Armstrong, to see inside.[55]

Silver closets were not only for the storage of silver but were also usually the place where polishing took place. Polishing silver and plated goods is the chore most often mentioned in footmen's autobiographies and unless a platemaid was employed it consumed a good deal of the footman's time, energy and dedication. The butler Eric Horne was aware of his own expertise in this field: 'I knew the trick of polishing and frosting silver, which is quite different from simply cleaning it. . . . It requires great strength to polish silver, also great care and endurance.'[56] He went on:

> It took me two years to get all the silver in good order, there was such a lot of it. When I first went there [an unnamed house] the silver plates and dishes were firstly taken to the stillroom to be washed, and then brought to the pantry to be washed again. They carried them in laundry clothes baskets, but that was knocking it about too much for me, so I stopped it, and they were taken straight from the dining room to the pantry. . . . One piece of solid silver, a wine cooler, took four men to carry it to the dining-room, there was also immense quantities of ornamental antique silver. . . . Blistered hands were quite a common thing.

The blisters were caused by polishing the silver with jeweller's rouge. Ernest King remembered his first encounter with rouge early in the twentieth century. He was set to clean a quantity of silver: 'cutlery, cruets, silver entrée dishes, serving dishes, salvers, sauce boats, soup tureens, teapots and kettles, and some two dozen silver plates . . . laid on a strip of felt'. The rouge was a soft red powder, mixed in a saucer with ammonia. The mixture was rubbed very hard over the silver with the bare fingers. The idea was that the heat generated by the fingers allowed the rouge to penetrate and remove fine scratches. After the rouge was dry, the silver was polished with a chamois leather. As King remarked:

Cleaning plate is hell. It's the greatest bugbear behind the green baize door, the hardest job in the house. When I began this work, rubbing the silver, the spoon and forks, occasionally getting a prong in my thumb, my fingers grew fearfully sore and blistered, but in those days if you complained you were just told to get on with it and you did. The blisters burst and you kept on despite the pain and you developed a pair of plate hands that never blistered again . . . they became as hard as boards. . . . Thirty years ago I would have three men working from eight to eleven every morning cleaning plate.[57]

It was said that you could always tell a footman by the state of his thumbs. Not surprisingly, the practice of polishing with rouge gradually declined. At Pilgrims' Hall it was used only occasionally 'to remove scratches and impart a deep, almost blackish shine'.[58] Peter Russell remembered that at Kensington Palace after the Second World War rouge was used once a year; they used a white rouge but still rubbed it on with fingers and thumbs. The regular cleaning was done with Goddard's Powder, a pink powder mixed in a saucer with water; this was rubbed on with a cloth, but occasionally bare fingers were used.[59] Even at this time, Russell thought polishing silver was an awful job – 'ten times harder than polishing buttons in the RAF'.

In the long term, hard and frequent rouging was not necessarily very good for the silver. Salvers were always getting scratched and so were heavily rouged, with the result that sometimes the crests and the engravings had almost disappeared. An experienced footman could also do routine maintenance jobs on the plate, such as pressing out minor dents. For more major repairs they were responsible for sending it off to the silversmiths in London.

Some wealthy households also had gold to clean. At Blair Atholl in the 1930s Mrs de Wichfeld had 175 toilet bottles in her room, all with solid gold tops, plus a gold shoehorn, cigarette boxes, matchboxes, gold-handled hairbrushes and clothes brushes. When it came to be taken to the pantry to be cleaned it made two full butler's trays.[60]

One domestic job which was specific to footmen was tending to the lights. Back in the 1830s in Thomas's day, most country houses were lit by colza oil[61] lamps and cleaning these took up a fair proportion of time. It was a job to be done as early as possible before breakfast as dozens of oil lamps had to be collected from all parts of the house. Lamp care brought Thomas into trouble with other servants, being castigated as a 'very careless person' by Mrs Kirke, the Lilleshall housekeeper, for spilling oil from a lamp which he was carrying from a carriage to the house; and getting into a squabble with another footman over which of them needed a particular lamp. Footmen also had to put the lights out at night. At Trentham, when Thomas temporarily replaced the under-butler who was needed in London, he recorded that he 'got to bed very early not having to stay up to put the lights out now as usual because I am under-butler'.

TO CLEAN LAMPS

Lamps were often neglected, especially in households where servants changed jobs quickly, since everyone thought they would last their time

Lamps should be emptied of oil once a week. Pour in boiling water, with a little pearlash, and shake it well; if the gummy part will not come away with this, scrape it carefully off with a wooden or steel knife; then take the lamps to pieces as much as you can, and clean every part thoroughly, paying especial attention to air holes. Do not use sand. Dry with a cloth and stand near the fire.

When cleaning lamps with several burners make sure you put the parts back together correctly by tying little pieces of coloured string to the parts.

Cleaning the glass parts of lamps with a damp sponge dipped in whitening, rub with a soft cloth or leather, and finish with a clean linen cloth or a silk handkerchief.

(After Anon., *The Footman's Directory*, pp. 25–6)

TO CLEAN SILVER AND PLATE

Wash silver and plate in boiling water, except for any handles of knives. Boiling water will bring off any candle wax on sticks. Dry whilst still warm and apply whitening, a little at a time, using a damp piece of sponge; rub small articles in whitening between the finger and the thumb, then finish with a soft, thick leather. Be careful not to let articles touch each other. Be especially careful with plated goods – polish as little as possible.

(After Anon., *The Footman's Directory*, p. 29)

TO CLEAN JAPANNED GOODS

Japanned candlesticks need extra care. Never use boiling water which will crack the varnish. Use hot water for cleaning, dry and if they are smeary use a little flour and rub it clean off.

(After Anon., *The Footman's Directory*, p. 29)

Until electrification, most houses had a separate lamp-room near to the pantry, fitted with a table, shelves around the walls and a locked cupboard for the more valuable lamps.[62] Every morning, up to 100 oil lamps might be cleaned, refilled and the wicks trimmed, with a thorough overhaul once a week. In addition Thomas recorded in 1838 that sometime during each day he had to prepare chamber candlesticks ready to hand to each member of the family as they went upstairs to retire. In larger houses, the footman only serviced the lamps during the day, the work of cleaning and filling being done by a 'lampman'. During the nineteenth century a candle boy was employed at the Marquis of Bath's household at Longleat in Wiltshire; he had to service 140 candles used in the chapel, and 400 oil lamps which were used in the house. Each day, after morning chapel, the candle boy snuffed the candles out, broke off the runnels of wax on the sides and repointed the tops into shape so they looked like new; the candles were replaced when they had burned down to the last two inches. In cleaning the oil lamps, he was helped by the hall boy, the steward's room boy and the odd men, who groomed the lamps in batches of twenty at a time. The great chandeliers had to be serviced *in situ* from ladders. Footmen lit the lights in the reception rooms, the hall boy did the ones in the basement rooms and corridors.[63]

Fire was an ever-present hazard in the country house and lamp-rooms were a notable source of risk. William Lanceley's memoirs, published in 1925, contained a number of descriptions of fires:

It was a large country mansion [unnamed] and over sixty lamps were required to light it effectually, which means sharp work for the servants, who must not take the lamps in too early or leave the rooms in darkness. . . . On this occasion the fire broke out in the lamp-room. The footman had set light to all the lamps he required . . . and had used a wax taper for the purpose. He blew the taper out, as he thought, and put it down on the shelf. Either it was not quite out, or a draught caused it to flare up again; however, it had been put near some engine waste that was used to wipe the oil from the lamps and this took fire in its oily condition, and soon the whole room was ablaze. A bracket just above the shelf, on which the lamp filler containing about a quart of oil was placed, was set on fire, and this in turn fell to the floor and carried the engine waste now burning furiously with it. Fortunately this was colza oil, so no explosion took place, but the oily waste floating on the top of the running oil made a most choking smoke and smell. The outbreak was discovered by the scullerymaid. We had all been warned that in case of fire in the lamp-room we were not to throw water on it, sand only. The girl kept her presence of mind, called out 'Fire', and ran for the coconut matting at the back door. . . . The mat was wet and it filled up the doorway, stopping the running oil; she then rushed to her scullery nearby, snatched two dinner plates from the rack and plunged them into a sack of sand which was used to clean pewter and copper utensils and threw the sand into the flames. The other servants followed her example and the fire was soon under control, but the smoke was dense and sickening. The footman, returning for more lamps, was dumbfounded . . . tying a lamp cloth over his mouth and nose he plunged into the burning room and brought out a four-gallon can of paraffin oil and a four-gallon can of colza oil. Had the paraffin oil exploded, another of the stately homes of England would undoubtedly have been burned to the ground, as the nearest fire brigade was five miles away.[64]

In another instance a footman was castigated by Lanceley for acting 'like a madman': immediately after lighting the gasoliers and side brackets with a wax taper, and still holding the burning taper in his hand, he started to draw the heavy curtains. He set fire to the inner lace curtains which blazed up furiously. He tried to tear them down, but could not put the flames out. Since country houses were usually isolated, servants were often formed into their own fire brigade, equipped and trained with hoses, pumps and escape ladders. They would turn out for any local fire, not just in their own house. In the case of the burning curtains, the house fire brigade was called out; but unfortunately all the members rushed to their rooms to don their uniforms, as trained. The fire was put out by the quick-witted odd man who was not in the brigade.

VALETING

In the 1830s George Granville, the 2nd Duke of Sutherland, had his own personal valet, but other male members of the family did not; this, and the job of valeting for guests, fell to the footmen. Our diarist Thomas wrote very little about this side of his work, except by implication or the occasional comment: 'I did not go out as I had a few pairs of gloves that wanted cleaning so I set to and put them to rights.' Footmen had to be skilled in personal services such as brushing, cleaning and folding clothes, polishing boots, cutting hair and shaving. Thomas did not find this onerous: 'It comes very easy to me for I have scarcely anything to do but clean the Duke's things and my own.' It could also be rewarding; valeting for Sir Charles Barry at Trentham earned him a generous 5s tip.

The nineteenth-century footman/valet looked after his gentleman's dressing-room, kept it properly dusted, the slops emptied and the fire lit. Most clothes were stored folded in fitted cupboards or presses rather than in hanging wardrobes, with drawers for gaiters, stockings and linen; boots and shoes were hung on pegs. The room might be equipped with an iron for pressing suits (after a single wearing) and the shoelaces of dress shoes.[65] Most items had their own covers or bags made of holland[66] to keep the dust off and to make packing easier. Like the laundress, the footman had to master the art of folding clothes skilfully and quickly. In 1825 *The Footman's Directory* gave elaborate directions for folding so that 'the coats may be packed up into a narrow compass for travelling without rumpling or creasing'. Hats had their own boxes and shoes their linen bags. Toilet items made of china or glass needed to be packed in boxes with straw or hay, slightly dampened to stop the contents from slipping around. The trick here was to pack tightly.

As far as possible any cleaning of clothes was done overnight or first thing in the morning by the footman, as everything had to be well aired before being laid out ready for his employer. There was a right way of doing this: the waistcoat, coat and breeches or trousers were wrapped in a cloth, about a yard and a half of brown holland; this was spread out, the required clothes carefully placed in the middle of the cloth, the two sides folded over to cover them. They were then laid over a chair or the bed. The footman also sent linen to be laundered and kept a laundry account or 'washing book'.

After the gentleman had washed, shaved, dressed and left, the footman cleaned up, wiping the razor dry, washing hairbrushes and combs in warm soapy water, emptying, cleaning and drying the hand basin and chamber pot. The length of time taken could vary depending on the habits of the gentleman – many changed their clothes two or three times a day.

Service in a hunting household could be particularly strenuous for a footman/valet, requiring long hours at night cleaning, drying and pressing muddy clothes. In the late nineteenth century William Lanceley's second post as footman was with a baronet who hunted six days a week: 'This made it very hard for me, as I had hunting kit as well as footman's duty to do. The clock . . . struck twelve most nights before I left the brushing-room; but still I liked the place.'[67] Slightly later in time, Ernest King had a similar experience and a particular way of cleaning a muddied scarlet hunting coat: 'When in this state we would ask the housemaid to save us the contents of the chamber pots, at least a bucketful. It was truly miraculous in getting the dirt out. That was immediately followed . . . by brushing with clean water. . . .'[68]

Stanley Sewell, a footman in a large house in Surrey in the 1920s, remembered the problem of cleaning discoloured hunting coats and buckskin breeches:

> They were washed every time they come in, straight in the tub, it's wonderful material. The Colonel, he could have hunted seven days a week in a different coat. You can't dry them quick; fresh air, then finish them off in an airing cupboard, knock them into shape when they're very wet, button them . . . Buckskin . . . that's a job on its own. I should think it took me nearly twelve months before I could say I was good at it, very difficult job. Well, it's not getting your water too hot, keeping it quite soapy but not too soapy, because when they were wet they were slipping about in the saddle. French chalk when they were nearly dry and keep polishing them with your hand on a flat table, dry them steadily else they'd be like a drying chamois leather; it would be as hard as a brick.[69]

Before houses were plumbed in, it was the footman's or odd man's job to carry water up to the gentlemen's dressing-rooms for personal washing, though the housemaids did this for the ladies. From the 1910s Viola Bankes described this in the nursery at Kingston Lacy:

> For ordinary washing, a man-servant carried up a huge can of hot water for the large white jug and basin in our room. At bathtime, a zinc hip bath, high at the back, low at the front, would be put down on the cold linoleum in front of the bedroom fire. Alice or Winnie . . . armed with coal tar soap . . . would check that the water was just the right temperature and then pour it over us as we rubbed and scrubbed ourselves. When we were out of the bath and snuggly swathed in huge, soft, white towels which had been warming before the fire on the towel horse, a man-servant, tactfully averting his eyes, would take the bath away.[70]

The water then had to be emptied into slop pails and carried away to a drain.

Some aristocratic employers could be extremely eccentric and tiresome about their clothes. Eric Horne recalled one for whom he worked as a footman/valet:

> He had about sixty suits of clothes. On Sundays he would make me carry them all downstairs, and spread them out in a large bedroom on the ground floor . . . he would come and begin to try them all on, in front of a long glass, one suit after another, which took hours. When he had finished there was a wagonload

of clothes to brush, fold up, and take back to his dressing-room, and stack away in their different classes and places. This was the Sunday clothes inspection. . . . When he went out for a walk he would put on four or five overcoats. As his blood began to circulate, and he got warmer, he would take one off and throw it down, on the ground or anywhere, and so on further on, till he had only one left. I had to go out afterwards . . . and collect the coats.[71]

Ernest King remembered Charles Chichester, his first employer in service (the same gentleman who enjoyed entertaining the cabbies of Barnstaple), who was somewhat odd:

He only shaved when the spirit moved him or he was expecting guests. On the latter occasions he would go to the kitchens, put an old iron saucepan on the range and hurry to his dressing-room and begin to change from country clothes into a dark suit and a black satin tie. Then he would remember he had to get the water to shave and hasten back to the kitchen. Many's the time I saw him holding his trousers up with one hand and the saucepan in the other. He liked doing things for himself. . . .[72]

Another early morning job for the footman was cleaning boots. If they were very dirty, the boots were washed late at night, and hung on hooks to dry. Then between 6 and 8 o'clock in the morning they would be polished. Boots were usually made of 'blacking leather', that is unpolished, dull-looking calf leather which required a great deal of effort to get a good shine on. Ernest King despised proprietary polish and made up his own mixture from blacking (bought as a solid cake, wrapped in blue greaseproof paper) softened with vinegar. This was worked or 'boned' into the leather, preferably with a bone from the front leg of a deer. Unlike boots cleaned with spit and tinned paste, boots cleaned in this way did not lose their colour when warmed by the foot.[73] Ladies' shoes needed a different approach – cleaned and polished with milk, with a little blacking put onto the edge of the sole.

OTHER DUTIES

There seem to be endless other jobs on which the nineteenth-century footmen's manuals gave instruction: how to shut the house up securely, to pay tradesmen's bills, to answer the door or answer demands for money, to hold a cane correctly, to

CONTENTS OF THE FOOTMEN'S PANTRY AT SHUGBOROUGH IN 1773

A Range sett in Brickwork

A Handiron Shovel, Tongs & Poker

A Deal Table with a Drawer

4 Beech Chairs with Matt Seats

7 Mahogany Trays

1 Japan Cistern

A Mahogany Knife Tray

2 Plate Baskets lin'd with Tin

1 Knife Basket lin'd with Tin

1 Brass hand Candlestick

1 Copper Plate Warmer

(SRO, Anson MS, D615/E(H)10)

CONTENTS OF THE UPPER PANTRY AT SHUGBOROUGH IN 1841

Coloured Counterpane, 4 Blankets, Wool mattress, Hair mattress, Easy chair with cushions, 2 flat mahogany trays (to turn up with hinges), 2 Mahogany trays, 3 tray stands, Oval oak table, 2 rush seated chairs, Sword, 2 Pistols, and Blunderbuss, Hearth Rug, Fender, fire irons.

(SRO, Anson MS, D615/E(H)11 and 12, extract from inventory attached to writ)

walk in front of a sedan chair, to pay turnpike tolls and generally to become familiar with the geography of London.[74] An interesting problem for manual-writers was the necessity of learning to tell lies; a whole section was dedicated to the importance of honesty, abstemiousness and religion, and this was hardly in accord with a footman's duty to tell unwelcome guests that his master was not at home; this was usually rationalised away as being only a white lie, told in the best interests of his service to others.

The 1830s household of the Sutherlands was highly structured, but Thomas's diary shows he was expected to be flexible enough to lend a hand wherever he was needed. He resented being told that he had to valet for Sir Charles Barry at Trentham and did so only after being ordered by Mr Vantini, the house steward. On the other hand, bored at Westhill, he was happy to help out at Stafford House when circumstances required it:

When I got there I found that James [the porter] had been drunk and the housekeeper had sent him out of the house, so as soon as I got there I dress'd myself and saw the housekeeper and she said I must stay there till James came back, so I was porter all day. His wife came and said James was at home very poorly. . . . I slept in James's bed.

Portering involved a new set of responsibilities which included attending to the front door and the visitors who came through it and cleaning 'the door and about' early next morning.

A manual first published in 1894 itemised footmen's duties into a 'daily round'.[75] This came to a formidable list which in a large household was divided between two or more footmen and/or butlers. An extract explains the way jobs were to be shared out:

Where two or three footmen and a butler are kept, the head footman, although in livery, is termed the under-butler. He does not go out with the carriage; it is the duty of the second footman to do so; it is the under-butler's duty to remain in the front hall to answer the door to visitors during the afternoon. . . .

What is termed the lady's footman is usually the second footman where three are kept. In the division of work . . . the third footman performs such duties as bringing in the coals and wood, cleaning knives and boots, etc., and in the country pumping or drawing water . . . while the under-butler and second footman clean the plate, trim and clean the lamps.

The hierarchy of footmen was even more complicated than this in great households like the Duke of Portland's at Welbeck Abbey. Even at the beginning of the twentieth century this employed four 'royal' footmen (presumably to wait on senior members of the family), two steward's room footmen (to wait on the senior servants), and a schoolroom footman – as well as a valet, a wine butler, under-butler, groom of chambers, master of the servants' hall, two page boys, a hall porter, two hall boys, kitchen porters and six odd-job men.[76]

Of course in many smaller houses theoretical job demarcations did not operate and servants were expected to do all sorts of jobs. This was especially true in the early decades of the twentieth century when servants were scarce. When engaged as a 'footboy' in a general's house, Eric Horne remembered: 'After I had put away the breakfast things I had to go into the kitchen garden and dig up large tracts of rough ground with a spade till it was time to lay the lunch, when I had to put on the livery and prepare for afternoon visitors.' Of the afternoons, Horne wrote: 'Pray do not think I was resting. . . . It was a large, new house and the lady was constantly rearranging the furniture. I had to carry it up and down stairs, try it here, try it there, so that by the time I had to go to bed I was as tired as a dog. . . .'[77] This is reminiscent of Mrs de Wichfeld in the 1830s, who, if she caught a chauffeur idling about would immediately 'start them moving furniture to and fro to suit some new arrangement she had in mind'.[78] In one household where he worked as second footman Horne had to scrub a pound's worth of silver coins in case they carried germs.[79] Geoffrey Worley, employed as third footman at Quenby Hall, Leicestershire, in 1949, had to skin, joint and cook rabbits for the household dogs.[80]

Even in larger households, a footman's job could be infinitely varied; employers could afford to indulge their preferences to the point of eccentricity. In some houses the footman's jobs were so various that written lists were read out to a prospective footman at his interview.[81] Sometimes, however, there developed a very strong *esprit de corps* within a household, resulting in servants helping each other out. In the late nineteenth century Eric Horne worked in one country house belonging to an extremely bad-tempered member of the aristocracy who kept an indoor staff of twenty-five: 'There was a goodly company of us in the servants' hall at night, as the groom and the under-gardeners would come in, and wash up all the silver and glass in the pantries; more for company than anything else, for there was nowhere for them to go for miles, in the evenings. So that by the time we had finished waiting dinner, all the glass and silver would be washed and put away.'[82] Sometimes a footman's service was very personal. At one time William Lanceley was footman to an elderly viscountess, whom he used to carry up and downstairs and lift into bed when she fell.[83]

It was the custom in wealthier establishments to employ young trainee footmen as steward's room boys, footboys or hall boys. This was how fifteen-year-old Stanley Sewell began his career in 1924, starting his first job in domestic service in Lincolnshire. He had to wait on both the upper and the lower servants, each eating simultaneously in a different room; also carry all the sticks and coal to over thirty rooms, scrub the yards and stone passageways, clean windows and generally act as dogsbody.[84] William Lanceley, writing in 1925, recalled the start of his career as a footboy, before promotion to a full footman after two years. Like all junior servants his main job was to practise his trade on other servants. His duties, which started at 6 o'clock in the morning, were as follows:

First light the Servants' Hall fire, clean the young ladies' boots, the butler's, housekeeper's, cook's and ladies' maids', often twenty pairs altogether, trim the lamps (I had thirty-five to look after . . .) and all this had to be got through by 7.30; then lay the hall breakfast, get it in, and clear up afterwards. Tea was provided at breakfast for the women servants and beer for the men. I was not rated as a man, but was allowed tea with the women servants, and was duly railed at by the other men. . . . My day's work followed on with cleaning knives, housekeeper's room, windows, and mirrors; lay up the Servants' Hall dinner; get it in and out and wash up the things, except dishes and plates; help to carry up the luncheon; wash-up in the pantry; carry up the dinner to the dining-room and, when extra people dined, wait at table; lay up the Servants' Hall supper; clear it out and wash up. This brought bedtime after a day's work of sixteeen hours.[85]

He was allowed some leisure in the afternoons, usually taken as a couple of hours' fishing on the lake. Similarly Ernest King's first job as a hall boy was hard work: 'More often than not, from the moment I put my foot out of bed till I got back into it at night I was hard at it.'[86]

Towards the end of the nineteenth century the shortage of menservants became such that many country houses set on parlourmaids to take over many of the duties of footmen. Mary Hunter started work at Cragside in Northumberland in 1920, a fourteen-year-old under-parlourmaid on a salary of £18 per annum. She gradually took on responsibility for washing and polishing all the silver, setting tables and waiting on with the butler, keeping all the writing desks clean and fully equipped, and even valeting for the gentlemen guests, as well as carrying water into the house and taking early morning tea to the senior servants. She also 'maided' the guest bedrooms – work which previously would have fallen to the housemaids. To distinguish her from the housemaids Mary wore a purple afternoon frock rather than black. She stayed with the Armstrongs for seven years, a crucial period during which the staff at Cragside was reduced from twenty-four to three.[87]

CHAPTER 3

'Dancing till Supper Time': the Footman's Lifestyle

The diary of the Sutherlands' footman Thomas shows a good deal of concern for his appearance and there are many entries in his diary relating to clothing. His livery was provided, including his mourning livery after the death of the Duchess Countess in 1838, but he had to provide a fair amount of his own clothing. His shirts were made up by a 'sempstress' outside the house and during the period when he was on board wages at Westhill his linen was washed and starched at his own expense by Mrs Clarke, a washerwoman who sent a man round to collect it. Laundry was something of a worry to him since he discussed it with a visitor, sister-in-law to the Sutherlands' seamstress: 'she said that if I had anything to be washed she would be happy to oblige me'. On several occasions he bought items of clothing second-hand from other servants – a pair of boots, gloves and a jacket.

Thomas was not short of money. His annual wage in 1838 was around £24 and was paid by banker's draft, so he had to go to Drummond's Bank to cash it; two days later he put £8 into the savings bank. He was given several gratuities, including his share of a pound given to the footmen by the tailor who made their liveries, presumably to ensure that they put in a good word for him with their master. Over the next few months he could afford several spending sprees: he bought a pair of dancing pumps from Barratts, a stock and 'something to keep my sewing in' and later he got himself measured for a morning jacket, a waistcoat, a pair of trousers and two pairs of winter gloves. He also bought several books, newspapers and journals as well as presents, including a doll for his young sister. He could even afford to lend money to other servants.

Given the variety of tasks in which he was involved, a footman needed at least three sets of clothing: clothes for early morning 'dirty' jobs; a set of livery clothes for normal family waiting; and a set of livery for formal or 'state' occasions. In the grandest London households, where footmen might escort family to royal functions, they also needed a court livery. 'Livery' was a term originally used to denote an allowance to servants from the employing family for food, drink or clothing; in this context it related to a family uniform supplied by the household. On leaving a job, the footman was expected to return all livery provided by the family within the last six months, including the silver and gilt braiding and lace, which had become a fashionable decoration for footmen's uniforms after the 1760s. Some well-run houses gave their footman an inventory of silver trimmings, so as to avoid arguments.[1]

Before the 1850s, footman's livery took the form of breeches and long coat cut in the style of the eighteenth century. After the 1850s these were retained only for dress or court liveries, which could be dazzlingly colourful. The Cavendish livery at Chatsworth consisted of canary yellow coats, blue breeches and white silk stockings.[2] The footman's trademark was the silver-tipped shoulder knot, copied from the shoulder knot which fashionable gentlemen wore between 1670 and 1700, and which itself was a vestigial 'flask string' for a gunpowder flask.[3] Court livery could be very valuable and was often not entrusted to the care of the footmen, but issued before the special occasion which needed it; so in the early nineteenth century in the household of the Herberts at Wilton House, Wiltshire, every 3 June the butler handed out court livery, including hats and cockades, to be worn the following day, the King's birthday. The next day, the butler checked that all the livery was clean and put it back in store.[4] Even a century later, livery could be alarmingly elaborate: Frederick Gorst, a footman in the service of the Duke of Portland in the 1900s, required two steel cases (5 feet × 3 feet × 2 feet) in which to keep his full state and semi-state liveries, two leather portmanteaux for smaller liveries and personal clothing, and six hat boxes.[5] Light-coloured livery could quickly become grubby-looking. Ernest King recalled how in a Paris household in the 1920s the fawn and red footmen's livery was sent to be professionally cleaned every week, whereas in an English household it would have been unusual to send livery out to be cleaned even once a year.[6]

Both court and family livery was, of course, deliberately expensive to provide, part of its function as a marker of wealth and status. In 1863 a single bill for livery items bought by the 2nd Earl of Lichfield at Shugborough totalled £120 7s 10d.[7] As late as 1896, Charles Booth recorded that it was usual to provide one or two livery suits a year, plus court livery.[8] In many houses it was the custom to wait for a few weeks before getting a new footman measured for livery; this was in case he turned out not to be suitable or not likely to stay. According to Peter Russell, in some houses new male staff were taken to a room and shown a variety of second-hand livery suits, hoping that one would fit.[9]

Extract from a bill for livery for a groom, footman and under-butler, from George Smith to the 2nd Earl of Lichfield in 1863. The Anson livery colour seems to have been scarlet and drab (a dark fawn). (Staffordshire Record Office, D615/E(H)14)

One feature of footmen's lives was the practice of powdering their hair. Like livery, this was a throwback to the fashions of the eighteenth century, when they wore a 'bag wig' – a full wig with queue or tail, enclosed in a square black silk bag drawn in at the nape with a drawstring concealed by a stiff black bow.[10] Powdering for footmen lasted well into living memory. It was universally disliked by the footmen, who held it responsible for premature balding and for continual colds. Eric Horne wrote in 1923: 'I constantly had a cold in the head through having to repowder after going out with the carriage, one's head is seldom dry.'[11] The problem was that the hair had to be dampened before stiffening with soap and powder. Adeline Hartcup described the process of powdering:

> The footmen took off their jackets, hung them up, and covered their shoulders with towels. Then they ducked their heads in water, rubbed soap in their hair to make a lather, and combed it stiffly through. Powder puffs came into action as they took turns to dust each other's hair with either violet powder [a form of toilet powder] or (in some cases) ordinary flour. This dried to a firm paste and it was important that it should not be shaken off and seen on a livery jacket.[12]

According to John James, it was necessary to wash and oil the hair every evening 'to prevent its becoming almost fox colour' and this too caused head colds. In many households the powder itself was provided, though sometimes the footmen were given 'powder money' with which to buy it.[13]

Not only were menservants taxed, but the powder on their hair was taxed also, on a per capita basis.[14] In 1799, the powder tax for the Trentham household was paid at Newcastle-under-Lyme by the house steward.[15] In addition to the Marquess and Marchioness of Stafford, the tax return covered twelve menservants (steward, valet, butler, cook, four footmen, porter and under-butler, and coachmen) and three women (two housekeepers and a lady's maid).

By the 1850s everyday livery had moved on from breeches to a morning suit before midday and a dark, evening-dress suit after, worn with a white bow tie but with brass buttons on the coat. After the Second World War, the usual daytime livery consisted of white shirt, black tie, striped waistcoat and a coloured tailcoat, for which maroon or bottle green were favourite.[16] To save time and effort the ties were bought made up and were cheap enough at a few pence each; one lasted a week before being thrown away.[17]

Like the Sutherlands' footman Thomas, all footmen were expected to find their own personal linen. Some families expected the footmen to find their own 'dirty' clothes too: a pair of trousers, with a waistcoat and a jacket made in some form of washable linen or cotton such as jean or fustian.[18] When cleaning silver they wore a dark green baize apron, for really dirty jobs a leather apron and a white linen apron for appearing before a gentleman in the early morning or for clean jobs such as washing glasses. As soon as these morning jobs were finished, they would have breakfast and then dress in their usual family livery.

Nineteenth-century footmen's manuals stressed the importance of hygiene, clearly with an eye on the comfort of the employing gentleman as well as the footman.[19] They recommended, for example, that the footman changed and washed before serving dinner. He needed enough shirts to last a fortnight, two a week being the minimum. In 1825 *The Footman's Directory* advised: 'Be particular in having your linen well washed, as it often happens that servants' things are neglected. Never wear them too long, or make them too dirty, before you have them washed. Always have drawers instead of linings to your small clothes [knee-breeches], that you may have them washed. . . . ' That these could be impossible standards in practice is shown by Lanceley's description from around 1900 of one footman who had been out of work for a month before starting a new job:

By this time the poor chap was on his beam ends, and when he came to me he only possessed one decent suit of clothes, half-worn-out boots, one shirt and two collars. . . . I had to complain to him at the end of a week on account of his shirt front – it was getting very grubby. He did not reply, but promptly turned his shirt. . . . The other men noticed it and asked him why he did not open his mouth and handed him over shirts, collars ties, and underclothing. . . . When I heard of this I advanced him sufficient to buy the necessary linen, and he was soon as smart as the others.[20]

In the 1830s, the Sutherlands' footman Thomas did an enormous amount of walking both indoors and outdoors and this seems to have been a common feature of the employment. One servant reckoned that in one London house there were 'eighty stairs from top to bottom, sixteen stairs to answer the front door, thirty-two to the drawing-room with tea'; another footman recorded a distance of 18 miles walked indoors in a single day during the London season.[21] Not surprisingly, *The Footman's Directory* placed particular emphasis on the care of feet. The footman was advised to use at least four ordinary pairs of stockings a week, preferably one pair a day, which he might have to buy himself; but he should always expect silk stockings to be bought for him. Shoes were crucial: 'You will find it necessary to have several pairs of shoes, as you will want thick ones for the carriage and to walk about in, and light ones to wait at table in.' Again cleanliness was encouraged: 'Keep your feet clean, and often change your stockings, particularly in summer . . . for if you do not, they will be very disagreeable to persons about you . . . keep a towel for this purpose, and dip it into water, and rub a little soap on, and wipe them every day, or as often as you change your stockings, which must be at least once if not twice a day.'

Physical exercise was important, for no one wanted a fat footman. In the 1910s the Duchess of Portland presented each of her footmen with a bicycle and a set of golf clubs and employed a Japanese judo expert to give them lessons in a fully fitted gymnasium.[22] For many footmen walking and rowing were more traditional methods of keeping in shape. At Trentham in 1838 Thomas and another manservant used to take a rowing boat out on the lake every morning before work. Thomas must have been fairly fit, for on his journey home to Cheshire he had to run most of the way from Trentham to the station at Whitmore, some three or four miles, on a very hot day and carrying a heavy carpet bag. Every day's entry in his diary ended with a short summary of the weather and the state of the roads, particularly detailed in the London phase of his occupation because he spent so much time walking from Westhill to Stafford House and back.

ACCOMMODATION

In the 1830s Thomas slept in a dormitory with other menservants. We know this, for one day he recorded that a manservant had mistaken the time and wakened all the room in a panic. In the restricted space of a town house, however, footmen usually slept in the servants' hall and later this practice seems to have spread to the country house. By the early twentieth century, for example, autobiographical evidence tells us that dormitory or single-bedroom accommodation was unusual. According to Eric Horne, 'Footmen generally have to sleep in let-down beds in the servants' hall, which outside of being unhealthy, is not nice for the servants when they assemble for breakfast.'[23] Footmen were the last servants to retire at night (Thomas counted it early if he was in bed by 12.15 a.m.) and even if the footman had been out on carriage duty till the small hours, he still had to get up early in order to vacate his somewhat public bed.[24] Confined sleeping quarters were the chief complaint of footmen, recorded by Charles Booth in London in 1896, when it was usual for menservants to sleep in the basement, well away from the women in the attic:

'This arrangement, though always desirable, often necessitates two or even three men using the servants' hall as their bedroom, while another sleeps in the pantry, and another beneath the stairs.'[25] At this time, even in such grand establishments as the Duke of Portland's house in Grosvenor Square, the hall boys slept on cots in the servants' hall. The practice was recalled by an army major who started work as a hall boy in 1930:

My bed was in a cupboard in the servants' hall and could only be let down at night after the other servants had finished their evening meal and had decided they had finished with the room for the night. Heaven knows where I would

Footmen in the household of Lord Leconfield at Petworth in West Sussex, photographed in 1904–5. Alfred Lee, T. Reed and William Watts are shown in their dress livery of dark blue tailcoat with silver crested buttons and black plush breeches. (West Sussex County Council)

have laid my head if I had been ill. There were no inside sanitary arrangements below stairs and after the doors were locked and barred for the night, the hall boy was forced to use a chamber pot which was emptied by the junior housemaid every morning very early.[26]

Despite the decline in country house accommodation at the end of the nineteenth century, footmen's bedrooms were usually better in the country than in town. Back in the 1770s the footmen employed by the Ansons at Shugborough had slept in a garret with two beds, each fitted with green hangings, a feather mattress and bolster, three blankets and a coverlet; the room also had an oak table and two chairs. In 1826 Trentham had a footmen's bedroom which was well appointed and even had a lead sink, though it was not as comfortable as the bedroom of their senior, the groom of the chamber, which had an easy chair and fitted carpet. Later in the nineteenth century, footmen at the Duke of Portland's country seat at Welbeck Abbey had comfortable bedrooms with fires and shared a bathroom fitted with large mirrors to act as a 'powder room'. Similarly, in 1913, when Thomas Henry Noel-Hill, 8th Lord Berwick, had an inventory made of Attingham near Shrewsbury, both butler's and footman's bedroom were comfortably furnished, though conveniently sited next to the pantry.[27] In 1905 the footmen at Kelmarsh in Northamptonshire had a room each, albeit in a dark basement.[28]

Even in houses where proper dormitories or bedrooms were provided there was often a folding bed or mattress in the footmen's pantry for extra accommodation, either for the hall boy or for visitors. Sleeping away from home in basement rooms could present problems even for senior footmen, as when William Tayler went with 'his people' to Brighton in July 1837:

9th . . . Had a very bad night's rest last night. I slept downstairs in a little room but, when I came to lay down, I found the bed covered with bugs. I began to kill them, but they were so numerous that I found it impossible to kill all. Therefore I shook the bedding and layed it on the floor. There a great many of them found me, so that I could get but little rest.[29]

THE FOOTMAN'S SOCIAL LIFE

There was a definite etiquette of servant behaviour outside work and for details of this we have to depend largely on footmen's diaries. In 1838 the Sutherlands' footman Thomas took every opportunity to visit other grand houses whether in town or country, and was often shown around them. He was a regular visitor to a family called the Wilbrahams in London and even on his holiday he went to Delamere House near Chester to see the servants there; from his friendly reception it seems likely that this was where he worked before joining the Sutherland household. His holiday was spent in an endless round of polite visits to old friends and relatives, and the habit of social calling colours the whole diary. Since escorting his employers on their visiting was part of his job, it may well be a trait which he copied from them. It seems to have been common among other servants, too, at least when in London.[30] William Tayler's diary for 1837 shows the same pattern of daily excursions, either on his employers' business or on his own and often filling in the empty hours between lunch and tea. Even when many of the household were confined to bed with influenza and Tayler had extra work to do, he still made time to go for a walk, which turned out to be very lucrative, as he called on a tradesman who gave him 5s for a Christmas box. A few days later the influenza was so bad that only he and one other servant had escaped it. He complained at the confinement this caused: 'I am obliged to stay within to help the sick. This is what I don't like as I like to get a run every day when I can . . .'.[31]

The Sutherland servants were themselves the recipients of visits, showing off their own domestic splendours to friends and relatives. When the Trentham household was visited by Lord Harrowby's under-butler, Thomas showed him round the house and gardens, through the ale cellars and up the belvedere to see the view. He also took him rowing on the lake and organised an impromptu dance: 'We got the porter to come and play the violin for us and we went up into our bedroom and had a very comfortable dance, there was about 10 or 12 of us all couples, we kept it up till after one. . . . '

Inside Westhill, the Sutherlands' house in Wandsworth, there was a polite etiquette of visiting between departments; Thomas was asked to take tea in the stillroom, for example, and he himself invited the two kitchenmaids, the stillroom maids and the dairy maids to tea in his pantry. But such visits were part of a formal structure, firmly based on the work hierarchy, which also gave rise to the rather strange habit of servants calling each other by a surname based on the position held – so Thomas referred to Sarah Dairy, Betsy Housemaid, Mary Sempstress, Thomas Porter, and Thomas Postilion, a useful custom when so many servants had the same Christian name. The senior servants he called Mr Brown or Mrs Galleazie or occasionally Mrs Housekeeper; the family he occasionally referred to as 'our people'.

A HARD-HEARTED FOOTMAN

29 January, 1837

'The Lady's maid is taken very sick today; I supose she has been eating to much or something of the kind. But she is very subject to sickness. Last summer when we were coming home from Canterbury, she actually spewed all the way, a distance of sixty miles and not less time than eight hours. The people stared as we passed through the towns and villages as she couldent stop even then. It amused me very much to see how the country people stood stareing with their mouths half open and half shut to see her pumping over the side of the carriage and me sitting by, quite unconserned, gnawing a piece of cake or some sandwiches . . . as her sickness did not spoil my apatite. It was very bad for her but I couldent do her any good as it was the motion of the carriage that caused her illness. I gave her something to drink every time we changed horses but no sooner than it was down than it came up again, and so the road from Canterbury to London was pretty well perfumed with Brandy, Rum, Shrub, wine and stuff. She soon recovered after she got home and was all the better for it after.'

(William Tayler, from Burnett, *Useful Toil*, p. 180)

More personal initiatives between servants were frowned on in the Sutherland household. The Westhill housekeeper, Mrs Adams, stopped Thomas from paying regular visits to the young French nursemaid to practise his French, in case the Duchess came to hear of it, but later herself arranged for him to have regular sessions with the more mature Madame Rousseau, one of the Duchess's personal maids. This was seemingly a great success, for she took pains over his pronunciation and also used him to practise her English. The Westhill housekeeper's job was not enviable, managing a houseful of bored young men and women with time on their hands. The formalised structuring of work and leisure was clearly an attempt to draw the teeth of potential problems, but was not always successful, as we can see from the following account of a series of servant celebrations at Westhill over winter 1838.

Formal servant dances were held on special occasions such as Lord Stafford's birthday, 20 December: 'All the talk in the house [Westhill] is about the Ball that is to come of on Wednesday and there is great preparing for it.' Thomas helped to organise the lights, the decoration and the drink; two bottles of brandy and two of rum were given to him by the steward, but no wine allowed, so he made a collection, putting 5*s* in himself and collecting 1*s* each from the rest of the servants, making a total of £1 16s 0d, of which he gave 16s to the violin players and with the rest bought extra drink. The household provided two sittings of a supper in the servants' hall, accompanied by unlimited ale; the dancing carried on till early morning:

> Some of the maids went away about 3 but there was most of them that stayed till the finish which was about 7 or half past . . . we had tea in the servants' hall about 8 as a sort of finish. I did not go to bed . . . I got my work done and got on as well as I could, but I was very sleepy. William Thomson was here all day and he assisted me to wash up all the glasses etc . . . the day passed over very heavy.

Five days later, Thomas recorded Westhill's Christmas dinner:

> All the servants and labourers about the place dined in the servants' hall except those in the steward's room and them in the kitchen. We had a very good dinner of roast beef and plum pudding and all a mince pie apiece and as much ale as we could drink. [Later] the housemaids made tea, the laundrymaids not having pleased Mrs Adams on Lord Stafford's birthday.

After tea they played whist and cribbage till 1 o'clock, when the housekeeper told them all to go to bed. Some of the men stayed on, becoming so noisy and quarrelsome that Mrs Adams came down again. This evening seems to have been the start of a general falling out among the servants: 'The laundrymaids, the stillroom, Dairy and Betsy Housemaid were offended at the gardeners taking so much notice of the nursery maids and they all protested that they would not come in the hall on New Year's Eve. . . .'

On 27 December, Thomas went with the Westhill housemaids to Stafford House, staying there till 3 o'clock dancing to a violin. Back at Westhill, the New Year's Eve celebrations got off to a bad start. The hosts this time were the gardeners who collected £2 to spend on drink. The disaffected Betsy Housemaid and Sarah Dairy told the housekeeper about these arrangements but she said nothing before the party. Thomas again sorted the drinks out: 'I made some grog, gin and water, brandy and water and rum, sherry and port. I did not make a punch but made it in glasses and it went off very well.' The dancing went on till 4 o'clock and since someone else had got into his bed Thomas went into the servants' hall and 'had a downer on the form before the fire till after six when I went and changed my clothes for breakfasting.' Since there were five bottles of rum and gin left, he planned to have another party.

However, reports of the dancing so dismayed the housekeeper that she threatened the gardeners with dismissal if they came up to the servants' hall again – so Thomas had to return the remains of their drink money. In a later conversation, Mrs Adams made it plain that she knew of the disagreements among the staff: 'she was sorry that we were not more united together'. Thomas himself put it all down to the maids: 'It is all done out of spite . . . against the Nursery maids because the Gardeners took more notice of them than the rest.'

The music at parties and dances was provided by the servants themselves. Singing is often remembered as a feature of servant life, especially by women, who used it as a means of getting through hard physical work.[32] The Trentham porter played the violin and another servant could play the flute. One reason for Thomas's trip home on holiday was to collect his clarinet which he sometimes played at dances and for which he bought sheet music. He seems to have been the instigator of many of the parties: 'All the lasses at Westhill said they were very glad to see me return . . . they had not had one dance all the time I had been away.'

There is a similarity of experience in the diary of Thomas, written in 1838, and the retrospective autobiography of Eric Horne, relating to a working period shortly before 1923. Horne, too, recorded dances, card games and punting parties and Horne himself could play both the concertina and the violin. Other sources show that many servants were amateur musicians and servant dances seem to have played an important role within the household. In some old-established families, they became institutionalised and went a long way to create a good servant morale, so that servants were loathe to move on. Eric Horne recalled one unnamed country 'castle' owned by an unnamed earl:

. . . we were allowed a dance on the first Tuesday in every month. The mason, who worked on the estate, played the cello, his son played second fiddle, the tailor played first violin. I played sometimes as well . . . it had been an acknowledged institution as long as anyone could remember. The under-gardeners, the grooms, and the two whips from the kennels, and perhaps a friend or two would come in, so there was no lack of partners for the maids. . . . The tables were put on one side, which formed a band stand. Our programme consisted of lancers, quadrilles, waltzes, schottisches, polkas, Valse of Vienna, Polka Mazurka and country dances. . . . Sometimes someone would sing a song between the dances. The young servants soon learnt to dance, and could dance the lancers with the best of them. I used to play my violin after supper for them to practise. . . . Sometimes the younger sons of the Earl, when home from College, would come in, but not before knocking on the door and asking if they may.[33]

Servants' halls were large and served well as dance rooms. Some became well known for their musical entertainment. According to William Lanceley in 1925: 'The Duchess of Connaught, who was very fond of music, encouraged her servants in this respect and a piano for their use was installed in the servants' hall. It was much appreciated and in a very short time even the newcomers could play very well. A few took music lessons and these helped the others in their first attempts.' More generally, Lanceley approved of music:

There are always good singers to be found in large or small houses, and everyone knows that singing with music makes all the difference to a happy evening. . . . I have often gone to the servants' hall to listen to a good song, and have been surprised at the talent that was under our own roof; two of the women servants were especially good and a footman and a steward's-room boy had both belonged to the choirs of two West End churches.[34]

Some houses had a tradition of more formal dances. At one of William Lanceley's places of employment in Scotland a formal servants' and tenants' ball was given annually. The dancing was 'opened by Sir H. and Her Ladyship, Sir H. leading off with the housekeeper, and my Lady with the Butler . . .'; and the two of them would stay dancing till supper time. In the Duke of Portland's household at Welbeck Abbey early in the twentieth century, the annual Twelfth Night servants' ball was even more formal. Twelve hundred guests were invited including all the staff, tenants and tradesmen. The scene was remembered by Frederick Gorst:

The rooms were beautifully decorated just as though the Duke and Duchess were giving a ball for themselves. An orchestra from London was engaged and a swarm of fifty waiters arrived because none of us were required to perform any duties that evening – this was the social event of *our* season. . . .

It was quite a revelation to see all the members of the staff in ball dress. Even the prim head housemaid looked quite chic in a velvet gown, and the head housekeeper, who wore a low-cut blue satin gown, was almost unrecognizable. . . . I found that we had acquired a new kind of individuality and gaiety for the evening, and, stranger still, that we were all seeing each other from a new aspect – as people, not as servants.[35]

The footman Horace Roome and the 'odd man' relaxing at Shugborough in the 1920s. (Staffordshire Arts and Museum Service)

By the 1920s mass-produced music was making inroads into these traditions. Wind-up gramophones replaced pianos in servants' halls and ragtime and the Charleston took over from the country dances. But the tradition survived of impromptu dances with the maids and footmen, as well as the annual servants' balls held in the Albert Hall.[36]

Did servants manage to have private lives outside the communal living of the household? In the 1830s at Westhill, Thomas certainly did. He kept in touch with relatives, especially his brothers William and David and his father in Cheshire, writing letters which he was allowed to have franked for posting by the house. The replies seem to have travelled a circuitous route via his friends, the servants at Delamere House in Cheshire and the Wilbrahams in London. He confided to his diary that he did not write often enough. It is not clear whether his father was a small farmer in his own right or whether he worked for someone else, though his parents' house near Acton in Cheshire was crowded, for when he went home he slept in the same bed as his father. Despite his new-found sophistication, Thomas still enjoyed the rural skills he was brought up with; at Westhill, near Wandsworth, he went out rabbiting and tried his hand at ploughing and was pleased to find he had not lost his touch. His parents were obviously enormously proud of their boy and of how well he had done. At the end of his short holiday at home, his mother walked along the road with him to see him off at the station: 'My mother cried and seemed very sorry at my parting, she gave me good advice etc. I saw the train coming I then put Mother a sovereign in her hand she thanked me and said I was very good to them.'

Other biographies show that the practice of taking holidays while the family members themselves were away was commonplace. William Lanceley wrote retrospectively in the 1920s:

After four years' service I was offered a holiday as the family were paying a round of visits lasting six weeks and those servants who cared to take a holiday did so. Very few did in those days [1880s] and no servant would dream of asking for one unless the family were away from home. The butler and the housekeeper arranged the allotted time for each. My first holiday was three days, quite enough at that time. Our cottage homes and food were no comparison to what we had left behind.[37]

Footmen were notorious for womanising and Thomas was no exception. He was, after all, a highly eligible bachelor who got involved with complex relationships with women. He was a favourite with the stillroom maid at Westhill, a cause of some disagreement with another footman. At the beginning of the diary he had a close relationship with Martha, usually referred to as 'M', a servant in another house. When she was waiting for her salary he lent her money and when he went home on holiday, the servants at Delamere House pulled his leg about whether he had married her. Later on, this relationship became strained; by the summer of 1839 Thomas was reluctant to invite her to Westhill, 'for I am sure I don't want her here' – obviously because of his developing interest in the women servants there. On several occasions he took out two of the maids, Anne and Sarah, together or individually; they walked in the park or went to the theatre and to Wandsworth Fair, Thomas spending as much as 3s a time on them. At one time he was caught by the housekeeper 'having a lark' with Sarah and Anne on the staircase. His favourite seems to have been Anne, for whom he bought a watch, costing £5 15s; yet not long after this he took Sarah on a day trip to Chiswick, confiding to his diary: 'Anne finds herself very much offended because she was not asked, and a nice bit of fun she is made of. She has been crying about something.' Shortly after this he paid a return visit to the watchmaker, seemingly to return Anne's watch. He was still visiting his 'M', however, and once took her a bouquet of flowers, though he seemed increasingly reluctant. Soon 'M' insisted on visiting Westhill; she stayed for dinner in the servants' hall and was invited for tea in the laundry. Thomas wrote after this visit: 'I have not spent a very pleasant day, the first place I did not want her come down at all but I did not tell her so. I treated her as distant as I possibly could saying I treated her civilly.' The relationship seemed doomed, for at the end of the diary Thomas spent a pleasant evening out with Anne and some friends, at the end of which he and Anne went for a midnight stroll 'to hear the birds sing in the woods'.

Thomas was by no means the only footman to make such admissions to his diary. The mid-eighteenth-century journal of John Macdonald is so annoyingly full of his conquests as to be unreadable.[38] Two hundred years later the highly successful and urbane Ernest King admitted that in one household he had got himself involved with the second housemaid: 'The lady had become too possessive. She used to give me a kick under the table, enough to break my shin-bone, in the servants' hall if ever I said 'Good morning' to any of the other girls. It was when she took her holiday that I took the opportunity to give my notice. She was due to return one evening and I left at midday on the same day.'[39]

In many households not only were servants not allowed to have 'followers' from outside the house, but courting between servants was strictly forbidden. As late as 1910, one footman, Gerald Horne, used to meet secretly with his beautiful Nellie, the head kitchen-maid who became his wife:

We hadn't to be seen talking, so we used to leave notes under the lamp room mat; or we'd get up at four in the morning and slip out for a walk in the woods. . . . It was sometimes possible for us to meet secretly outside for a few minutes in the evening and neither of us will ever forget the time when Nellie, having as usual nipped out of the larder window, went to cross a five-foot plank which the builders had left to cover a trench. It had been a very wet day . . . Nellie (in pale blue) slipped in and I'd a devil of a tug o' war with the mud before it would let her go.[40]

Footmen were by no means uneducated by working-class standards. Even in the seventeenth century, they had to be able to read and write as they often made small purchases for the household out of their own money and so had to be able to make out bills to recoup their expenses.[41] Certainly in the 1830s Thomas was keen to be educated. He learnt French, and bought books and journals. He enjoyed inspecting the interesting technological features in the places he visited and there were many of these in Shropshire and Staffordshire at this time – the new steam engine installed at Lilleshall, the inclined plane 'where they wind the boats out of one canal into another', and the pump house at the new reservoir at Trentham. Invited into one of the lodges at Lilleshall for a meal of 'peas and cold mutton and gin and water', he was taken by a novel sort of grate with a 'fireplace in the middle and a boiler at one end and oven at the other so as the fire would keep both hot at one time. . . . ' Thomas's contemporary William Tayler was also full of curiosity about the world around him, as is shown by his account of a stay in Brighton in 1837, when his sleep was marred by the bedbugs: 'Been walking about seeing all I could . . . some large ships going past here in full sail going out to India. . . . Went to the pier. This is a kind of bridge projecting into the sea a quarter of a mile. It's a great curiosity as it's hung on chains. . . . '[42] As we have seen, Tayler felt confined when not able to go out each day. He summed up this feeling:

> December 30th. Have been very busy and at home all day. The life of a gentleman's servant is something like that of a bird shut up in a cage. The bird is well housed and well fed but is deprived of liberty, and liberty is the dearest and sweetest object of all Englishmen. Therefore I would rather be like the sparrow or lark, have less houseing [sic] and feeding and rather more liberty.

Footmen were reputed to be heavy drinkers. At the begining of his diary in June 1838 Thomas rather priggishly claimed that he drank nothing stronger than ale and not much of that. Later he recorded with relish the many occasions when he took whisky or brandy and he developed a habit of buying the odd glass of brandy for himself and friends when out in London. He was at the top of a slippery slope and there was no shortage of dire examples before him. His friend, James Porter at Stafford House, was consistently the worse for drink, or, as the household jargon had it, 'going for a jury', meaning he was absent with a hangover. Almost a hundred years later, William Lanceley thought that drink was still the 'chief ruin' of menservants, especially when beer and ale allowances were normal practice. This survived in some households well into the twentieth century.[43] Ernest King described an incident during the Second World War when his employer's wife suggested stopping the menservants' beer allowance as part of the war effort. He explained that if a footman had to drink cold water after a long day's work, serving all sorts of spirits to the gentlemen and working until two in the morning, it should not come as a surprise if they took to helping themselves to the gentlemen's drinks. The idea was hastily dropped.

The Chichesters' household in which Ernest King worked in the 1920s was in the charge of a butler who was very fond of drink:

Whenever Mr and Mrs Chichester went out for the day, the moment their carriage was out of hearing, down to the cellar the butler would go and ring the bell to summon all stablehands, gardeners and workmen. . . . And the beer would flow. . . . I know that both the butler and a footman died of drink. Many an insurance company then would refuse to insure a butler because of his ready access to drink.

A FAMILY VIEW OF A FOOTMAN'S DAY AT PILGRIMS' HALL

'The pantry staff's day started with my father's call at 6.30 and they would bring down any clothes needing attention. They opened up the heavy wooden internal shutters with which all the principal rooms were equipped, brought in our breakfast, had their own and then saw him off to the station at 8.30. Washing up and valeting work took till 11, when with the rest of the staff they adjourned to the servants' hall for bread and cheese. From then until they started luncheon preparations they cleaned silver, a task to which quite an extraordinary amount of time and skill was devoted . . . Everything that had been cleaned was washed in hot soapy water and put away in drawers and cupboards to exclude the air, which tarnished silver within a few days. There was a strict rotation for everyday things, and those only used for special occasions were put away in tissue paper or green baize bags. . . .

Peace descended on the pantry in the early afternoon, with only one of the men sitting by the fireplace in an armchair, only occasionally disturbed by the front-door bell or by my mother needing to be seen off somewhere in the car or carriage. Activity set in again for tea, the return of my father from the station at 6.30, dinner and the shutting up of the house for the night.'

(Lewis, *Private Life*, pp. 137–9)

This was a house where, contrary to usual custom, even the wine cellar was never locked. Charles Chichester was a mild-mannered, very generous gentleman whose nearest approach to a reprimand was to pin a notice in the cellar saying 'The same man who took a bottle of my very best port has now taken a bottle of my very best brandy.'

King also recalled an occasion in the more elaborate household of the de Wichfelds at Blair Castle, where two temporary footmen, described one evening as 'up to their eyebrows with whisky', got tired of washing up dessert plates, coffee cups and glasses and so tipped both trays and precious contents through the window to a 200 foot drop to the river below. Mrs de Wichfeld being a formidable housekeeper in her own right, the two footmen were quickly on the station at Blair Atholl, bound for London, while two replacements were already on their way north.[44]

According to Lanceley, the second most common road to ruin for menservants was betting, a great temptation to servants who were brought into contact with racing by their masters. He recalled one valet who was in the habit of placing bets of up to £5 a time:

> This man was soaked in racing, it was his life. He prided himself in remembering the winner of every big race for the past twenty years . . . but when I left the establishment where he had been all his life, and he was then 65 years of age, he had not sixty-five pounds saved up for old age, although he was a bachelor and had no poor relations to help as so many servants have. . . .[45]

Albert Thomas took time out of service to run various hotels and clubs. During one of these phases he began running accounts with three bookmakers on behalf of his club members, taking a commission on £30–40 turnover a week. It was a habit which remained with him when he went back into service.[46]

CONCLUSION

Returning to our stereotypical image of the footman, Lady Greville's article on the footman as a 'magnificent fellow' which was quoted at the beginning of chapter 2 was answered at the time by a riposte appearing in the magazine *The Nineteenth Century* in 1892, written by a butler named John Robinson.[47] He must have been an unnerving butler, for he was highly intelligent, well educated and literate. He accepted that many of Lady Greville's criticisms were justified, that by the time he was writing the average manservant had been demoralised into 'a very poor creature indeed', given to idleness, insobriety and dishonesty. But Robinson attributed this to the behaviour and attitudes of employers rather than servants. His argument went as follows: the living-in manservant is poorly supervised, set inappropriate examples by the employing classes, bored and under used, given no incentive to better himself. He is fed with inadequate, poorly cooked food and given unlimited access to alcohol. In many respects he is living a life of deprivation in the midst of plenty. A manservant's duties might appear light, but a conscientious servant has to be on the alert all day and every day, so there is no time for 'fruitful application'. Shunned and belittled by the outside world, if ever he makes a suggestion 'he at once evokes a more or less direct reminder of his position'. He is not trusted to keep accounts, so 'he argues that he is not trusted, therefore there can be no breach of confidence in taking all he can get'. Robinson concluded that 'If employers really wish for improvement among their servants, it lies for the most part with themselves to effect the change.' It should be recognised that there is nothing inherently degrading in manservice; but it must be seen as a respectable trade and given improved conditions of service; then higher expectations would be matched by higher levels of performance.

Writing four years later than Robinson, Charles Booth was also inclined to blame the employers, especially for their ignorance and carelessness about the conditions of their servants: 'In the large houses in which men are employed, it may be said that those masters are the exception who know more than the bare name of the men daily engaged in their service.' Even the reality of the name may have been in question. Tradition has it that footmen's names were changed to suit the position or the household. It is difficult to be sure how true this is, but certainly John James happily changed his name to William in one household where a member of the family was confusingly named John; and according to the memoirs of Albert Thomas all the third footmen where he worked were called John.[48]

If even the apologists of footmen were ready to admit the footmen's faults, does the picture which emerges from the first-hand accounts by footmen agree? As we have seen, the evidence is conflicting. To a contemporary visitor from abroad, English menservants seemed lazy.[49] To the modern reader one feature of the footman's life which seems universal was the amount of spare time he had – time which could be spent idly, playing shove ha'penny and watching the world go by in the street, or constructively, learning to speak French or exploring the wonders of the developing industrial world. Our two footmen of the 1830s seem to have been more constructive and inquisitive in this respect than their counterparts a few decades later. The general impression of plentiful spare time, however, may be misleading. Like all live-in servants, they were on call all day and all night; but their routine work took up mornings and evenings, extending often into the early hours of the following morning; they were less busy in the afternoons. In effect they had the problem of a split shift. Combine this with a job which required hours of waiting and it is no wonder that boredom and demoralisation set in.

The amount of spare time varied with circumstances. Thomas, left at Westhill with the nursery staff and young children, was hardly overworked. By his own admission he spent part of his days there 'sauntering about the house all morning' and 'at my own leisure as usual'. Some households were easy disciplinarians, some were strict. In the 1930s, Mrs de Wichfeld, though extraordinarily wealthy, expected a full day's work from her staff: 'If she saw a footman gossiping, even if he had just come off duty, she would tell him to find a cloth and polish some glass. . . . A footman had constantly to be on duty to open the front door the moment her car drove up or she'd become almost hysterical with rage.'[50]

Another feature is the range of work which footmen were expected to do. Their duties varied according to season, the size of the household and the numbers of servants kept; work for a footman who was one of four and had the assistance of a lamp-man was very different from that of a single-handed footman. The variability of footmen's work relates to the origins of the post, when they were part of the outdoor staff, involved with carriage and escort duties. As time went on the indoor duties grew, so that by 1660 at Woburn, the footmen belonged partly to the house and partly to the stables. This meant that they came under the authority of both the steward and the gentleman of the horse. In her study of Woburn, Gladys Scott Thomson described this as being 'a highly complicated arrangement which . . . led to considerable friction'.[51] It was only resolved by a rota system but it was never a very happy management structure.

Footmen were also in the unfortunate position of being 'voyeurs' of the life of luxury and extravagance led by their employers. More than any other servant, their duties required them to be privy to the more intimate side of their masters' behaviour – at dinner, in the drawing-room and even in the dressing-room. They above all were in a position to know that their masters had feet of clay. True deference needed to be earned and it is clear that many employers failed to do this. As an escort received into other great houses, the footman was both instrument and audience of a life of conspicuous luxury. It would be unreasonable to expect that he would not be affected by this in some way or wish to share to some extent in the lifestyle of his employers.

Footmen were certainly dressed in luxury, but in a particularly cruel way. The archaism of family and court livery marked them out for what they were in a most extravagant and effete fashion – servants 'dressed to kill'. They were never allowed to forget this fact and even Thomas, still proud of his achievements, resented going to church only to find that he had to sit in a special part of the congregation reserved for livery servants.

Eric Horne thought that appearance in livery could be very important for a footman, even as late as the 1900s:

> A servant must be absolutely perfect in form, disposition and action. He must have no sweaty, smelly skin, or feet. . . . There used to be an old titled lady in Eaton Place who was very prowd [sic] of her two tall matching footmen. When she was engaging them she would make them walk backwards and forwards across the room to see if she liked their action, just as though she was buying a horse.[52]

Lack of height was one of the things which Horne thought had held him back: 'Had I been three inches taller, a six-foot man, I could easily have got to the very top of the tree.' Ernest King said that before 1914 when there was no shortage of menservants, a footman was unemployable unless he were 5 feet 10 inches or 6 feet.[53] As Hecht has pointed out, the better the physique the greater the 'waste' in employing it to do unproductive work and therefore the greater the social status.[54] According to Charles Booth in the 1890s, the practice of paying footmen according to height was widespread. He gave a scale:

1st footman:	5 feet 6 inches– up to £30 per annum
	5 feet 10 inches – £32 to £40 per annum
2nd footman:	5 feet 6 inches – £20 to £22.
	5 feet 10 inches – £28 to £30[55]

The wage records of footmen show structures which could relate to this practice, rather than to the intricate hierarchy of age and experience used for other servants. The four footmen who worked for the London establishment of the Duke of Sutherland in the 1840s were all paid exactly the same amount – £25 4s a year – so perhaps they were matched in height; the steward's room boy, an apprentice footman, was paid half a full footman's salary – 12 guineas.[56]

TO BRUSH CLOTHES

In the brushing room you will need:

> A table long enough to spread the clothes out on;
> A solid wooden horse to put them on;
> A small cane to beat the dust out of them;
> Two brushes, one hard for great coats and one soft for fine soft coats which have a nap.

Make sure the coats are dry before brushing. Rub out the spots of dirt between your hands. Then spread the coat on the table, holding the collar with the left hand, the brush in the right. Brush the back of the collar first, then between the two shoulders, then the far lapel and arm, and then the skirt. Make sure you brush the cloth the way of the nap, towards the bottom. Do the other side, then the inside and last of all the collar. Use the brush lightly and quickly.

   You will find it necessary to beat coats thoroughly once a week, but this does wear them out and knocks the buttons.

(After Anon., *The Footman's Directory*, pp. 45–6)

As with other servants, board wages in lieu of food and drink allowances were paid to footmen when they were left in a household with the family away. These could readily accumulate and if paid regularly could effectively double the servants' remuneration. In 1865 footmen at Woburn were paid a salary of £28 plus 10s 6d a week board wages for those times when the family was absent.[57] Board wages had the further advantage of being reckoned on a weekly basis and paid in cash. They figured in the disputes about servants in the eighteenth century; not only were they expensive, they encouraged male servants to take their meals in local inns where they fell into bad company. In practice, though, footmen did not do as well as other servants out of board wages, because they often accompanied the family away from home.

   There were many other forms of remuneration in kind or cash which were available to domestic servants, but most important to the footmen was the practice of tipping.[58] Ernest King's tips when working for Mrs de Wichfeld in the 1930s (valeting for her husband and any guests who came without a valet) totalled £16 a week.[59] Autobiographies often mention tips left by visiting guests or tradesmen anxious to keep in with the household. In 1929, however, Dorothy Marshall found evidence to show that tipping had become a necessary part of a servant's income, the basic wage having become inadequate.[60]

In the 1830s a footman's remuneration seemed to provide Thomas with a good standard of living. As we have seen, he could afford to buy drink for his friends, or lend them cash, give money to his mother and go out to the theatre, as well as buying himself clothes from good quality outfitters. He was young and single, of course; the situation for an older footman with a wife and family to support was very different. The footman's wage structure offered little scope for progression, so the only way he could better his wages was to gain promotion to under-butler and eventually butler, or to move to a better-paid post in another house. In the long term, if promotion was not forthcoming, an ageing footman was lucky to be demoted to 'odd man'.[61] Thomas's contemporary, William Tayler reckoned: 'There is money to be made in service, but the person must be luckey enough to get in good places and begin service when very young. I was very much too old when I began service, therefore I shall never be worth a jot.'[62]

Writing almost a hundred years after Tayler, Eric Horne thought that, even as a relatively well-paid butler, manservice was not a bad life but neither was it especially rewarding:

> . . . If a man has a family and wife to keep, and house rent to pay, there is not much left out of a wage of seventy or eighty pounds a year, finding his own clothes. . . . Though I have never had to borrow a penny in my life, I cannot say I am much better off than when I began in gentlemen's service.[63]

This was perhaps not true of the other footmen recorded here, most of whom had working-class, sometimes impoverished, origins and many of whom ended up as stewards or butlers, at least one rung higher up the social ladder.

The footmen's autobiographies show they moved positions frequently. In this they were like the vast majority of servants who were notoriously mobile, always moving on in search of a better place. This became a particular problem late in the nineteenth century when fewer youngsters were coming into the trade, but it had been a feature of domestic service from at least the eighteenth century and probably long before that; between 1746 and 1779 the footman John Macdonald worked for twenty-seven masters.[64] Using a wages book, it is possible to chart the turnover of staff in the Sutherland household during the 1840s. Some menservants were relatively steady – there was not much movement in the posts of butler, lamp-man or upholsterer; but the positions of third footman and second steward's room boy had a faster turnover. These were both jobs at the bottom of the hierarchy, from which the ambitious manservant would try to move on as soon as possible.[65] The record shows some individuals rising within the same household but only to a very limited extent; only one out of ten second steward's room boys became first boy and only one of the four first boys became a footman.

This pattern was probably widespread among menservants. In 1896, Booth identified the promotion route as being from steward's boy to footman; from footman to valet or butler; and from butler to steward. Each step required a change of master, for 'a jumped-up man', a footman who was promoted in the same house, 'is eyed with little favour by the other servants'.[66] Most moves were made to better oneself, either in terms of money or to gain further experience. A footman at St Fagan's, Cardiff, recognized the need to change jobs regularly every year as did Ernest King: 'I do not think it took me very long to grasp the fact that a man-servant, to learn his business, must move from job to job, from place to place to widen his experience, to pick up all he can.'[67] Mobility among servants was also a form of safety valve. There was always a chance that for whatever reason a servant would become unhappy in a household and the ability to move on to another post without too much angst was highly desirable.

Money aside, Thomas's account records an active social life which is a curious parallel of aristocratic social niceties. We do not know whether the traditions of visiting, dancing and music were common to his home as well as his workplace, but he certainly had plenty of opportunity to indulge these within servant society and to learn to copy elements of his employers' lifestyles.[68] That this was by no means an isolated case is borne out by both William Lanceley and Eric Horne's later accounts.

Perhaps such emulation coloured employers' attitudes to liveried servants. On the one hand they went to great lengths to bedeck them in luxurious uniforms, to require them to look handsome and elegant and wait upon their every need; and on the other, they resented the fact that menservants might learn inappropriate gentlemanly habits such as wasting time and spending money on drink and clothes. Such extravagance, they believed, tended towards the destruction of class distinctions and attacked the very heart of the deference society. Simply for this reason, the whole area of the lives of footmen deserves close attention.

CHAPTER 4

'Unseen and Unheard': the Housemaid and her Work

Of all the servants in the country house, housemaids were perhaps the most important in seeing that the inhabitants lived comfortably as well as in a grand manner. Yet their work is difficult to reconstruct through the archive, because, unlike the kitchen or laundry staff, their workplace was the normal interior of the house. This, perhaps, is the reason why even in retrospect housemaids have achieved invisibility. As Lilian Bond wrote in 1956, modern depictions of the country house paint 'dream worlds' run entirely by kitchen and pantry staff: 'A pompous butler and attendant parlourmaid, with some assistance from the cook's department, between them do the work of non-existent housemaids.'[1]

We can represent the 'invisibility' of housemaids statistically. In 1864 Robert Kerr reckoned a house worth £40,000 or more would have a total floor space of some 41,800 sq ft or almost 200 rooms.[2] Of this, 17,000 sq ft (97 rooms) needed to be domestic offices. This 17,000 sq ft was divided thus:

Function	Sq Footage	%
Food and drink storage and preparation	5,254	31
Laundry and linen	1,804	11
Footmen	1,086	6
Housemaids	320	2
Servants' bedrooms, sitting-rooms, etc.	2,800	16
Administrative functions, fuel, corridors, wcs, etc.	5,736	33
Total	17,000	99

By this criterion, housemaid's figure very low indeed in importance; yet they were the largest single group within the domestic household. The larger country houses employed four or five housemaids, even sometimes as many as eight, structured into a hierarchical framework. Shugborough in 1828, for example, had five; the head maid was paid an annual salary of 13 guineas, the second and third were paid 10 guineas, the fourth 8 guineas and the fifth 5 guineas; all were entitled to the same board wages of 9s a week.[3] What is perhaps amazing is that a hundred years later at Shugborough the number of housemaids was exactly the same: Mrs Courtenay, housekeeper at Shugborough, began working there in the 1930s as a housemaid with four juniors under her. The house was in upheaval as it was having electricity put in and it was only after this that the numbers of housemaids started to decline.[4]

Equally intriguing is the invisibility of the housemaid in the long-distant past. Did she even exist? According to students of the great medieval households, these were run almost totally by men; women were employed as personal servants to women but both household chores and household management were the preserve of men. Even as late as the 1630s the Cecil household at Hatfield House employed ten full-time women but five times as many men.[5] In contrast, by 1840 the Sutherland household employed less than one male for every female servant.[6] So the gender balance of the great households changed radically over the centuries. Extraordinarily, we can catch a glimpse of earlier patterns of work distribution in the sometimes bizarrre rules and regulations which governed practice in nineteenth-century service.

Here, the central importance of housemaids within the nineteenth-century household is illustrated by describing the nature of their duties within day-to-day routines, and the degree to which their methods and materials contributed to the good order and long-term stability of the house contents.

A HOUSEMAID'S ROUTINE

The easiest way to get a picture of the housemaid's duties is through a daily timetable. The example given on the opposite page is a summary of a timetable given to Mrs Scoot, who went to work as an under-housemaid, aged fourteen, at Ackleton Manor, Bridgnorth, Shropshire, in 1926.[7] This was not a large servant household; it kept no footmen, for example. In a larger country house there would be less carrying of dishes and serving of food and less washing-up; to compensate, there would be more room cleaning. The general structure, however, was fairly

SUMMARY OF A HOUSEMAID'S TIMETABLE, 1926

1. 6.30 to 10.30 a.m. – set duties

6.30 a.m.   Draw back curtains and open windows in Day Nursery. Shake rug outside, clean grate, light fire, put out coal buckets. Wash floor, dust furniture and lay table for Nursery breakfast. Clean children's shoes. Repeat cleaning in Morning Room.

8.00 a.m.   Take up Nursery breakfast. Have own breakfast.

8.35 a.m.   Strip beds in Night Nursery and leave to air. Empty hot water bottles, fold night clothes and tidy room. Repeat in own room and front bedroom. Clear Nursery table and take down dishes. Help Nurse carry in Baby's bath. Make beds, empty slops and sweep floors in all bedrooms, while Parlourmaid dusts furniture. Brush top landing and stairs, dust furniture and doors etc., except every other Monday when wash landing and clean stairs.

10.15 a.m.   Wash Dining Room breakfast dishes and Nursery dishes.

2. 10.30 am to 12.15 – weekly routine

Monday: Get ready laundry. Turn out own bedroom or landing and stairs (alternate weeks).

Tuesday: Turn out Dining Room or front bedroom (alternately) .

Wednesday: Turn out Night Nursery, North Room and spare room.

Thursday: Turn out Day Nursery.

Friday: Turn out Drawing Room or Morning Room.

Saturday: Clean hall brasses. Turn out Servants' Hall, sweep cellar steps and outside lavatory.

Sunday: Change all bed linen. Give Cook a hand.

3. From 12.15: set routine

12.15 p.m.   Clean bathroom, lavatory. Lay table for Nursery lunch.

1.00 p.m.   Take up Nursery lunch and have own. Wash up in scullery. Lay Nursery tea.

2.30 p.m.   Push second pram, except Tuesdays and Sundays when free.

4.15 p.m.   Lay tea in Servants' Hall, clear away and wash up.

5.00 p.m   Bring down Nursery tea things, wash and take back.

6.00 p.m.   Sewing and mending for Mistress, except Fridays when own mending to be done.

7.30 p.m.   Lay table for supper in Servants' Hall.

7.45 p.m.   Help wait at table with Parlourmaid. During dinner go upstairs and turn down beds. Wash up in Pantry.

10.00 p.m.   Bed.

(Ackleton Manor, Bridgnorth)

standard – a set daily timetable until mid-morning, then a weekly rota of 'turning out' rooms until lunchtime, then a set timetable again.

It was standard practice to issue one of these timetables when engaging a new housemaid.[8] One can only sympathise with the anxious teenager presented with it. Lavinia Swainbank, born in Newcastle upon Tyne in 1906, worked in her second job as an under-housemaid of two:

> I had never before seen one of these and on first sight I could not see how one could possibly perform these duties in one day. This proved a splendid basic training, turning an ordinary human being into something resembling a well-oiled machine whose rhythm and motion ran smoothly like a clock. To this day I have not lost the clockwork precision instilled into me by a succession of head housemaids and timetables forty-eight years ago.[9]

A 6.30 a.m. start as advocated on p. 75 seems rather late by comparison with the memories of many housemaids. Two women working as housemaids at Shugborough between 1925 and 1928 recalled how the maids had to be waiting at the front of the main house at 6 o'clock sharp every morning, with themselves and their workboxes clean and neat. They had to pass the housekeeper's room on their way and she would check them as they passed; anyone who was a few minutes late was in trouble. One of the maids remembered that her first job each morning was to clean Shugborough's wide front steps; as she swept under the portico she occasionally stopped to watch hares racing across the front of the house in the early morning mist. In winter, of course, this early work was done in the dark, using a candle lamp kept in the box, deemed to be safer for maids than an oil lamp.[10]

The cleaning of grates and the downstairs floors had to be done before 8 o'clock when the family might be up and about. Coal fires in particular made a lot of work around the house. In smaller houses the housemaids carried all coals and cinders to and from the fires, but in most country houses the houseboy filled the scuttles outside and the footman carried them to the rooms; but housemaids had to clean and polish the fireplaces and light the fires first thing in the morning. House guests could mean as many as twenty fireplaces had to be cleaned; a maid at Thorpe Lubenham Hall in the 1930s started on the grates at 5 a.m. and had to be finished and all cleared away by the time she took a cup of tea to the housekeeper at 7 o'clock.[11] The head housemaid at Shugborough in 1926, later to become the housekeeper Mrs Courtenay, remembered the strict demarcation which was still in operation: the head housemaid did not clean grates; the second

An early photograph of the maidservants at Elford Rectory, near Tamworth in Staffordshire. The image comes from an album which contains several photographs of the family in the garden taken at the same time and dated 1860. It was obviously a special occasion and the maids were dressed in their best frocks, though the one on the right also wears a pinafore. (Staffordshire Arts and Museum Service)

housemaid cleaned fireplaces in the public drawing-rooms and the third did those in the dining- and sitting-rooms.[12]

There was, too, a set way of cleaning fireplaces. The first thing was to lay a cover in front of the hearth to protect the carpet. The second was to make sure all ashes were cleared away safely. Wood ashes were treacherous; even though they looked cold they could burn up again in a draught. More than one fire was caused by a housemaid putting ashes into her work box and forgetting them. For this reason, some houses which burnt logs left the ashes in the fireplace from one spring-clean to another.[13] The following description for cleaning a coal-fired grate or range which was to be leaded is based on an instructional book published in 1880:

Take out the ashes, if necessary sprinkling them with wet tea-leaves to stop them flying around. Pick out the larger cinders and sift the rest of the ashes . . . retaining all the cinders as a base for the new fire. If there is an oven attached, clean out the ashes from under this. Sweep the grate from the top with a hand brush and sweep the inside of the oven. Fill the boiler while grate is still cold.

Next mix some powdered black-lead[14] with enough cold water to make it as thick as batter; put it on the grate with a small round brush, beginning at the top and working downwards. Brush off the black-lead with another brush and then polish the grate vigorously with a dry brush. Three brushes are thus used.[15]

The bright steel fireplaces which are such elegant features of many country houses were a different matter. These were cleaned with an abrasive powder (bath brick or emery)[16] mixed with some sort of oil. A housemaid recalled how in the 1920s steel fire bars were rubbed with emery paper first, then with a burnisher, a small square of leather covered on one side with fine chain which burnished the steel until it looked like silver. Another way was to rub the steel vigorously with a large pebble.

After cleaning the fireplaces, the housemaid lit the fires using sticks brought in her box and then she cleaned the hearths. Marble hearths were washed with soap and water and dried with a linen cloth or cleaned with a frothy liquid made from bullocks' gall. Freestone hearths were scoured with soap, sand and cold water. Slate slabs were polished with hot mutton fat.

Next were the floors – wooden floors were dry-swept and dusted every day, taking care to turn the edges of the carpets over so as not to damage them. Carpets, common from the eighteenth century, were brushed on hands and knees at least twice a week, at other times just gone over quickly to pick up bits. To prevent dust from flying about all sorts of easily available materials were used – sand, rinsed-out tea leaves, damp salt, pepper, grass cuttings or shredded cabbage leaves, even dryish snow were scattered over the surface and swept up with the dust. After sweeping, the room would be left for at least fifteen minutes to settle before dusting was done, so rooms were always swept in pairs. Manuals might recommend covering furniture with a dust sheet or turning pictures to the wall while sweeping, but no such practice appears in servants' accounts – there simply was not time.[17]

From the eighteenth century onwards carpets were protected by druggets or strips in places where they would show wear and 'crumb cloths' were placed under tables. These were usually of green or drab baize or linen canvas. Other locations which took hard wear or were subject to spillages, such as entrance halls, passageways, closets and under the sideboards in dining areas, were covered with floorcloths made of painted and oiled canvas – the predecessor of linoleum.[18] In the 1920s housemaids were still cleaning huge carpets at Shugborough with a

TO CLEAN WALLPAPER HANGINGS

Blow all the dust off the paper with a pair of bellows. Cut a stale loaf into eight pieces. Beginning at the top of the wall, wipe lightly downwards with a piece of the bread, covering about half a yard with each stroke, until the upper part of room is cleaned all round. Then go round again cleaning the bottom. Do not rub the paper hard, and do not rub it across or horizontally.

(After Adams., *Complete Servant*, p. 100)

TO CLEAN A CARPET

1. If the carpet is very dirty generally, shake well, spread over it with a brush some grated raw potatoes. Brush clean and leave to dry.
2. Beat the carpet well, then stretch it out and cleanse it with a hard brush, dipped in soft water, in which bran has been boiled. Whilst wet, rub the carpet over with fuller's earth, laying it in the sun to dry, and repeating the process two or three times. Then beat the carpet until the fuller's earth is quite out; next rub it with a soft brush dipped in alum water, and lastly dry it in the shade, when the colours will appear bright and new.

MRS WHATMAN PREFERRED TO TURN CARPETS RATHER THAN BEATING THEM

'I think she had better have the carpets in the Library and the Eating Parlour turned on the wrong side. It gets out the dust much better than beating them, and let them remain so after we come back a little while.'

(Hardyment, *Susanna Whatman*, p. 56)

TO CLEAN FLOORCLOTHS

Sweep and wipe with a damp flannel. Then wet them all over with milk and rub with a dry cloth until they are bright. This will not make them slippery.

Turning them upside down once a week stops them from curling up at the edges.

If you make your own floorcloths, choose a fine-textured cloth or use an old carpet upside down. Make sure the layers of paint are dried thoroughly before the next coat.

(After Adams., *Complete Servant*, p. 100)

hand brush and dustpan, but the wooden surrounds were polished with beeswax and a 'donkey' or 'jumbo' – a solid stone block with a thick felt pad underneath and a long handle to push and pull it. A version for stone floors was made of a heavy wooden block with four scrubbing brushes attached.

The dressing-room to bedroom No. 3, at Castle Ward in County Down, complete with hip bath in front of the fire, dressing table and weighing machine. (John Bethell, National Trust, 1979)

According to Mrs Courtenay, the experienced housekeeper could tell whether a floor had been swept properly; the dust was collected at specified points – near the door and in front of the fireplace – and she knew how big the piles of dust should be. Each pile of dust was to be checked over by the housemaid in case she had swept up something of value. The housemaids cleaned all the floors at Shugborough, except the saloon when it was cleaned and chalked for dances by the footmen.

When the dust had settled from floor cleaning, furniture and fittings would be dusted and rubbed, either by the housemaid or the footman; if the latter, he needed to time his work to suit the housemaid. 'Rubbing' furniture was strongly advocated – this meant rubbing vigorously with a silk cloth or a chamois leather; polish was applied only a few times a year. Housemaids always dusted with two cloths, one in each hand, in some cases one slightly damp.[19]

At 8 o'clock the housemaids took off their 'dirty' aprons, made of hurden,[20] or a heavy grey drill-like cotton, and went to call the family. At Shugborough in the 1920s and '30s his Lordship and her Ladyship were called with a tea tray by the head housemaid; the second maid called the other married family members or visitors and the third called the single ladies; bachelors were called by a footmen. Each tray carried a cup of tea and a biscuit or some thin bread and butter. The timetable at this point was very tight and the housekeeper Mrs Courtenay remembered the hurry: 'It was a rush around, everybody was running, you didn't have time to live.' Each bedroom had a specific 'calling china' which matched its decor. The housekeeper laid it all out according to who was staying in which room and each girl would know exactly which tray was hers. So what at first sight seems an extravagance was in practice a useful system of colour-coding, essential if there were twenty or thirty bedrooms. To make sure, some houses had a list of bedrooms mounted outside the housekeeper's door; each room had a slot by its

An updated dressing-room at Lanhydrock House, Cornwall, incorporating a plumbed-in bath, a washstand and weighing machine. The toilet service includes several water jugs and the obsolete hot-water cans stand decoratively in the hearth. From the 1850s or '60s even the most outdated country house had at least one huge cast-iron or slate bath, but plumbing was often inefficient, as recalled by Lord Ernest Hamilton: 'A call on the hot-water supply . . . did not meet with an effusive or even a warm response. A succession of sepulchral rumblings was succeeded by the appearance of a small geyser of rust-coloured water, heavily charged with dead earwigs and bluebottles. This continued for a couple of minutes or so and then entirely ceased.' Lanhydrock's bath looks much more successful. (From Girouard, Country House Companion, *p. 173) (John Bethell, National Trust, 1973)*

name in which was written the name of its occupants. This ensured that considerations of status were respected and embarrassment avoided.

Bedrooms were to be tidied while the family were at breakfast, which usually started at 9 o'clock. Here again there was a set routine: the window was opened, the bedcovers thrown back over two chairs placed at the foot of the bed, and the washstand 'slopped'. This last was a complicated routine because of the intricacy of its equipment. The Victorian washstand in a country house was furnished, according to Hippolyte Taine, with 'one large jug, a small one, a medium one for hot water, two porcelain basins, a dish for toothbrushes, two soap dishes, a water bottle with its tumbler, a finger glass with its glass'.[21] Underneath on the shelf would be a sponge in its dish and a footbath. The chamber pot would be under the bed. Three sets of water were provided on the stand. The cold water for washing was preferably soft, kept in the large jug or ewer; hot water was brought by the housemaid first thing in the morning when she brought the calling tray; drinking or mouthwash water was also provided – this was spring water and kept in white ceramic bottles.

Contrary to cartoons showing servants walking downstairs with chamber pots in their hands, the nineteenth-century convention was that when cleaning the washstand no basin or chamber pot was to be taken out of the room. The maid took two buckets into the room, one pail filled with clean water, and a porcelain slop bucket, empty but clean; she also needed a bottle of drinking water. The chamber pot was emptied into the slop bucket and thoroughly rinsed out with whatever clean water remained on the washstand, either in the water bottles or ewer; the wash basin was emptied and rinsed similarly. All the rinsing water went into the slop bucket and everything was rubbed bright with a cloth, taking care to use the right cloth of three – for the mouth glass, the basin and the chamber pot. The ewer was refilled with clean water from the pail and the water bottles also refilled. Twice a week the chamber pots were to be taken out of the room to the housemaid's closet and scalded; the slop buckets were to be scalded every day. In the eighteenth century, 'chamber chairs' were preferred to chamber pots, but presumably the pans from these were cleaned in the same way.[22] In the 1920s during Mrs Courtenay's time at Shugborough the routine of 'slopping' the washing water in the bedrooms had to be done before and after every meal – breakfast, lunch, afternoon tea at 3 o'clock, dinner and bedtime. By this time flush toilets were in use so the slop water was put down these.

Next, the bedroom fireplaces were cleaned and polished, ashes removed and the fire laid or lit. All the bed hangings were lifted onto the bed so the maid could sweep the floor, including under the bed, occasionally mopping it with a damp mop. The maid then had to wash her hands, change her apron to a clean one and with the help of another maid, make the bed, shaking and beating the feathers in the mattress and pillows. She then dusted the rest of the furniture. Clothes were folded neatly and left out, and towels changed.

All this was done to a tight schedule. While the senior maids were cleaning the family bedrooms the two juniors made the servants' beds and swept and dusted their rooms – a considerable chore when one realises that even a middling-sized country house like Kelmarsh in Northamptonshire contained a minimum of ten servant bedrooms. Another of the junior's jobs was to wash all the equipment used during the day – dusters, brushes and chamois leathers – and clean water cans.

After bedrooms came the cleaning of interminable passages, staircases and landings; where floorcloths were laid they were wiped over with a damp cloth. After this routine daily clean, the housemaids would then move on to the weekly rota – the rooms which were due for their general weekly 'turn out'. This would mean a more thorough cleaning than could be done during the quick daily tidy up; furniture would be moved and drapes 'whisked' with soft brushes; in the eighteenth century, when wooden floors were not polished, boards were scoured. Picture frames were dusted, brushed or had the dust removed with a pair of bellows or cotton wool. This 'turning out' took up the time until servants' dinner at 1 o'clock. It might be slotted in evenly throughout the week but many houses had special days when extra time was given to it – traditionally Tuesdays and Saturdays.

After 2 o'clock some houses allowed their housemaids a period of rest to be taken in their rooms; more usually they spent the afternoons mending in the housemaids' room, or in the case of Mrs Scoot, the under-housemaid from Bridgnorth, walking the pram. After servants' tea at 4 o'clock, the maids worked on in the housemaids' room. In the days when households made up most of their linen requirements from home-made or bought lengths, housemaids patiently seamed sheets and pillowcases, decorated huckaback towels and carefully hemmed cleaning cloths. Mending was ever present, sometimes so much that some housemaids sent it home for their mothers to help out. Neither was their work limited to linen; one housemaid remembered: 'We did all sorts of jobs, repairing lampshades if they were going, mending the chairs with cane.'[23]

Everything had to be timed to perfection. As the family moved out of one room during the day, so a team of housemaids would move in to tidy it. When the bell for dressing for family dinner sounded, the maids waited a few minutes before going into the reception rooms to tidy up, check the fires and the blinds, plump the cushions, remove any dead petals, then return to the sewing until they were sure the family had gone into dinner. A housemaid working in a large house near Peterborough in the 1930s recalled:

> We each had our allotted tasks. In this house with three housemaids, Annie, the head, would straighten the newspapers and magazines . . . Florence, the second housemaid, shook up the cushions and emptied the ashtrays. I, being third, swept the ashes into a pile under the grate, and folded the towels and cleaned the washbasin in the cloakroom.[24]

Housemaids waiting to have their warming pans filled with cinders. Undated pencil and wash drawing attributed to George Dance, part of a series illustrating the seasons. (Fitzwilliam Museum, University of Cambridge)

During family dinner bedrooms had to be tidied, slops emptied, new water put out, beds turned back, counterpanes taken off and the lady's dressing gown laid on a chair and over that her nightgown. Her day wear was picked up, folded and laid on another chair and covered with a silk, cotton or embroidered cover, ready for attention from the lady's maid. Finally at 10 o'clock they warmed the beds. Before the days of stone bottles, this was done with brass or copper warming pans, which were filled with a scatter of embers from the kitchen fire; a sprinkling of salt was used to prevent them smelling.

House guests made extra work for the housemaids. Those female guests who did not bring their own lady's maid with them had to be 'maided' by the housemaid, according to a strict rule of precedence: the head housemaid maided the married ladies and the second maid attended the single ladies. This meant more routine work was passed down to the junior maids. According to a housemaid who worked at both Eaton Place and Kensington Palace, 'maiding' involved unpacking all their luggage on arrival and repacking when they left; calling them in the mornings and taking them hot water for washing and if necessary preparing their baths, even sometimes putting toothpaste on the toothbrush and laying out their day clothes on a chair. The same routine was gone through before dinner, the evening clothes laid out neatly and folded into a soft calico cover.[25] In recompense for such labours, it was usual for the guest to leave a tip for her housemaid, discreetly tucked under the pillow.[26]

In households like Trentham, guests were coming and going all the time, making a good deal of extra work, such as airing beds. In the 1920s at Pilgrims' Hall:

> unexpected guests were not approved of . . . probably because mattresses really did need airing. . . . The room would therefore be opened up at least two days before, a fire lit in winter and two or three stone hot-water bottles put amongst the mattresses and blankets. Beds were never left made up so sheets and pillow-cases came ready-aired from the linen cupboard . . .[27]

A bed needed airing if it had been out of use for a week or more. For this reason the simplest expedient for airing was for the housemaids to sleep in unused beds periodically. This was the system advocated by a little undated handbook published for the education of maidservants sometime in the mid-nineteenth century, which recommended 'sleeping in them once a week, which is the place of the housemaid'.[28] Other manuals disapproved of this tradition, as it was hard on the housemaid 'to make a warming pan of her' and gave 'opportunities for great impropriety of conduct' – a housemaid should keep to her own bed where the housekeeper knew where she was.[29]

Like footmen, housemaids were sometimes responsible for serious accidents, in the following case recalled by William Lanceley from the 1920s, the result of airing mattresses for a house party:

> Several mattresses were placed in a circle around the fire-place, and the housemaid had piled up the coals and carelessly forgotten to hook on the fireguard, leaving it leaning against the bars of the grate. A large piece of burning coal fell off the fire and, lodging on the hook of the guard, caused it to fall backwards. The weight of the coal overbalanced the guard, which in turn fell over the fender into the mattress, setting it alight, and it was a long time before it was discovered. The house-carpenter was sent to a bedroom in this part of the house to repair a looking-glass, and when passing this room he noticed a smell of burning and on opening the door, found the room was a mass of flames.[30]

The fire was put out by pouring water from the bedroom jugs and by bringing up a hose, but not before a large part of the floor had been burnt through and most of the furniture destroyed.

Another of the housemaids' duties was keeping the beds free from infestations of various sorts. Bedbugs were common when the linen change was less than rigorous, and in some situations they could be difficult to eradicate, especially when the bedsteads were old and wooden and topped by the usual layers of mattresses – first a straw palliasse, then a wool or hair mattress, then a feather bed. Manuals exhorted housemaids to dismantle the bed as soon as bugs were discovered, give the bed frame a good scrub and pour boiling water into the joints. There were many recipes available; in 1830 *The Servant's Guide* recommended brushing the bedstead with 'petroleum oil', the smell of which would drive the bugs away – though thankfully it did warn the servant not to do this by candlelight. Even the best-kept houses could have problems of infestation. Nesta, a laundrymaid at Shugborough in the 1920s, recalled an occasion when, returning to her bedroom late at night, she put the light on to find the floor covered in a dark moving mass of cockroaches. From then on she had the carpeting replaced by linoleum and always slept with the feet of her bed in jam jars filled with water.

The main bedchamber floor usually had a housemaids' closet built near to the service stairs. Here all equipment was kept on shelves and pin rails. In the

BEDBUGS

Cimex lectularius is a blood-sucking insect which plagued the domestic house for centuries. They were well established in England by the sixteenth century and widespread by 1730. An obvious hazard for overnight travellers, everyone came into contact with them even if one's own house was free. Normally flat and able to live in the tiniest of cracks in bedroom furniture or panelling, when fed with blood they swelled. They loved to lay eggs in wallpaper paste.

Bedbugs were canny creatures. They would allow you time to go to sleep before attacking, but once started nothing distracted them, not even a strong light. They did not usually go under the bedclothes but attacked the area around the head, face and neck. Their bite was painless so you might not be aware of their presence until next morning when a large red, painful, swollen area appeared on your skin, rather like a severe case of nettlerash. Sometimes this would develop like boils.

Inns were notorious, of course. The experienced traveller refused a bed and, like Lord Herbert, preferred to take 'two Tables, very greasy and dirty, put a clean sheet over them and upon this hard bed, I had a very comfortable sleep'. The bedbug was no respecter of persons. It could be imported into even the most aristocratic house in second-hand furniture or with servants. Many of the splendid new houses built in the London squares – Hanover and Grosvenor – were infested with bedbugs even before they were first occupied. They loved elaborately carved four-poster bedheads and the feather and wool contents of mattresses, which could be crawling with them even when new.

Thomas Carlyle's wife Jane Welsh Carlyle recorded in her journals many encounters with bedbugs, especially in her Chelsea house: 'I flung some twenty pailfuls of water on the kitchen floor . . . to drown any that might attempt to save themselves; then we killed all that were discoverable, and flung the pieces of the bed . . . into a tub full of water, carried them up into the garden, and let them steep there for two days; and then I painted all the joints, had the curtains washed . . . and hope and trust there is not one escaped alive to tell the tale. *Ach Gott*, what disgusting work to have to do!'

Contemporary writers advised all sorts of precautions or remedies – insisting on close examination of all trunks and boxes brought into the house by friends and servants, washing or cooking the contents of mattresses three or four times a year, setting wicker bug traps under the bed, anointing the bed with infusions of various herbs or with mercury mixed with egg white, or fumigation with sulphur or arsenic. Or you could employ a professional bug-catcher such as Mr Tiffin, who advertised himself in 1814 as 'bug-destroyer to Her Majesty' and claimed 'I have noblemen's names, the first in England, on my books'.

✳ ✳ ✳

According to newspaper reports in September 1998, a new resistant strain of bedbugs is on the march.

(After L.O.J. Boynton, 'Bedbugs', *Furniture History Society*, vol. 1, 1965, pp. 15–31) nineteenth century many households had a sluice or slop sink connected to a foul drain, but before these were fitted inside houses the drain could be as far away as the basement or even an outhouse. At Pradoe in Shropshire, a stone-built outhouse still has a perforated drain leading into the compost heap, and, through a hole in the wall, a large sloping sheet of iron bars over a pit, used for separating cinders from ashes. Most houses also had at least one larger housemaids' closet in the basement or on the garret landing near their rooms, where brushes and boxes could be stored.

Pails were supposed to be scalded after use and periodically scoured with sand, or salt and turpentine. They needed to be plentiful, so that each could be kept for a particular purpose; slop pails were white and distinctive. Similarly cloths should be used only for one job; this was especially important when cleaning steps with whiting as this would cause smearing if later used for washing floors. Cloths for dusting furniture were soft and carefully hemmed so as not to catch in bits of ormolu.

The heating of water caused a lot of problems in the country house. Back boilers could be installed behind kitchen grates even in the eighteenth century, filled by ladle and supplying hot water through a tap at the side of the grate. Later smaller ranges were fitted with a boiler at the side, but these were mainly for kitchen use. Even when larger independent boilers were fitted from the 1850s

Left: Slop pail made of plain white earthenware with a perforated lid and a wicker handle. About 10 inches high, they were also supplied to match decorated 'toilet services'. Right: Hot-water can, carried to the bedrooms by housemaids and footmen. Cans were supplied either in brass for the best bedrooms, or painted in red or, peculiarly, in a brown wood-effect finish. These painted ones gave off a very evocative smell when filled with hot water. (P. Sambrook)

onwards, the supply was by no means adequate. As late as the 1920s William Lanceley complained: 'I have known as many as forty baths required twice daily at the same hour and they do not take into account that for every can of hot water drawn off another can of cold water has to be heated in its place. The old-fashioned cast-iron bath with painted surface is in most cases too large and is a great waste of water.'[31] Lanceley calculated that each bath used between 15 and 45 gallons and as even a modest-sized country house would have eleven baths, the consumption of both water and fuel was very great.

Before the days of piped washbasins in dressing-rooms, footmen and housemaids carried hot water for washing in brass or painted cans with lids and spouts, covered with a towel to keep them warm. Some houses had special 'watermen', as recalled from 1905 at Belvoir Castle, Leicestershire, by Lady Diana Cooper:

They were the biggest people I have ever seen. . . . They had stubbly beards . . . wore brown clothes, no collars, and thick green baize aprons from chin to knee. On their shoulders they carried a wooden yoke from which hung two gigantic cans of water. They moved on a perpetual round. . . . They seemed of another element and never spoke but one word, 'Water-man', to account for themselves.[32]

Some jobs housemaids were not allowed to do. Usually they did not clean chandeliers and windows or wind the clocks, as these were the work of footmen, butler or clockman, or clean the lady's dressing table as this was done by the lady's maid. In the reception rooms, most housemaids were forbidden to touch the writing desk which was dusted by the butler. Millie Milgate, the housemaid from Eaton Place in London, mused: 'We would clean the whole of the room except one item . . . odd isn't it? They had all these unwritten rules.'[33]

Restrictions on cleaning go back to at least the eighteenth century. In the 1770s Susanna Whatman instructed her housemaids at Turkey Court in Kent 'never to dust pictures, nor the frames of anything that has a gilt edge'.[34] She was similarly specific about any paintwork on ledges, window frames or furniture – these were to be brushed with a painter's brush and then a duster. Susanna Whatman understood the running of her house better than her servants, which was not necessarily the case in nineteenth-century households, which relied more on the professionalism of servants. Mrs Whatman laid down detailed orders for each room – at what time the blinds should be lowered to protect the furniture from strong sun, how the carpet should be cleaned and the furniture rubbed; the cut-glass candlesticks she cleaned herself. Tending towards obsession, she foresaw all sorts of disasters in her absence, such as the laundrymaid helping the housemaid and damaging the furniture because she was 'not used to the care of it'. She understood that care was in the minutiae of routine: 'One of the most useful common directions next to carrying a candle upright is that of putting away chairs, tables and anything that goes next to a wall, with a hand behind it. For want of this trifling attention, great pieces are frequently knocked out of the stucco, and the backs of chairs . . . leave a mark on the wall.'

Susanna Whatman was a strict taskmaster who worked her housemaid hard and set down very clear rules. When cleaning fireplaces 'The Housemaid should never fail sweeping down the sutt every morning as high as she can reach' and in winter 'Always to turn up the carpet round the fire and sweep under it every day. . . . ' Her housemaid seems to have had little time to herself. Her evenings were spent ironing her own clothes and mending towels and 'her Master's common stockings'. She was not expected to mend bed linen, though she could if she wanted to. When she had finished her own housework she had to help the laundrymaid fold linen and keep the linen cupboard in order. On alternate weeks she was to clean out the sink and the yard at the back, including climbing up a stepladder to clean a gutter which was not set slanting and so tended to block. Sundays were not days off; she had housework to do and she and the laundrymaid were required to take turns to go to church. Every evening she had to sit up to make sure the master's bed was warmed properly with a pan, except on Mondays, when she was allowed to retire early as on Tuesdays she had to get up earlier than usual to wash her own clothes.

The standard of cleanliness which resulted from such regimes must have been high, surely no less in the eighteenth century than later. At Pilgrims' Hall in the 1910s 'the beautiful cleanliness and fragrance of the house' was remembered long afterwards and Ernest King paid tribute to the housemaids in the house where he worked as a butler: 'How they worked, those girls! Up at five to clean and light the fires, to polish the steel grates in the Adam fireplaces, to whiten the hearths and later to take up the brass cans of hot water to the bedrooms. We men only started at seven and could sit down in the afternoons, but the girls had to darn and repair the linen – and all for eight pounds a year.'[35]

The care lavished on the household goods of others may seem remarkable and illustrates the degree to which servants came to identify with 'their' family. In 1925 William Lanceley recalled an old head housemaid who had worked for the same family for thirty years:

She was always proud to relate that for twenty-five years she had been in charge of the best dinner service and nothing had been broken or chipped. She would allow nobody to handle the plates and dishes, but washed and wiped them herself and she alone would carry them to the dining-room door and wait there to bring them back to the housemaid's pantry where they were washed. She was quite sure that each plate had cost £5. This no doubt was an exaggeration, though probably they were not bought under £2 apiece, as they were old Worcester ware with the coat-of-arms painted in the centre of the plates.[36]

With a similar sense of identification, one old servant recalled how she, as head housemaid, would often return home from a walk feeling furious because she could see all the blinds on the sunny side of the house were up, rather than at the proper level appointed by her.[37]

SPRING CLEANING

Despite the routine of daily and weekly care, annual spring-cleaning was still a necessity. At Pilgrims' Hall in Essex in the 1920s it lasted about a fortnight and took place in May when no more fires would be needed. Organised by the housekeeper, a time was chosen when the family would be absent, except perhaps for the children who joined in the fun. Extra help was sent for – washerwomen or general cleaners from the village – and gardeners and grooms were asked to help with heavy lifting such as moving furniture and taking carpets outside, or awkward jobs such as washing paintwork in high or inaccessible places. Estate carpenters and contractors such as locksmiths or plumbers were also organised.[38] Lesley Lewis recalled the spring-cleaning at Pilgrims' Hall as a very happy time for a child looking on: 'There would be a lot of cheerful banter between the men and the maids, between those on the top of stepladders and those holding them steady, and though curtains were sometimes dropped on people's heads and buckets overturned nothing seemed to matter very much. . . .'[39]

Starting at the top of the house and working downwards, curtains were taken down and brushed, sponged and perhaps calendered[40] in the laundry. Case covers, counterpanes, blankets and pillows were washed. Bed hangings were changed into the summer suite, usually muslin. Chests of drawers were dismantled and the carcases damp-dusted. In the Victorian house, paper or muslin decorations were made to fill the empty fireplace.

Before the nineteenth century, wooden floors were scrubbed during spring-cleaning, using warm water, a coarse flannel and sand,[41] or soft soap applied with a scrubbing brush. Too much soap could leave a white deposit on the boards and Susanna Whatman preferred regular dry-rubbing with fuller's earth[42] and sand.[43] Wet scrubbing could cause dampness, as was discovered by the inspecting committee of the Stafford Infirmary in 1833, when they ordered that the wards no longer be scrubbed, but dry-rubbed instead.[44] Floors made of inlaid blocks were never wetted but dry-rubbed with sand. Rubbing with sand rather than soap was generally recommended by Hannah Glasse in her manual published in 1760: 'Sope is not proper for boards, and sand and water shews the grain, which is the beauty of a Board.'[45]

Wooden floors were often not stained but left a silvery light brown; or they could be stained to match mahogany with a mixture of blacking and small beer; or rubbed hard with tansy, mint, balm and fennel which gave a sweet-smelling 'brown and bright' finish.[46] For oak floors which had been neglected a long time, an old remedy was to rub them hard with a handful of fine iron chain; used only on oak and rubbed with the grain of the wood, it produced a lovely grey-brown lustre which needed no polishing.[47]

White paintwork was washed first with water and then rubbed gently with fuller's earth and finished off with a chamois leather. A stronger scrubbing mixture for any white wood was made from soft soap, whiting and sand mixed together with cold water.

Brocaded wall hangings were dusted with soft brushes and then rubbed carefully with tissue paper and given a final soft rub with silk cloth.

At spring-cleaning carpets and rugs were taken outside and shaken. Mrs Boscawen's instructions to her villa household in 1787 were detailed: 'let it be turned out upon the lawn as soon as this rainy weather has given place to sunshine and dryness. Then let it be shook and beaten without mercy by the strong hands of both gardeners.'[48] In this case when the carpet had been removed the floor under it was to be scoured twice and then dry-rubbed by the gardener's wife. The carpet was not to be put back because during summer the floor would be covered only with mats. This was a common habit during the eighteenth century: a house had winter and summer carpets, curtains and bedspreads and one reason for the annual spring-clean was to replace winter with summer hangings. A less vigorous version of the spring-clean was gone through in the autumn, when summer hangings were replaced by heavier winter curtains. Grass was an efficient carpet cleaner. One housekeeper who retired before the First

World War recalled an emergency cleaning of a carpet from a room where the oil lamp had been left smoking all night, with the result that the carpet had strings of soot all over it. The gardeners took the carpet out into the garden and dragged it pile downwards over the grass, which took all the soot off it.[49]

The extent to which servants cleaned pictures beyond the routine cleaning of frames is not clear. The advice of early specialist literature on the care of pictures was not to allow servants to touch them for whatever reason as they did not have the necessary 'sensibility'. The very existence of this advice, of course, implies that servants did sometimes rub picture surfaces over 'with a wet greasy cloth'. Some domestic manuals did advise housemaids on dusting pictures with a silk handkerchief, a painter's brush or bellows and cleaning the surface with a variety of available fluids ranging from urine, warm beer, laundry blue and lye (see chapter 6).[50] In the wealthier houses picture cleaning came into the province of the groom of the chambers, who was required to be trained in upholstery – a word which had much wider connotations of furniture-care than today.

The overall effect of spring-cleaning was startling even in a house like Pilgrims' Hall which was cleaned regularly:

> It was extraordinary what a difference the annual spring-cleaning made to a habitually well-kept house. The opening of doors and windows for a good blow-through with curtains removed probably had much to do with it and it was perhaps not purely fancy that furnishings put out of doors on a fine sunny day retained some of the scents of the garden. The air really felt as though it had been renewed, and newly cleaned paint, lamp-fittings and picture glasses retained their sparkle until the fires started up again in the autumn.[51]

Ventilation was regarded as being of primary importance to the cleanliness of the house. Up until the beginning of the twentieth century there persisted the widespread belief in the 'miasma theory', according to which, disease was caused by noxious fumes collecting in unventilated areas. So in 1880 spring-cleaning was seen by manuals as the time when 'the very atmosphere . . . requires washing, by streams of fresh air'.[52] Late nineteenth-century manuals recommended that drains, cisterns and waste pipes be inspected and scrubbed out during spring-cleaning, as 'there are few servants who do not look upon them as metallic boa-constrictors, capable of swallowing and digesting anything'.[53] Yards, outhouses and basement passages were whitewashed at least once a year.

After the spring-clean, houses might be 'wrapped up' for the early summer when the family were either travelling or staying in town for the London season. This meant the furniture and fittings were wrapped in their protective sheets and 'case covers'. Pamela Clabburn has made the point that the tradition of allowing respectable visitors to view the interior of country houses when the family was away was rather pointless: 'The visitors saw little as they would find the chandeliers tied up in a bag to keep the flies from the glass drops, the furniture in their cases, the beds with their curtains drawn and probably the window curtains taken down and the shutters closed.'[54] Yet visitors expected this and far from being dismayed, were impressed by the housekeeping care it showed. Celia Fiennes, visiting Ashtead Park, near Epsom, around 1712, described several bed chambers with 'well furnish'd good damaske beds and hangings and window curtaines of the same, and so neatly kept folded up in clean sheetes pinn'd about the beds and hangings'.[55] Covering up furniture in this way was primarily protection from dust. Jenny Rose, researching traditional housekeeping practices in relation to picture care, found equivocal evidence about the extent to which country house managers understood the importance of protection from light, but references in autobiographies to the discipline of window blinds are not uncommon, so someone must have understood about damage by light as well as dust.[56]

One reason why spring-cleaning was a happy time and the work entered into with gusto was that it was usual for the housemaids to fit in their annual holidays after they had finished. A week or a fortnight's holiday was taken in turn. So this was seen as a sort of reward for those maids who stayed behind for the cleaning.

One of the elements of both spring and autumn cleaning was the very important one of chimney maintenance. Fuel consumption in a country house was enormous. Fireplaces which smoked were common, especially the gracious but inefficient hob grates of the eighteenth century, and the ever-present threat of fire was very real. In an effort to reduce this, most houses had a regular routine for sweeping chimneys, at least twice a year. Often the very largest households employed a full-time sweep. William Lanceley recalled that a timber-framed house where he had worked still employed a full-time sweep and a boy in the 1870s. The house had two huge brick chimney towers, each with fourteen flues which were built with projecting stones on the inside to form steps for the sweep's boy. To the other servants the boy seems to have had a disembodied, ghostly life around the house, for he would pop up in unexpected places or completely disappear when anyone was looking for him. On one memorable occasion he accidently interrupted family prayers: 'A small black boy with a hangman-like cap on his head, two shining eyes, red lips and white teeth peeped timidly round the door.'[57]

Other houses had a regular contract with a local sweep, so payments appear in the household disbursement books. At Little Crosby, Lancashire, in March 1710, Nicholas Blundell paid 3*d* a chimney for nine chimneys.[58] Shugborough employed not only a sweep for the main flues but also a local 'chimney doctor' for problem flues; in the 1780s the household also paid a blacksmith regular amounts to sweep the kitchen flues and service the hot-air mechanism which powered the spit inside the chimney breast.[59] Following the legislation which banned the use of climbing boys in 1855, local associations were set up to buy equipment for the 'humane sweeping' of chimneys and to employ inspectors. At Shugborough, the chimney plan used at the inspection in 1855 details 27 chimneys containing a total

TO CLEAN PICTURE FRAMES

To clean the frames, take a little cotton wool and rub the frames with it. This will take off all the dust and dirt without injury, but never use a cloth, as this will damage the gilding. Never wet frames. If they are varnished you may rub them over with alcohol.

(After Anon., *The Footman's Directory*, pp. 43–4)

TO PREVENT FLIES DAMAGING GILT FRAMES

Boil 3 or 4 leeks in a pint of water. Brush the liquid over the frames. Flies will not alight on it.

(After Drury, *Victorian Household Hints*, p. 78)

TO COVER PICTURES AND CURTAINS WHILST THE FAMILY IS AWAY

To prevent pulling the curtains out of shape when you cover them when the family goes out of town, cut and paste strong paper together as nearly to the shape of the curtains as possible. Put this under the curtains and pin it to them. Then fasten the dust sheet to the curtain rail and pin it to the paper on the inside. Make sure before you cover curtains that you have brushed and draped them properly.

(After Anon., *The Footman's Directory*, p. 44)

of 105 flues, all of which were specified according to the method of cleaning (hand brushing or machine brushing) and the number and location of trap doors.[60]

Others had a more do-it-yourself approach; both disbursement books and oral history refer to the practice of 'firing' the chimneys of lesser buildings such as wash-houses with a charge of gunpowder. In the early nineteenth century, London washerwomen regularly cleaned their chimneys by 'throwing in, in rapid succession, small quantities of gunpowder'.[61] Within living memory country householders commonly fired chimneys with a shotgun, a system which worked best with furnace fires which had a door which could be wedged closed with a bar. Both methods had the benefit of clearing stray dislodged bricks as well as soot.

CLEANING MATERIALS

How did the materials used in country house cleaning change over time? Household disbursement books show that housekeepers or stewards bought cleaning materials as well as using generally available domestic products. Even in the seventeenth century the wealthy house was far from being self-sufficient in this respect, buying in cleaning materials in a crude form rather than made up into branded goods.

In 1634, the highly prestigious Cecil household living in London at Salisbury House (in the Strand) bought soap for scouring floors and furniture once month. They also paid several shillings a time for extra cleaning at their Hertfordshire houses, Hatfield and Quickswood.[62] At Gorhambury, also in Hertfordshire, in 1638–9, the Wortley household bought soap in large quantities, one and a quarter firkins costing £1 10s; this was used at a regular rate of an eighth of a firkin, or 3s worth, each week. The house also made regular purchases of brushes (including 'fower long brushes for cobwebs – 6d'), brooms, mops, scouring sand by the peck, whitening[63] and 'flanders tyle' (a form of hearthstone[64] made of powdered stone and clay), as well as making extra payments for women to air the chambers and beds and for chimneys to be swept.[65]

In the 1670s, the London house of the Levesons bought a range of materials in a routine of purchases. Regular weekly purchases were made from one supplier: fuller's earth (of which 3d worth was bought every week); sand (bought in enormous quantities – up to 21 pecks at a time, costing 1s a peck); and mops (one a week, costing 11d each; presumably the stone floors wore them out quickly). Less frequently, but still regularly, the same household bought whitening, brooms and brushes – 'a hair broom', 'a flag broom', 'a rubbing brush'.[66] There were monthly or bi-monthly purchases of red lead and 'lamb's black', probably 'lamp black'.[67] Hartshorn[68] was bought in large and small quantities – 5s to 6d a time, sometimes in the form of 'burnt hartshorn'. More occasional purchases were made of neatsfoot oil[69] (by the quart); bran 'to wash the dishes with' (5d); and sack 'to wash my lady's swansdon [sic]' (a pint and a half costing 1s 6d). Soap was bought in large quantities, up to 18 lb a time. A few years later in 1681 in their country house at Trentham, the same household continued to buy large quantities of soap, in one case two firkins of soft soap were bought 'against Christmas', for scouring. Sand was again purchased by the peck, the total amount for the year being 14 pecks at 1s a peck. In the country mops were bought by the dozen at 12s a dozen, and brooms cost 15s 6d for fifteen. Sweeping the chimneys at Trentham cost 1s a time, which was paid once every two or three months, so they appear to have had a regular routine for this.

Eighteenth-century accounts from almost any estate will reveal a similar variety of cleaning materials. The Shugborough household, for example, bought abrasives in the form of 'sand for the kitchen'[70] emery 'for making up mattresses' (probably for sharpening upholstery needles to make up the mattresses); and 'scoweren paper', paper with sand or emery stuck on to it. They also bought 'brewms' and 'besoms',[71] hartshorn, bladders by the dozen,[72] boxes of salts of lemon,[73] mops, linen for rags, and pounds of beeswax. They even bought protective clothing in the form of strong grate gloves and housemaids' gloves. The Shugborough household also paid hourly for a variety of jobs such as beating and sweeping carpets, scouring pewter, cleaning and oiling the smoke jack, dressing feathers and filling mattresses, calendering bed and window curtains and sweeping the chimneys; as well as washing and 'charin'.[74]

Even by the nineteenth century things had changed little. The Trentham housekeeper, Mrs Ingram, kept receipts for 1874 showing her purchases for basically the same materials – brushes of various descriptions which were priced and bought by the dozen: scrubbing brushes (£1 16s); blackleading brushes (6s); brooms made of hair (2s each); and mops (£1 8s).[75]

Unfortunately, the earlier records tell us nothing of who supplied these materials. For the country house of the 1870s, intent on its charitable reputation, the supplier of such goods was often a local institution. Then Shugborough bought doormats made at Stafford gaol and the Trentham housekeeper bought her brushes from the local boys' home. More specialist items were supplied by what were known as Italian warehouses. In 1864, a firm called R. Nicholson & Co.

The servants at Oxley Manor, Staffordshire. The housekeeper is in the centre, flanked by three housemaids in their afternoon frocks. To the right is the coachman and to the left a garden labourer who was famous in the area for his hedge-laying skills. (Staffordshire Arts and Museum Service)

in Maidenhead supplied the Leveson-Gowers at their rented house at Cliveden with a standard monthly supply of soap, two qualities of candles, matches, emery cloth, bath brick, tobacco, blacklead, chair blacking, hearthstones, salt and pepper, sulphur and greaves.[76] The total bill for one month was £13 10s 3d. The record was kept in individual account books supplied by the firm, often elaborate leather-backed books, complete with advertisements and carefully interleaved with tissue and blotting paper. Once a housekeeper had identified a satisfactory supplier of this sort, she could expect a regular visit from the proprietor to check her requirements; the materials would be delivered later at the door. She would keep her stores under lock and key in the cupboards in her room, in a system which had 'a place for everything and everything in its place'. Thus stocks could be checked at a glance and pilfering and waste reduced to a minimum.[77]

Housemaids were usually issued with cleaning materials on a Friday morning, as was laid down in the rules for liveried servants at Hatfield House from 1896.[78] Many years after her employment, in her eighties, the housekeeper at Shugborough in the 1930s had good cause to remember Fridays:

Friday was store day and it was a very busy morning. Everybody brought their cans to be filled and a list of what they wanted for working – soaps, brasso for cleaning the brass, black lead for doing the grates, and all the general working stores as well as the food stores. . . . Each one was allowed a quarter of a pound of butter per head per week for the staff. And you got so much jam – so many housemaids got so much jam, maybe a 2lb pot of jam. . . . And the same with the linen . . . all the beds were changed on a Friday. . . . Anyhow you had to have all this ready for the morning. And you know when I was housekeeper sometimes I was till midnight getting all this out. . . . Unless you'd got into a routine it was very complicated. . . . Underneath each window was a folding table. . . . It was pulled out on store day. . . . Outside the stillroom there was a cupboard, well that was soaps, all the bathroom soaps, toilet, large tablets and small tablets for the basins, and there were long bars, just plain yellow soap . . . you had for scrubbing, washing clothes; the laundry maids got a couple of those every week. They used to send away for the soaps, get it in hundredweights. . . . I remember one year it was 28 pound of different things, brushes for the housemaids, dustpans, soaps and various things . . . it was just like an ironmonger's shop, with all these things stored.[79]

CONCLUSION

From the detail of routines and materials we can recognise the essentials of good cleaning. It depended on three features: strict timetabling; good communications and teamwork; and individual hard work.

Evidence of strictly-regulated timetabling comes mainly from the later eighteenth century onwards. How far it was adopted in earlier households is difficult to judge. Family mealtimes changed over time, so housemaids' timetables would inevitably be different. Before the eighteenth century, theoretically servants were more a part of the extended family and privacy of family members was not considered so important, so perhaps such a strict regime was not considered necessary. Later, daily timetabling was crucial if cleaning was to be fitted in around the family's need for quiet and privacy. A mid-nineteenth-century *Catechism* for housemaids emphasised this point: a housemaid should never sing or talk loudly and ought to complete her work 'thoroughly, unseen and unheard'.[80] This feature of their work was recalled by many housemaids with vivid reality: 'You had to be out of the [bed]rooms by a certain time. . . . You weren't to be seen there, you had to work quietly; if anybody came you had to make a bolt for it.'[81] Some households were ruthless in pursuit of the ideal of the 'invisible' housemaid. At Crewe Hall in Cheshire a visitor was puzzled to see a host of housemaids at chapel, but only a flash of black dress disappearing round a corner at other times. The housekeeper enlightened her: Lord Crewe's strict orders were that housemaids who were seen by visitors should be instantly dismissed from his service.[82] Similarly at Woburn Abbey in the 1880s, any servant seen by the Duke of Bedford after twelve noon was liable to instant dismissal and a generation later even the electricians wiring the house used to bundle hurriedly into a cupboard when their lookout reported the Duke's approach.[83]

For this reason communications within the house were critical. It was not only the family, guests and kitchen staff who needed to know when dinner was about to be served. The dinner gong was important for the housemaids too, so that they could put down their sewing and go to tidy the sitting-rooms without fear of bumping into the family.

The timetable dictated what housemaids wore. In the mornings this meant 'washing dresses' – printed cotton, often striped or with a small flower pattern – with long white aprons and caps, and aprons of hurden for dirty jobs. Before lunch they went to their rooms, washed their hands and faces, straightened their caps and put on clean aprons, ready for their main meal in the servants' hall. After this they usually changed into black frocks with smaller aprons and caps with goffered fronts. This related partly to the nature of the work to be done in the afternoons – sewing and tidying rather than heavy cleaning – and partly to the long-standing general convention of formal wear after midday.

The household had to work well as a team; the housemaids and the footmen needed to coordinate their cleaning and dusting of the public rooms. Often the housemaids worked as a pair (as with making beds) or as a group (as with tidying sitting-rooms during family dinner). As each maid had her own individual duties, this joint work had to be timetabled in.

The junior housemaids were among the hardest-working of all country house servants. Oral history tells us that many girls started as housemaids aged thirteen or fourteen and their lives were as hard as any general servant working in a small household.[84] Their only comfort was that they were at least on the bottom rung of a ladder and with luck things would get better for them. Hannah Cullwick started work in service aged eight in the 1830s. She worked in small country households, moving up the ladder to the point where, aged fifteen, she was employed in the house of the daughter of Lord Liverpool. Yet even here, as a young girl she had poor accommodation, sleeping in 'a rough outhouse next to the kitchen . . . with no windows to look out for anything'.[85]

A letter from the 1870s, written by a fourteen-year-old girl named Harriet to her step-mother to thank her for making up aprons for her, reminds us how tough domestic service could be even in an élite household: 'I must try and finish them [making her print dresses] this week for I am sick and tired of seeing them about. I have been so driven at work since the fires begun I have had ardly [sic] any time for anything for myself. I am up at half past five and six every morning and do not go to bed till nearly twelve at night and I feel so tired sometimes. I am obliged to have a good cry. . .'[86] The tragic irony was that twenty years after this letter was written, Harriet's daughter went through exactly the same experience. She set off to her first job in service, carrying her wicker basket, so inexperienced that she needed a label tied on her lapel. She became the eighth of eight housemaids, working from five in the morning till late at night, doing all the roughest work, scouring the wooden floors of the servants' quarters with soft soap and silver sand until her hands and arms up to the elbows became red raw. Like her mother before her, many nights she cried herself to sleep.

Louise Jermy was a servant who survived an impoverished and hard-working childhood in the late nineteenth century, which affected her health; she found her time as a housemaid too much for a seventeen-year-old: 'But oh, it was dreadful, it really needed a big strong woman to do all that had to be done, and the stairs, there were nearly eighty of them. . . . I had to share a bedroom with two other girls, and there was only just a space between our beds . . . certainly no privacy.'[87]

The lot of part-time day labour charwomen or cleaning girls could be even worse, for these did all the jobs the permanent staff did not want. A Lancashire woman remembered starting work in 1914:

I'd to brush the carpets, and I'd to take the stair carpet on the lawn and drag it up and down the lawn. It was hard work for a girl of fourteen . . . I'd to stand outside on the bay window and all those tiny little windows I'd to clean every one of them . . . and I'd to chop firewood of course and I'd chop m'finger and m'hands were chapped with cleaning these outsides. . . . My hands were sore and I was tired. . . .[88]

There were compensations, of course, to country house service. It offered many poor girls better food than they were used to at home and, in Louise Jermy's case, provided an escape from an inept father and a violent mother. Mrs Milgate, working at the very top of the servant hierarchy at Kensington Palace in the 1930s, felt she was living in enormous luxury compared with factory girls.[89] Many households must have developed a strong sense of community, of shared hardships and pleasures. This certainly appears in the reminiscences of later years in service; housemaids at the Yorkes' house at Erddig in the 1920s, for example, recalled evenings spent having 'a good natter' in one of the housemaids' attic bedrooms, or sitting in the moonlight on the roof outside their windows, watching rabbits and waiting for the grunts of badgers.[90]

There must have been compensation, too, in the relationship between servants and children. The concept of servants being part of the family was old-fashioned in the nineteenth century, but it could survive in some households where there were children in the family to break down the barriers of status, albeit temporarily.[91] Viola Bankes, for instance, recalled how she loved to spend time with the Kingston Lacy servants, especially when her mother was away from home. She used to share their games of whist and billiards, and slide on the carefully polished floors, much to their annoyance: 'I climbed on Edith's strong, broad back whenever she was on all fours dusting the oak boards, which cannot have helped her in her work.' But even here the memories were bitter-sweet, for Viola's father had left her mother, and the children were dependent on the household servants for stability and comfort, even to the extent that the butler, Copper, gave them their pocket money.[92]

Such servants were in a position of great trust, as were housemaids who were privy to all sorts of domestic secrets. Manuals attempted to deal with this; the housemaid's *Catechism* required her never to 'pry into the secrets of the family, by reading letters or papers that may be left about – or repeat any family affairs I might chance to overhear – I should not open drawers or desks out of curiosity, and I should never make game of the family, or speak against them'.[93] On-the-job training concurred, as one retired housemaid recalled: 'You were always told to mind your own business and keep your mouth shut. Don't converse with anyone much in the village. . . . You hadn't to repeat what you heard.'[94]

FOR THE RELIEF OF CHAPPED HANDS

'Take Small-beer and Butter, heat them, wash your hands [in it], wipe them, and draw on a pair of Gloves; this will make them fine and smooth and is proper to be done every night.' The gloves were to be worn all night.

(Hannah Glasse, *Servant's Directory*)

Like the footman, then, the housemaid was privy to secrets and intimacies in a world to which she did not belong in any capacity except to service it. Discretion was needed, to the point where the recipients of her services could pretend she did not exist and to this end an elaborate structure of work was created which relied on its own system of household time.[95]

CHAPTER 5

'Very Old and Very Worn': the Use of Linen

Women have always been launderers, even in the great medieval households where men were the cooks, scullions, servers, managers and record-keepers. Yet although laundering has been one of the main sources of income for working women for so long, in the past it was barely recorded; Gervase Markham, who published an early manual for housewives in 1615, wrote not a single word on the subject, though he did give instructions on how to finish and bleach new linen.[1] Even in present times it has been little researched until recently.

Despite this, people generally have had fixed ideas about laundry work and the people who did it. These perceptions usually went as follows: it was a low-technology and low-skill activity, requiring hard physical labour rather than dexterity or technical ability; little if any training was needed, as women somehow knew instinctively how to wash. For these reasons it had a low status which attached itself to the operatives. Even the term 'washerwomen' has slightly pejorative undertones and many of the word-pictures drawn in literature have been touched with ridicule. In the nineteenth century it was a useful occupation for low-status women – orphans, prisoners, paupers and reformed prostitutes.[2] In a country house context, work in the laundry was sometimes used as a form of punishment for some misdemeanour committed by other maids.[3] Laundrymaids were suspected of being subversive and up to no good, usually with the groom or the gardener. Even the modern eminent architectural historian Mark Girouard has fallen into this trap: 'The independence of the job tended to bring pretty girls into it, and the position of the laundry to make it easily accessible to outside workers – especially the groom in the stable. As far as sexual segregation was concerned, the laundry was the Achilles heel of the Victorian country house.'[4]

The nineteenth-century use of washing as a punishment for social failure has made it of interest to the new breed of women's historians, so at this level it is

Illustration of a public washing ground in 1582, from the Harleian MS,3469. It shows the processes of hand-washing, batting clothes, rubbing clothes in a stream and hanging and stretching clothes out on the grass. (Rural History Centre, University of Reading)

beginning to be researched.[5] At the level of country house laundry, however, it has usually been viewed as an unimportant addendum of the élite household and of little general interest. The next chapters aim to take a much closer look at the work and lifestyle of the country house laundress, addressing issues relating to washing systems, material culture and the organisation and management of the laundrymaid in the country house. But before coming to any of these areas, we need to ask two related questions: how many washable textiles did the country house possess, and how often were they washed?

AMOUNT OF LINEN

The late medieval household may appear to have owned a limited range of household textiles. In 1515 the regulations governing the two Yorkshire castles of Algernon Percy, 5th Earl of Northumberland specified a total of only forty-nine linen items. Yet this appearance is probably misleading. All of the listed items in the Percy archive related to ritualised public dining; no mention was made of any bedlinen, for example, so the list is obviously incomplete.[6] Santina Levey, in a detailed and fascinating study of the textiles at Hardwick Hall in Derbyshire, found evidence to show that it was the usual custom for linen inventories at the end of the sixteenth century to exclude bedlinen and the more workaday items of household linen which were in daily use; only the very best cambric and fine holland sheets usually kept in store were included in an inventory taken at Hardwick in 1601, though made-up table linen is listed in detail and unused lengths of linen, waiting to be made up into cloths and napkins, were listed according to quality, width and purpose.[7] Levey concluded that bedlinen was not inventoried as it had a limited life and inventoried goods were listed for posterity. In the Hardwick inventories, it was not until 1764 that ordinary quality sheets were included, 1782 before miscellaneous items used in the kitchen and laundry appear and 1811 before most items were measured for the inventory.[8]

Even given incomplete records, a 1553 inventory of the household of Sir William Cavendish at Chatsworth showed a lavish wealth of linen, including a matching set of tableware consisting of a 6 yards long cloth made of diaper woven with the story of Abraham, valued at 12*s* a yard; napkins costing 2*s* 6*d* each; and towels to be used by the servers costing 4*s* a yard. The set cost £9 16*s* – at a time when the annual salary paid to the Chatsworth butler was £2.[9]

By the sixteenth century the fully operative élite household was very well supplied with linen and spent large sums of money on its replenishment. In the humble household, it was the later seventeenth and eighteenth centuries which saw an increase in the amount and variety of household linen and other textiles used, part of a general increase in both the quantity and quality of possessions. The change is indicated by both the amounts recorded in probate inventories and the stock of textile distributors such as mercers and chapmen.[10] Using a simple indicator – the ratio between the numbers of pairs of sheets and the number of beds in a house – Barrie Trinder has shown there was an average increase in numbers of sheets of almost three and a half times between the 1640s and the 1740s among the inventories studied from the small town of Wellington,

Shropshire.[11] The same study shows that in the late seventeenth century there were five mercers in Wellington, each in competition with each other, but each wealthy and thriving and showing a degree of specialisation by serving slightly different markets. That the trade was growing is indicated by the fact that two of the five were new businesses, set up in new premises against the competition of existing mercer families.

Of course the change from numbers of sheets which are barely adequate to enable a change of bedlinen to an over-abundance might well indicate stored wealth rather than functional wealth, but the increase in both quantities and varieties of textile possessions is so widely evidenced that it surely must have been accompanied by an increase in the time and money spent on textile care in the home.

Much of this increased amount of household textiles was of imported goods, both linen and cotton.[12] In the sixteenth and seventeenth centuries complex weaves such as damask, huckaback and diaper[13] were made by weavers in Lancashire and elsewhere in the north of England, but the better-quality goods were imported from Holland, France and Ireland. Yet the older tradition of making one's own household linen, especially sheeting, survived until the end of the eighteenth century. Indeed it may well be this tradition which is responsible for the exclusion of most bedlinen and working cloths from earlier inventories; perhaps they were not listed because they were home-made, not because they were short-lived. Documentary evidence for the home production of linen in élite households is well established from the sixteenth and seventeenth centuries, employing estate workers and the wives of menservants for the time-consuming processes which flax-processing required.[14] The extent of home production varied with climate and agricultural practice, but certainly the disbursement books of Trentham in Staffordshire in 1645–6 included amounts paid by the housekeeper for day labour for weeding flax, dyeing and spinning linen yarn and weaving napkins and bagging.[15] On the other hand the Trentham household of 1645 was far from being self-sufficient in textiles. It bought better-quality imported cloths – fustian, calico and silk – as well as specialist products such as tape, ribbon and sewing thread. Thirty years later, the situation was little changed; in 1679 the Trentham housekeeper paid for the weaving of hempen and flaxen cloth at around £1 12s a batch, at the same time as buying speciality textile goods, such as 'thrums for mops' and 'cotton and linen candles'.[16] In 1681, the disbursement book shows even more payments for weeding, pulling, rippling and dressing flax, as well as for bleaching a previous batch of finished cloth. At the same time the household was buying in an increasing variety of both cloth and speciality items.

Late in the next century, though, it seems likely that the Trentham household had stopped making linen, for by 1799 all qualities of linen were being purchased.[17] That many households continued to grow flax well into the eighteenth century, however, is shown by the publication of handbooks such as *The Weaver and Housewife's Pocket-Book* written by David Ramsay, a weaver of Dalkeith, published in 1750, giving guidance to the housewife on 'how to prepare her yarn and have it right woven into cloth'.[18] Barrie Trinder's study of inventories also showed that both hemp and flax cultivation and spinning were common in Shropshire in the eighteenth century and as late as 1796 William Pitt reported that the home production of flax was still common in Staffordshire, though there was no commercial production in the county.[19] Disbursement books from Shugborough show that the Anson household was producing flax until the 1790s and the Hardwick inventories contain evidence of household production of coarse linen sheets from the 1760s and 1780s.[20]

The home-made tradition coexisted alongside a much more sophisticated trade. Many of the items purchased by the Trentham housekeeper were bought in London but the more ordinary quality goods were bought from mercers' and drapers' shops in country towns local to Trentham such as Newcastle-under-Lyme, Market Drayton, Uttoxeter and Eccleshall. By 1799, the Trentham household used three regular suppliers, one of whom specialised in furnishing goods, the other two supplying household linen, cotton and wool. The prices paid for individual goods varied, reflecting the purchase of different qualities.[21] Much of the fabric bought was imported from Wales (flannel), Ireland and Russia. Even cheap sheeting was bought. In some cases fabric was bought in large pieces, such as a single purchase of 225 yards of huckaback. The most valuable purchases were best quality sheeting and blankets, bed ticks, quilted bed covers and striped bed 'furniture' (hangings for four-poster beds.)

The strength of the general demand for household textiles at the end of the eighteenth century is shown by the existence of merchants who came into the area offering one-off sales of a wide variety of goods at prices which undercut the local shops. Such a sale was advertised in the *Staffordshire Advertiser* in April 1800; this was a fourteen-day sale of linen, mercery and hosiery goods of great variety, and of 'the latest and most modern fashions'; the sale was to be held in the Talbot Inn, Stafford, at 20 per cent under the regular price.[22]

For those who needed to buy household fabrics, as early as 1696 one cloth merchant wrote a guide to the purchase of linen, aimed at 'both Rich and Poor', with the intention of helping them to avoid buying 'damaged cloth, which most

ITEMS FROM THE HOUSEHOLD DISBURSEMENT BOOKS OF THE LEVESON FAMILY

1. Trentham, 1681. Selected items for the home production of flax

May	Paied for weeding flax		7*s*	3*d*
June	For hempseed 2 strick		8*s*	
July	For whineing cloth		10*s*	
	6 lb of turmerick for dieing the chears		6*s*	8*d*
Aug	For whitteing [bleaching] 8 score and 6 yards of cloath		14*s*	6*d*
	For pulling flax	£1	10*s*	3*d*
	For ripling flax att 3*s* a day		14*s*	
Sept	10 days dressing flax		2*s*	6*d*
	Whiteing cloath 26 yards		2*s*	6*d*

2. Trentham, 1681. Selected items relating to the purchase of textiles

Dec	Tape for brawne		1*s*	
Mar	For two peices of kenting for hancheiffs	£3	10*s*	0*d*
May	Half a lb blew thrid		4*s*	
	For 4 ounces of thrid to mend cloaths		2*s*	
	Due to me for cloath bought	£2	17*s*	9*d*
	2 yards of blew callicoe		2*s*	
June	2 yards of coars cloth for dish cloaths			6*d*
	9 yds of cloath for shirts for Mr.Beckwith		12*s*	6*d*
	4 yds ferritt ribing [narrow ribbon made of wool or silk]		1*s*	3*d*
July	2 ounces of thrid for mending napkins		1*s*	4*d*
	For 26 yards of cloath for napkins	£1	11*s*	8*d*
	For cloath 6 yards for aprons for Mall		7*s*	
Aug	For ells of hollond 4 att 5*s*	£1		
	For 5 ells of hollond att 3*s* 6*d*		19*s*	6*d*
	For a callicoe for making up a sheet		6*s*	6*d*
	A yard and a half of muslin for my mr.		4*s*	6*d*
	For a nounce of thrid			6*d*
Oct	For 42 yards of hugaback att 1*s* 2*d* a yard	£2	9*s*	0*d*
	One coars cloth			6*d*
	For 2 bedticks and boulsters	£4	1*s*	0*d*
	A yard of coars cloth for bruar			8*d*
	For the carage of hugaback		1*s*	
Nov	For 21 yards and a quarter of callicoe	£1	11*s*	10*d*
	For 7 yards of flannell for an iring cloath		7*s*	
	For thrid one pound for to mend cloaths		4*s*	9*d*
	Paied Martha for 4 ounces of thrid		2*s*	

(SRO, Sutherland MS, D593/R/1/64)

people buy, it looking well to the eye, but when it comes into the Water falls into pieces, and are in as much want the week after it is washed as if they had not bought any'.[23] He also aimed to teach people how to distinguish one type of cloth from another; and to warn people of the dangers of buying cloth from pedlars who purveyed substandard goods, revealing perhaps an ulterior motive in his publication. His book gave a description of over a hundred different types of linen, hempen, ramie[24] and cotton cloth. Each description gave the name, the width and length of the finished piece as sold off the loom (in yards or ells), the weight (for example 1,600 was the lightest weight of diaper, 4,000 the heaviest), how it wore (for example 'will wash white'), what it was best suited for ('pillow fustian' was good not only for pillows but also for waistcoats and lining men's breeches), and any obvious characteristics of the selvedge (for example best quality 'alcomore' holland had strings in the selvedge). Some linens carried a maker's mark, so the author was able to advise his readers to ask for a specific weaver.

The choice of linen and cotton described in the linen guide is bewildering and one can see why a housekeeper would need assistance. The management of a country house to the exacting requirements of the day necessitated a consumption of textiles which was huge, in terms of amount, variety and value. At Erddig in 1726 the list of linen covers four pages, all of which was handed on by a new housekeeper into the care of the laundrymaid.[25] Among almost any collection of country house papers there will be housekeepers' inventories of linen of similar size. The linen inventory taken at Trentham in 1803 included among other items 461 napkins (of two qualities in various condition), 172 tablecloths (of three qualities and one horse-shoe shaped), 109 sheets (in three qualities), 441 towels (of at least four qualities), 189 domestic cloths of various sorts, and 78 pillow 'coats'.[26] Hartcup noted a housekeeper's list from Harewood House in Yorkshire in 1836 which runs to over 600 towels and nearly as many cloths, marked and distributed for use among each of the household departments: china cloths for the stillroom; rubbers (polishing cloths) for the kitchen; pocket cloths for the footmen; glass cloths for the butler; lamp cloths for the pantry; dusters and china cloths for the housemaids; and horn cloths for the servants' hall.[27]

The Workwoman's Guide, a book of instruction on needlework published in 1840 for the use of housekeepers, endorses this picture of the household textiles which the efficient manager was expected to supply and the laundrymaid to maintain.[28] What was called 'house linen' was divided into several types – for bedroom, table and pantry, housemaids, kitchen and stable. The guide went on to give full lists of what was required of each for a gentleman's household.

THE CHARACTERISTICS OF LAUNDRYMAIDS

Mrs Ingram

Stafford House
St James's
London

April 26th 1876

Dear Madam,

I cannot understand what you mean about the new Laundrymaid. All I can say about her is, that she had a most excellent character as a good strong hardworking and willing young person. If she had not been so I would not have engaged her.

In the meantime I shall be glad if you will not listen to what Janet McDonald or anyone else says against her for the short people often work better than the taller ones. After I had engaged this young person one of Janet's friends applied for the situation: but if I had not been settled I should not have engaged her as she talked too much.

So Janet must make herself comfortable as I shall not think of discharging the girl without just cause.

Trusting you are quite well,

I am Yours Truly

pro. J. Whittaker

(SRO, D593/R/10/3), letter to the Trentham housekeeper)

This complexity was the result of three requirements. The first of these was the need to use the fabric best suited for any particular use, in terms of texture, weight and coarseness. Perhaps because of the lack of cleaning fluids, the Victorian household manual laid great stress on having the right cloth for the right job: 'There are, or ought to be, cloths separate or exclusively for each thing you have to use them with . . . if you have not a sufficient number for use, always speak to the master or mistress for more, as they cannot know unless they are told.'[29]

The second requirement which added to the complexity of textile goods was the need to vary the quality of fabric according to the social hierarchy of the household. The guests, family, nursery, senior servants and servants were all equipped with a specific texture of weave, fineness and weight of towels, sheets, pillowcases and toilet-table cloths suited to their position.[30] The best quality was reserved for guest rooms, the second quality for general family use and so on down the hierarchy. Best tablecloths, for example, were made of damask, second-best of diaper and lower quality of huckaback. Invalids, infants and young children were often supplied with sheets and pillowcases of fine calico, which was warmer than linen. Servants had sheets made of the coarse hempen cloth called 'hurden', or of coarse creamy calico or unbleached linen which until well washed had the texture of cardboard.[31] Each sheet was made of two lengths of fabric because of the difficulty of getting a sufficient width; they were seamed down the middle and had the advantage that when the sheet got worn in the middle, the seam could be easily unpicked and the sides turned.

In the late Victorian era, good sheets were made long – up to 4 yards in length, to allow the bottom sheet to be well tucked in at the bottom and then rolled around the bolster.[32] As Pamela Clabburn has pointed out, however, the tradition of long sheets is much older than the nineteenth century; sheets of 4 or even 4½ yards were mentioned in sixteenth-century inventories.[33] What one did with the extra length of the top sheet remains a mystery; sheets were invariably inventoried as pairs, which presumably means they were the same length – or does it?

It is probable that cotton sheets did not come into use until the nineteenth century. Certainly by the late nineteenth century cotton sheeting had become acceptable for family use, even preferred to linen in some households, though pillowcases were usually still made of linen, since this kept the head cool and aided sleep. Best-quality towels were always of linen, and usually of a huckaback weave.

Blankets were also graded. Early blankets were made of fustian, either all wool or a wool and linen mix and were up to 5 yards long so that they could be used doubled. They were allocated to beds in pairs, usually one pair per bed. By the seventeenth century a wide variety of materials were used: best-quality blankets were made from Spanish merino wool, but Pamela Clabburn quoted one household inventory from 1623 which includes fustian, cotton, cloth and linsey-wolsey blankets, some of which were coloured.[34] By the late seventeenth century most blankets were made out of white all-wool blanket material, often still processed and spun at home and put out to a local weaver. By the eighteenth century, many houses were buying blankets from specialist areas like Witney in the Cotswolds. Best-quality blankets were identified by a rose motif in all four corners; these were embroidered in crewel wool by the workers at ½d per motif and marked the place where the length was to be cut up into individual blankets.[35] 'Rose blankets' figure in the Trentham textile bills for 1799 and the practice ended when blankets became machine-woven in the 1850s.

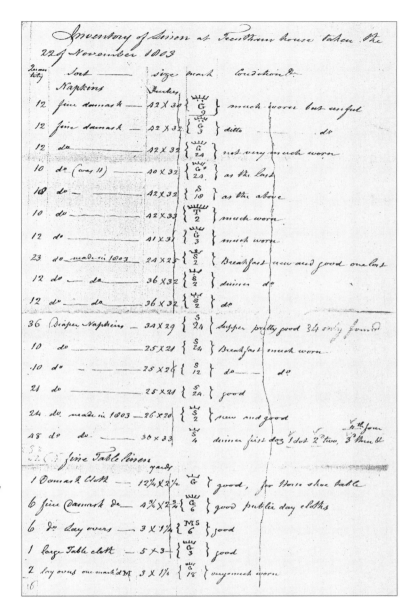

Extract from a lengthy linen inventory taken at Trentham Hall on 22 November 1803. The 'S' and 'MS' probably refer to the senior title of the Leveson-Gowers at the time, the Marquis of Stafford and 'G' to the heir's title of Earl Gower. (Staffordshire Record Office, D593/R/7/2)

The third element in the complexity of household linen was the long tradition of covering things up. This was not the result of some sort of Victorian prudery; it was a tradition which pre-dated the nineteenth century, was usually founded on good practical sense relating to the care of household goods and is retained today in most country houses. Everything had its purpose-made covers – furniture had loose 'case

One of the most superb restored laundries is at Castle Ward in County Down. As is usual, the ironing tables are ranged in front of the windows, the ironing stove situated in front of one end wall. The stove has good top surfaces for heating different sizes and types of irons and for boiling a kettle. On the opposite side is a box mangle showing the Howland 1807 patent system (p. 170). The system of racking is unusual and simple; because of the two galleries which run the length of the room, racking is made from removable lengths of timber propped on the gallery rails, dispensing with the need for a windlass. (Lord Rossmore, Irish Architectural Archive, Dublin)

covers' to protect it from dust when not in use, as did pictures, mirrors and curtains. Work tables of various sorts had covers of a suitable type – bedchamber tables had 'toilet covers' – shaped cloths of fine diaper, Marseilles or Manchester quilting, dimity or muslin or pastel-coloured silk, complete with matching pincushions with removable covers and matching bags for combs. Bedroom washstands were covered in oilcloth, the edges bound with ribbon. Kitchen and pantry tables and dressers were covered with cloths of huckaback or coarse diaper, made to measure so they were long enough to fall over the edge by a couple of inches, protecting the pristine scrubbed surface of the table and the paintwork of the dresser. Clothes, gloves and shoes were stored in individual bags made for quick packing. Washable watch pockets were provided for the bedside and removable covers for the stools to washstands. Holland, chamois or cotton covers, the corners bound in ribbon, were made to protect favourite or valuable books. Any item which might be taken travelling was fitted with protective linen or baize covers. Even the travelling trunks had canvas covers on which was fastened a direction card.

Loose covers for furniture were used from at least early Tudor times, made out of both cloth and leather for protection when being transported.[36] Expensive furniture was provided with covers by the makers; for example the suite of fourteen chairs and two sofas made in 1793 by Charles Smith for the Red Drawing Room at Shugborough came complete with smart case covers to protect the red silk upholstery and fine burnished carving.[37] Though the practice of making case covers lasted throughout the nineteenth century, later ones tended to be used as much for style as protection, so one eventually arrived at a situation where case covers had covers made for them.[38] Valuable tester beds had a special set of protective curtains made which could completely shroud the bed. Sheets were pinned to bed and window curtains for the same purpose. Carpets were protected by druggets and chandeliers were wrapped in bags to keep them from fly spots and dust.

In this complex system of differentiated goods, it was important that both laundress and maids were able to identify items. Where hygiene was concerned, the fabric itself was distinctive (as with the slop-bucket cloths); and the ability to sort out all the other types of cloths came with experience. To make sure, everything was marked. The marking system of some households was in itself an elaborate code. Sheets, for example, were marked in one corner with the master's initials, or sometimes the initials of both master and mistress, or sometimes the family motif and perhaps a coronet if the family were entitled; then would follow the initial of the set to which it belonged (for example, B for best, F for family, S for servant, P for pantry, K for kitchen, H for house, and so on); then the number within the set; and finally the date. The example given in *The Workwoman's Guide* is:

H.M.S.

F.

4

38

meaning Henry and Mary Saville, family, fourth pair, 1838. Sets of sheets were allocated to specific beds and so might be marked with the name of the bedroom. The marking was done either in ink or embroidered in silk thread and *The Workwoman's Guide* gives exact instructions as to the choice of embroidery writing styles to be used. Pocket handkerchiefs and finer quality items, for example, should be marked using a slanting Italian style of writing. These styles were practised by girls, of course, on their samplers.

Linen inventories show that houses did use laundry-marking systems. In the mid-nineteenth century, the Kingston Lacy linen was marked with a system of dots, indicating the quality of linen, five dots being the best and one dot the coarsest; servants' and working linen had no dots.[39] Within this system, each piece was allocated to a set and numbered according to the number of items in the set. Surviving examples of linen also show marking systems – a napkin from the collections at Hardwick Hall carries a mark embroidered in blue silk with a coronet, H, 27, 1872.[40]

At least once a year the linen was counted over and inventoried into a book, the traditional time for this ritual being winter. The age was noted, as were missing items, repairs or replacements needed. Many households made a regular purchase of new linen items every year and these were entered into the inventory. Items which were too far gone for repair were set aside to be used for some other purpose such as bandages.[41] The linen inventory taken at Trentham on 22 November 1803 was organised into columns headed quantity, sort, size, mark and condition. Most of the items were marked with a coronet above an initial; then followed a set number. Fabulously wealthy the Leveson-Gowers might have been, but the 'condition' column reveals that old sheets and table-cloths were cut down and reused for children's sheets, dresser cloths and powdering sheets for protecting the shoulders when dressing the hair.[42]

In many households laundrymaids worked with the housemaids in the task of keeping the linen in good repair.[43] Back in the 1770s Susanna Whatman had required her laundrymaid to mark with a pin pieces which needed mending and to 'look over linen in the storeroom Monday morning, put stitches or buttons in all her Master's shirts. If more is wanting, as new risbands [sic] and collars, she is to put them by for the Housekeeper. If any tablecloth wants more than a few stitches, to put it by for the Housekeeper to mend the end of the week.'[44]

Chamber linen was stored in linen rooms, usually sited near the bedrooms or the housekeeper's room. Table linen was usually in cupboards near the butler's pantry. In the seventeenth and eighteenth centuries linen not in regular use was stored in chests, but by the mid-nineteenth century these had been replaced by linen rooms whose furniture ideally consisted of a table for folding, with presses (cupboards) fitted with shelves and drawers below.[45] The linen cupboards needed to be warm, ideally backing onto a chimney flue, locked and ventilated perhaps with a perforated door. Proper sliding linen shelves had sides to them and on the front edges had enough space to stick labels carrying the name and numbers of items on the shelves. The inner carcases of linen cupboards were often lined with brown paper or, as at Dunham Massey in Cheshire, with glazed holland. This was to protect against dust, damp and mildew. The shelves too were lined with paper or calico, big enough to wrap over the

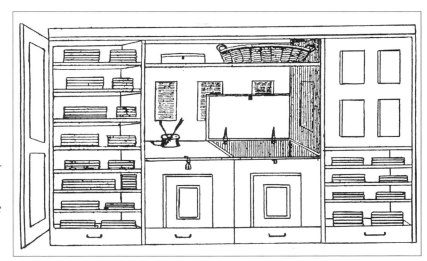

Design for a linen cupboard or 'press', incorporating bins for soiled linen, to be lined with calico bags which could be sent direct to the laundry. (From The Workwoman's Guide, 1840, plate 21, fig. 5)

top from the back and turn up over the linen from the front. Wherever possible linen was stored in complete sets – napkins in dozens or at Hardwick up to fourteen dozens, tied round with ribbon. Inside the door would hang washing lists and inventories. The linen room also needed baskets or boxes for soiled linen. Soiled table linen had to be handed to the housekeeper by the footmen every morning.

To keep track of washing as it was sent out, a washing record was required. Early versions were wooden tally sticks or horn books. A seventeenth-century tally from Haddon Hall in Derbyshire was in the form of a horn-covered piece of wood, on the front of which was marked all the types of linen; each name had a disc which could be rotated to an appropriate number.

In addition to the household linen, laundries had to cope with personal or body linen. During the mid-nineteenth century the quantity of this increased greatly and the switch to cotton fabrics like calico, which people thought needed more frequent washing than linen, must have added to the problem. Flannel was also used in quantity in underwear and was particularly popular in the late nineteenth century. In the 1880s most handbooks on domestic economy were advocating wearing wool next to the skin all the year round, including woollen stockings and flannel petticoats. The amount of underwear worn seems enormous today, but one only has to experience the icy blasts which haunt most country houses even now to realise how much this wrapping was needed.

The nursery in particular generated large quantities of washing. According to *The Workwoman's Guide* in 1840, an infant's wardrobe consisted of a minimum of

113 textile items and it is hardly likely that a child of a country house would be limited to the minimum. Women's linen, too, consisted of a formidable array of clothing: shifts or chemises of fine linen or calico; drawers made of calico, twill or cambric muslin, with flannel or wash-leather drawers for riding; nightgowns and nightjackets; waistcoats of flannel (rather like liberty bodices); stays in canvas, flannel, linen or silk; a wide variety of day and night caps of lawn or muslin;[46] dressing gowns of flannel, dimity, calico or silk; winter petticoats of flannel, and summer 'washing' petticoats of fine calico, twill, dimity or cambric; pockets to tie round the waist; and a wide variety of aprons, pinafores, walking capes, collars and tippets. Most were decorated with crimped frills, flounces, ruches or fine pleating. Some of this would not have been washed, of course; stays, crinoline and bustle supports were usually sponged rather than washed and were regarded by the wealthy as disposable when dirty.

HOUSEMAIDS' LINEN

Dusters were of soft linen or a blue cotton check; scouring flannels of strong close-weaved flannel; paint cloths (for cleaning paintwork) of old softened linen; chamber bottle cloths (for cleaning water bottles) of soft, fairly thin linen; chamber bucket cloths (for cleaning the slop-buckets) of blue or lilac checks or stripes (different from any other cloth to prevent them being used for anything else); clothes bags (for storing clothes) of good quality linen or cotton; housemaid's pinafore of soft calico (worn when making beds).

FOOTMEN'S LINEN

Knife box liners needed to be made of thick but soft linen; pantry knife cloths (for drying knives) were of coarse but strong linen; pantry dresser cloths (for laying on the top of the dressers to prevent their paint from being scratched) were of coarse damask or medium fine huckaback; plate basket cloths (bag-shaped removable cloths made to fit the inside of plate carriers to keep them clean) were of strong linen; pantry china cloths were of soft and thin linen or cotton diaper; pantry glass cloths needed to be thinner than china cloths; pantry lamp cloths could be of fine flannel or linen; pantry aprons of strong linen or calico; and waiting gloves of woven cotton.

(After *The Workwoman's Guide*)

Fashion in underwear changed, as did other garments. The edition of Cassell's *Household Guide* published in 1911 referred to the Victorian practice of wrapping the body in layer upon layer of 'stuffy unventilated clothing' which was also cumbersome and unshapely.[47] The guide claimed that a change to lighter, fewer undergarments resulted in a considerable reduction in the washing bill. The illustrations of the lighter combinations, however, show that even these more rational garments were covered with time-consuming white-work embroidery, frills, pleats and lace inserts.

Museum collections show that as with 'washing dresses' (dresses which can be washed) underwear was made with no raw edges visible – seams were either French or overlaid. One long-established practice was the use of linings, made of cotton or linen and sewn into the inside of garments to protect them from body soiling. These were particularly used for corsets and mens' breeches, in the latter case originally instead of separate drawers; the lining could be unpicked and washed.[48] Other forms of clothes' protectors were 'brush braid', sewn to the bottom of hems, and underarm 'dress protectors', in use from the 1840s.

Of course many items of clothing were unwashable, especially menswear and women's dresses. The cleaning of these was part of the responsibilities of the valet and ladies' maids, who accumulated a body of skill and experience which was different from the laundrymaids', who needed to know only how to remove common stains such as blood and ink from boilable linen and cotton. The Victorians in particular were fussy over the cleanliness of their dress and body servants were expected to know all the various techniques for sponging and dry-cleaning, taking the shine off trousers, removing stains from silks, fixing dyes, restoring finishes and stiffening and even making fabrics waterproof.[49] Many of these recipes used raw materials which were available around the house, such as lemon juice, vinegar, pearlash, rhubarb, dry bread, bran, hay, gin, coffee, tea, black pepper, linseed oil, borax,[50] Epsom salts, whitening, even scraps of bacon rind (for rubbing on velvets). Many had a sound chemical basis for their use.

Because of the complexity of dress and the absence of effective mothproofing, the storage of clothes was important. Body linen was stored in cupboards with other clothing in the appropriate dressing-room rather than with the household linen. Items which were used regularly were hung up on hooks, but all the rest was folded and wrapped in unbleached holland cloths (linen is naturally moth-resistant) or brown or blue paper. Oddly enough, coat hangers were not used until the 1890s, which is why old wardrobes have hooks rather than brass rails. For long-term storage, dresses might even be unpicked and stored in flat pieces.

Given the size of houses, the number of bedrooms, the number of pieces needed for each bedroom or table, the number and variety of persons living and working in the house, it is clear that a huge quantity and variety of linen was needed. Each weight of damask, holland, calico, diaper and huckaback required slightly different washing or ironing temperatures and each item had a traditional, recognised method of finishing, folding and storing suited to its particular role. This is the context which has to be borne in mind when exploring the day-to-day world of the country house laundress.

HOW OFTEN DID THE COUNTRY HOUSE WASH ITS LINEN?

Most writers on domestic organisation accept that the great households of the seventeenth century indulged in 'quarterly orgies of washing of huge stocks of dirty linen'.[51] Later, the interval between washings was reduced to six weeks, then to three weeks, and finally, by the mid-nineteenth century, to one week. Is this pattern supported by what we know of the country house?

In 1515, the Percy households in Yorkshire paid an annual sum for washing all the linen belonging to 'the Chapell the Ewery the Sellar the Pantre the Kechynge and the Wardrobe'; the payments were made to Richard Gowge, the comptroller of the household, in four quarterly sums, at Christmas, Lady Day, Midsummer and Michaelmas.[52] Launderers do not figure in the detailed lists for breakfast in the same household, so the comptroller was probably subcontracting the work to outside washerwomen. The record tells us how often the payments were made to Gowge, but not how often he paid the washerwomen or how often they washed. Was it quarterly in line with the payments?

By the seventeenth century there is ample evidence that some élite households were washing more frequently than quarterly. In 1638–9, the Wortleys' household accounts for Gorhambury in Hertfordshire refer to both 'landrymaids' and 'washmaids' who were probably not the same people; the distinction was perhaps between personal body servants who washed, starched and ironed small items and maids who did the heavy washing. These were washing once a month for at least part of the year.[53] In addition, the household made extra payments (6d a day) to Goodwife Mason for helping to wash during a concentrated washing period in August and September, lasting seven weeks for two or three days a week. So regular washes were combined with one great wash at the end of summer.

In 1634 the Cecil household employed a laundrymaid at their Hertfordshire house, Hatfield. They also made extra payments for washing in London, mainly to 'Bettres

A RECIPE FOR SOAP

'First you must take halfe a strike of Ashen ashes, and a quarter of Lime, then you must mingle both these together, and then you must fil a panne ful of water and seeth them well, so doone, you must take foure pound of beastes tallow, and put it into the lye and seeth them togeather untill it be hard.'

(Thomas Dawson, *The Good Huswife's Jewell* (London, 1596/7), reprinted by *The English Experience*, (1977), p. 68)

Some substances lather naturally. Some were frequently mentioned in manuals and were probably fairly widely used in various cleaning processes – such as bullock's gall for de-greasing wool and making into a paste for marble. Plants which lather, such as soapwort, ragged robin, carnations and clove pinks are an unknown quantity; we simply do not know the extent to which they might have been used originally.

Hickman' who tendered a bill for eight weeks' washing, starching, smoothing and perfuming shirts, bands and aprons priced at 6*d* a week.[54] Both the Wortley and Cecil households bought ashes for washing and the Gorhambury accounts also show purchases of powder blue, white starch and regular bills from a cooper for the repair of washing tubs (see chapter 6 for explanations of washing substances).

In the disbursement books of the Leveson household we can see evidence of washing patterns over a longer time period. At Trentham, Staffordshire in 1645–6 the family employed a washerwoman, a widow called Alice Madder, on day work at 4*d* a day.[55] It is perhaps surprising that the pattern of payments shows a concentration of washing in December. Occasionally payments were for a single day, more often for three or four days at a time. There are payments also for powder blue and a single payment for two heaters for a smoothing iron (a box iron) made by the smith for 6*d*. Some thirty-odd years later, in 1677, the Leveson-Gower disbursement book was kept all year for London, where the household was again paying a laundress by the day. Again payments were grouped into a seasonal pattern, but now with a concentration in the summer and autumn.[56] The going rate for a day's washing in London in 1677 was very much more than in the country in 1645 – 1*s* a day. Similar materials were bought, but more regularly and in smaller quantities: starch at 6*d* a time; stone blue at 2*d* or 3*d* a time (2*s* 6*d* a pound); and ashes at 3*d* a time. Laundering equipment bought included: 'a board to wash points, 1*s*'; lines for clothes, 3*s* 3*d*; a total of 5 yards of calico cloth to smooth clothes on (i.e. to cover the ironing table); a clothes horse – described as 'a thing to dry cloaths on'; and repair of the wash tubs, costing 1*s* 6*d*.

In 1681–2, the Leveson-Gowers lived mainly at Trentham and the disbursement book again recorded payments for day-work washing, in sessions which could last from two to eight days, with one intensive week when two women were employed for seven days. Again the pattern is clearly seasonal but different – one great wash in the spring, smaller washes over the summer and another concentrated wash in the autumn. The rate of pay in Staffordshire in 1681 (3*d* a day) was less even than in 1645 or that paid by the Wortleys in the 1630s. The Trentham household bought ashballs, rather than simply ashes, in fairly regular amounts throughout the year, at times which did not necessarily coincide with the washing sessions, but perhaps reflected those times when ashballs were obtainable. They were bought usually 100 at a time, at a variable price of 2*s* 6*d* or 3*s*. The fact that they were bought for laundering is made clear by one entry which states 'ashballs to wash with'. The Trentham household also bought stone blue, and 7 yards of flannel to make an ironing cloth.

Frequency of Washing at Trentham

No. of days washing[57]

	1645–6	1677–8	1681–2
December	22		
January	4	5	0
February	0	0	0
March	4	0	0
April	2	0	7
May	1	2.5	28
June	3	5	10
July	1	4	4
August	0	2	6
September	4	7	12
October	0	8	6
November	0	4	0
December		0	0
Total no. of days	41	37.5	73

As we can see the total number of days washing in 1681–2 was almost twice that in the 1640s and '70s; is this an indication of the increasing ownership of textiles or simply a change in the fortunes or habits of the Levesons? The timings were probably a fine balance between the movement of individual members of the family, the ecclesiastical calendar, the weather and, perhaps most importantly, the seasonal pattern of migration of the family.

The effect of this last point can be seen at the Duke of Bedford's house in London in 1675. In addition to the 'great wash', Bedford House was thoroughly cleaned prior to the family's arrival:[58]

Before the Great Wash

Extracts from the Housekeeping Accounts at Bedford House

July 1675

For washing sheets and napkins . . .

when the two masters was in town	2s	0d
For four pounds of soap	1s	0d
For six pounds of candles	2s	6d
For three women one day to wash	4s	0d
A woman two days to help dry up the linen	3s	0d
For oil, ashes and sand to scour	1s	8d
A woman to scour two days	3s	0d
For washing of twelve pairs of sheets at 4d a pair	4s	0d
For two pounds of soap to scour the great room		6d
For nine pounds of soap	2s	3d
For four mops	4s	0d
For fuller's earth and sand to scour the rooms	1s	8d
For removing the goods from Mr Robert's chamber and the other rooms	2s	0d
For removing them again and setting up	2s	0d
A woman six days to help to wash all the rooms after the workmen left the house	6s	0d
A woman six days for scouring and washing the rooms and cleaning the irons against the family's coming to town	6s	0d
A woman to help to air the bedding when the family came to town	2s	0d

Shortly afterwards the family went back to Woburn and the housekeeper, Mrs Bruce, again had Bedford House cleaned and proceeded with her great wash:

Beningbrough, North Yorkshire, has a self-contained laundry block to the side of the main house. Shown here with a car parked close against the door, it incorporated a wash-house, ironing room and, on the first floor a laundress's bedroom and dormitory for the laundrymaids. The enclosed court in which it stands formed the drying green. (Robert Thrift, National Trust)

July 1675

For soap for the great wash when the family left London	4s	6d
For two women to wash after his Lordship's being in town	3s	0d
A woman four days to help to make clean the house when the family went out of town	4s	0d

As well as the upheaval caused by family moves, there was much coming and going of individuals (sons, daughters and grandchildren) between Woburn and Bedford House, as the latter was a convenient stopover for a couple of days in London. Each visit is marked by cleaning and washing bills from Mrs Bruce.

All the households mentioned above bought soap, sometimes a few penceworth at a time, sometimes by the firkin. Some was used for washing linen, but as the purchase pattern often differs from washing payments, much was probably used for scrubbing floors.

To summarise this admittedly very partial evidence, the pattern of washing in both town and country in the seventeenth century seems to have been that washing took place on irregular days or sometimes over several consecutive days within a week, for part of the year; in addition, there were more intensive sessions lasting several weeks concentrated into specific seasons, which could vary with family habits. Washing certainly was not the regular weekly occurrence all the year round, as it became later, but neither was it subject to a standardised quarterly pattern.

A record from West Coker, Somerset, however, supports the quarterly pattern. Up to the 1750s, the clerk of the household received between 6s and 7s for 'washing the linning four times a year'.[59] He was subcontracting this out to a washerwoman who probably came into the house to do her work, as according to an inventory it did possess a laundry in an outhouse. Sometimes evidence has been misunderstood by historians: as late as 1840 *The Workwoman's Guide*

The Beningbrough laundry, showing the ironing tables fitted around two sides of the room, the laundry stove to the right, the ceiling racks and box mangle in the centre. (Robert Thrift, National Trust)

advocated washing 'by the year, or by the quarter, in places where it can be done', advice which has been taken out of its context to refer to quarterly or annual washing. In context, though, it is clear that the author was referring to paying for contract washing rather than the actual washing.[60]

It is worth examining for a moment the term 'great wash', which seems to have been in widespread use over centuries. This obviously refers to the size of the wash but it had more complex connotations. Several sources, including Hannah Glasse as late as 1760, refer to 'great clothes', meaning large items of linen such as sheets and tablecloths, in contrast to 'small linen', meaning items of clothing. Confusingly enough, 'great clothes' could also mean outer garments (as in 'great coat'), as opposed to 'small clothes' which usuually referred to breeches. Small linen might be washed more frequently than the great clothes, often singly and overnight, in what Hannah Glasse referred to as 'little slop washes'. Of washing coloured linens, she advised: 'Such things as these are best done with the small linen, such as must not be either sop'd or wash'd after other great clothes.'[61] So in the eighteenth century at least we have a distinction between different types of linen, different types of washes and different timings.

Infrequent washing was possible if you were rich enough to accumulate large reserves of linen and was thus a status symbol. Caroline Davidson cited evidence for an inverse relationship between frequency of washing and wealth: the poor washed weekly, the gentry monthly and the rich quarterly.[62] According to Davidson, this difference began to break down in the eighteenth century, when the élite household started washing more frequently, firstly perhaps in town – where their clothes would get dirtier – and later transferring the habit to their country estates. This is not entirely borne out by the disbursement evidence above; the rich were washing more frequently and in more complex seasonal patterns than quarterly before the eighteenth century and this applied to both town and country.

It is likely though that regular weekly washing first developed in town households. In 1743 Lady Griselle Baillie, for example, stipulated a weekly wash for her Edinburgh household: 'one week the body linnen is washt, the second week table and bed linnen'.[63] By the mid-nineteenth century, weekly or fortnightly washing had become the norm and the general rule established that a respectable household never allowed soiled clothes to remain unwashed longer than a fortnight.

When washing finally became weekly, Monday was not invariably the designated day. One handbook dated 1881 said that Tuesday was the usual washday in large households, as this gave time to prepare on Monday for collecting, sorting, mending (all mending except of stockings was done before washing), removing stains and soaking.[64] A Monday wash certainly gave problems in this respect; in the 1920s at Shugborough, sorting and mending was done on the previous Saturday and the laundress had to go into the laundry on Sunday afternoon to put the linen to soak overnight. Some households had other reasons for choosing an entirely different timetable: in mid-Wales, the laundry at Powis Castle, for example, had to wait for the family's London wash to arrive at dawn on Friday mornings, so Friday was the start of their wash.

How often did people change their domestic linen? Unfortunately, we have little or no evidence on these matters before the reach of oral history. The housekeeper at Shugborough recalled that in 1930, the family had all their bed and bathroom linen changed on Fridays, with an additional change of one sheet on Tuesdays; sometimes family sheets were changed every day. The family tablecloths were used for one or two days and family socks and underwear were changed often three times a day. The servants had clean towels each week and clean bedlinen once a fortnight.[65] At Tredegar House in South Wales in 1911, a laundrymaid wrote to a friend, complaining of the extravagance of the house:

> My Lord has a clean table cloth for every meal. Is it not ridiculous? Sometimes when he is alone we have twenty-three table cloths in the wash in a week and when he has a lot of company we have anywhere from thirty-six to forty . . . The sideboard cloths are changed three or four times a week and my Lord has a clean cloth, on every tray taken up to him.[66]

CHAPTER 6

'Preparing for the Great Wash': Early Processes of Washing

Most people have a clear image in their mind's eye of the traditional washday. Centre stage are a dolly tub filled with hot soapy suds and an upright mangle. Yet these objects are themselves of recent invention and are not representative of washing technology before the nineteenth century. Although earlier laundry techniques consistently depended on labour-intensive methods involving heavy manual work and skill, the detail of those methods was complex and changed over centuries.

Caroline Davidson identified four methods of washing in use before the introduction of the washing machine: pounding or batting; steeping in urine; steeping in lye; and rubbing with soap.[1] These were seen as separate techniques which marked a definite line of progress. This is a little simplistic, for the boundaries between methods were often indistinct, one developing into another or used in combination, or used with other important techniques, such as boiling linen. Methods varied geographically, too, as explained by Mrs Hannah Glasse writing in 1760: 'Different . . . Places have all a different manner or Way of preparing for the great Wash.'[2] Given this proviso, we can identify four basic techniques, which are slightly different from Davidson's.

POUNDING

The most primitive method involved the action of pounding or batting the washing in a running stream or on a wooden bench to loosen dirt, using a stone or a ridged wooden beetle, with no soap. From as late as the eighteenth century, Davidson found many accounts of this type of washing and its Scottish variant of trampling the washing with the bare feet instead of with a wooden beetle. Country houses, however, had moved on from this method by the seventeenth or eighteenth centuries, except when used in conjunction with other techniques.

STEEPING

Steeping in some sort of cleansing liquid was a traditional method of washing linen. This could be either stale urine or a vegetable-based lye, or perhaps most frequently a mixture of the two.

Urine was a useful household product which was collected into small tubs in the backyard. It had a variety of local dialect names ('lant' in Lancashire, 'weeting' in Yorkshire, 'wash' in Scotland) testifying to its widespread use in laundering, textile-bleaching and leather-making. In the 1840s, in colliery towns of the north-east, urine from several houses was collected into large communal tubs, from which each household was supplied on wash day, a practice which according to Davidson survived until the late nineteenth century.[3] As early as the seventeenth century, the Yorkshire coast near Whitby was the centre of a large-scale trade in urine, for the manufacture of alum for leather-dressing. Deliveries were made of both 'country urine' and 'London urine' – the latter brought as return cargo for the collier boats.[4]

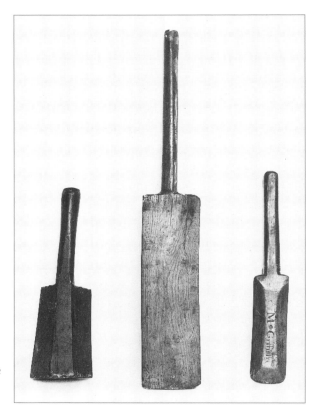

Three shapes and sizes of nineteenth-century washing bats from the collections in the Museum of Welsh Life, St Fagan's. (National Museum of Wales)

Lye was also a household product, made by steeping wood ash in water to extract the potassium salts which acted as a powerful alkali cleanser. Very often this was strengthened by adding bran, stale urine or water in which dung had been steeped, especially chicken or pigeon dung, of which larger households had an ample supply. This was used for steeping or pouring over the linen, a process called 'bucking' from the name of the large tub, or 'buck', used for the process (the smaller tub placed under the larger one was called a 'bucket'). The use of lye survived into the nineteenth century in both cottage and middling households probably because all the constituent materials were household waste products. It was retained very late for particular types of washing, notably white linen goods.

One of the problems with lye was that it had to be made of wood ashes. Some woods were better than others – ash, apple and pear wood gave a very strong bleaching action, oak tended to give a bad colour. Coal ash or mixed ashes would not do at all, so when households changed from wood to coal for their domestic fires they created a problem for themselves, the size of which can be gauged from the fact that as early as 1700 coal supplied over half the nation's fuel requirements.[5] For this reason households bought wood ashes which were sold in various forms. In 1678, the household of Swarthmoor Hall, Lancashire, bought 'bucking ashes' by the pound weight.[6] Ashes could also be consolidated with warm water into round balls – called ashballs or washballs – which were easier to market and store than loose ashes. As we have seen these figure frequently in household disbursements books of the seventeenth and eighteenth centuries.[7]

The making of ashballs was a small-scale cottage industry, providing useful supplementary income for women and children, especially in areas of rough waste where ferns grew abundantly, for fern ashes were particularly rich in potassium salts. In Staffordshire, for example, the ashball trade was recorded both by the antiquarian Robert Plot in 1686 and by Celia Fiennes on her journey through Cannock Chase in Staffordshire in 1698:[8]

In this Country they burn all this tyme of the yeare, July, their fern and make the ashes up in balls and so keep them to make Lye for driveing thier Buck of Cloth's, which whitens them much.

and:

When its [the fern] at its maturity which happens just before the harvest or hay tyme the whole Country are employed in cutting it up and burning it in heapes

The Fern Gatherers, *mezzotint of painting by George Morland, 1799. Both the man and the children have hooks for cutting fern which is being burnt on site. (Colonial Williamsburg)*

for the sake of the ashes, which they make fine and rowle them up in balls and so sell them or use them all the year for washing and scouring, and send much up to London, the ashe balls being easily sent about . . .

The fern ashball trade was also commonplace in Scotland and Ireland, where James Hall recorded in the early 1800s that thistles, docks and all sorts of weeds were added to the ferns; the burnt ashes were sieved, mixed with water and 'formed into a kind of loaves, shaped like brick-bats, with a hole in the middle of each, through which a string is put with a view to hang them up to dry'.[9] Some households cut and burnt bracken for their own use, not to sell. In 1612 the Shuttleworths at Gawthorpe Hall in Lancashire paid 6*d* a day for eight days for burning bracken and collecting the ashes for a year's supply of lye.[10]

If the home supply of ashes were plentiful, the easiest way to make lye was to set up a tub on a stand. Ash, sycamore or deal tubs were used, or a barrel with the top knocked out (not an oak barrel, though, as lye would strip the surface in a matter of hours). The bottom of the barrel was filled with straw and a piece of coarse linen or sheepskin was pinned above as a filter; this was filled with ashes. Soft rainwater was poured over, a gallon at a time, and the clear yellow lye dripped out of the bottom of the tub.[11] Many households set up a barrel permanently by the back door and routinely emptied slop water and chamber pots into it. Another way was to use a lye-dropper, a wooden hopper-shaped vessel with holes in the bottom, lined with straw and set over a tub. A method described in the nineteenth century was to add ¼ peck of wood ash to 3 gallons of water; boil for 20 minutes, put into a tub, then add a further 2 gallons of cold water, stir and let settle till clear.[12]

Clothes washed in lye or urine had to be well rinsed afterwards but even then they had a peculiar, characteristic stale smell, which could be masked by a rinse in a herbal infusion. Herbs which were used for this included sweet marjoram, costmary, rosemary, mint, hyssop, lemon balm, bay and angelica. Lavender was used for the same purpose, but more usually made up into small faggots or bags and put among the clothes when they were stored in the press. It was also thought that lavender deterred flies and moths.

The vegetable lyes used in bucking were purely potash based. After around 1815, washing soda, or sodium carbonate, began to be used for both softening water and pre-wash soaking, as well as in the soap industry. The ability of washing soda to cut through grease must have come as a tremendous step forward; for the first time there was available a cheap, easy and effective method of cleaning greasy kitchen cloths. Steeping remained a regular part of the pre-wash routine for most laundrymaids well into the twentieth century, using mainly soda but also borax or salt for handkerchiefs, or just plain water for loosening dirt or bloodstains in white cotton or linen.

SOAP-WASHING

The third type of washing was rubbing with soap. A crude form of soft soap could be made at home by boiling lye with mutton fat, bacon grease, pig fat or suet. It needed to be boiled for at least three hours and stirred more or less continuously. The process involved not just a physical mixing of ingredients but also a chemical reaction called saponification. The mixture would gradually thicken; salt was added to help coagulate it into a jelly. This home-made soap was soft and rolled into balls. It was very strong in action and therefore not much use in laundrywork except for cleaning workmen's overalls, but it was good for scouring floors or pots. The hard soap used in laundrywork needed a mixture of vegetable-based lyes plus caustic lyes made with urine and unslaked lime. Making hard soap at home was extravagant of both time and fuel and recipes varied from the economical to the excessive.

Commercially made hard soap was mentioned as early as the twelfth century in Bristol. Other centres of the soap-boiling trade were Coventry and several areas of London, while best-quality soap was imported from Castile. In England, the first patent for soap-making was taken out in 1662 and by the late seventeenth century soap was made in many qualities as the soap-boiling trade expanded.[13]

Soap-washing was an expensive system relative to bucking. Not only was hard soap difficult to make at home, but soaping needed warm or hot water, so more fuel was needed. Soap-washing also needed some form of agitation – rubbing with the hands or using a mechanical device such as a washing stock or dolly. Nevertheless, London households turned to soap-washing relatively early because their fires were generally of coal; they therefore could not make lye themselves and ashballs for sale were limited in quantity.[14] Bought soap was expensive, however.[15] Some types used high-quality oils, fats or wax, much of it was imported and all of it was taxed.

Excise duty on soap was levied first in the 1640s, on the basis of each household consuming a pound of soap a week.[16] This sounds a lot of soap, but it was the amount calculated by a contemporary authority which a 'respectable family' would use if all their washing was done at home.[17] A century later another authority calculated that a young bachelor earning an annual income of £238 would spend £12 of it on soap, starch and blue.[18] Soap was taxed until 1853, producing an annual revenue income for the government of just under £1 million in 1835. The tax was an effective discouragement to the expansion of both a large-scale soap industry and a commercial laundry industry based on it.[19]

Nevertheless, by the eighteenth century a wide variety of soaps could be bought if money was no object: common black soap was a transparent, very dark green jelly soap and, like a popular soft blue-mottled soap, was used for domestic cleaning and scouring; Crown, Joppa, Genoa, Castile and Marseilles were high-quality hard soaps sold in cakes and made with olive oil; green soap was made with vegetable oils for toilet use; there was also imported Irish soap, grey Bristol and even brown Windsor soap.[20] Davidson cites many examples of evidence of the

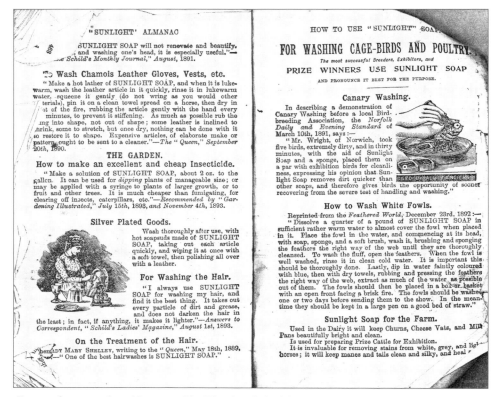

Extract from an advertising pamphlet The Sunlight Almanac for the Home, *published in 1899, which laid great emphasis on the versatility of Sunlight soap. According to the pamphlet, the soap could be used for washing anything from underwear to canaries. (P. Sambrook)*

widespread purchase of commercially produced soap by the later eighteenth century and not only by wealthy households. Home soap-making was a laborious, smelly and fuel-expensive process and housewives gave it up as soon as possible.[21] Yet laundry manuals of the late eighteenth century still included recipes for making home-made soap using waste fat material; whether they were widely used is debatable.[22]

In the nineteenth century, a hard yellowish resin-based soap was bought by country households in large quantities, dozens of 18 inch long bars packed in soap boxes or bought by the yard.[23] The bars were cut into tablets, trimmed and hung up to dry to make them last longer. The trimmed bits were dissolved in water to make a jelly for laundrywork. Country houses generally bought all their soap in quantity:

Ordered by the Trentham Housekeeper, 28 April 1875.[24]
From Greenhill and Co.

		£	s	d
Best yellow soap	@ 37/-	18	12	4
Best mottled soap	@ 38/-	19	2	5
2 doz. tablets Rose soap	@ 1/6	1	16	0
2 doz. " Windsor soap	@ 10d	1	0	0
2 doz. " glycerine soap	@ 10d	1	0	0
8 doz. " white toilet	@ 2/-		16	0
8 doz. " honey soap	@ 3/-	1	4	0
1 firkin of soft soap		1	4	0
Total 11 boxes in all		44	14	9

European soap-makers obtained their lyes from burnt kelp and barilla from Spain, but this trade was severely dislocated by the Napoleonic Wars. An alternative source was pioneered by a Frenchman named Nicolas Leblanc, who developed a cheap method of extracting soda from sea salt. This process was taken up by James Muspratt, and England's first commercial soda plant of this type was built at St Helens, Lancashire, in 1814. The large-scale industrial production of soap developed and after the removal of soap duty annual consumption began to rise quickly – from around 7 lb per head in 1853 to 8 lb per head in 1861 and 17 lb in 1900.[25] The first branded solid soap was Sunlight Soap, launched by W.H. Lever in 1884. This was still sold by the length, cut and wrapped by the retailer in Lever's own paper.[26]

BOILING

The fourth technique, boiling, became an integral part of soap-washing but it was also used from an early date with lye to accentuate its cleansing properties. Long before the general acceptance of the idea that microscopic germs spread disease, people understood the usefulness of boiling household linen not only for its appearance but also for sterilisation against fleas or even cross-contamination by disease.[27] Clothes were usually boiled with shredded soap and perhaps a whitener like washing soda, borax, pearlash or, for a time in the late nineteenth century, paraffin.[28]

Towards the end of the nineteenth century the first of the new so-called 'chemical' soap powders came onto the market, intended for use with boiling. The first of these for laundry use was Hudson's Soap Extract, initially marketed in 1863. By 1895, Harrod's was also marketing its own soap extract powder; in

An advertisement for 'Sunlight Soap', undated but late nineteenth century. The 'old system of washing' referred to is probably hand-washing with old-type soaps, rather than bucking or batting. (P. Sambrook)

1907 the Army & Navy Stores carried a wider variety – 'Y.Z.', 'Gospo' and 'Sicco'.[29] These, and the soap flakes and powdered soaps of the 1920s, were made by the further processing of conventional soap; truly synthetic detergents took over from them for all laundry purposes in the 1940s.

COMBINATION AND CHANGE

In practice many élite households used a combination of several washing methods over a long period. According to the writer of *The Laundrymaid, Her Duties and How to Perform Them*, published in 1877, bucking worked well only on linen goods.[30] A form of bleaching, over time it rotted cotton and flannel goods and faded dyes. This last did not matter with linen which did not take dyes easily and so was usually left undyed. This explains the early eighteenth-century laundry routine of Elizabeth Purefoy, who stipulated that her Buckinghamshire household should use alternate processes: 'One day Soap and another day ye Buck'; she was using different methods for different types of fabrics or garments.[31] This alternating system was probably far from being an idiosyncrasy of the Purefoy household and according to *The Laundrymaid* had been usual 'in byegone days', when 'it was a regular practice in farm houses to wash for all the servants, men and women, as well as for the boys and girls who were parish apprentices. Washings would then have been very weighty matters, had not the "soapwash" and the "bucking wash" been set apart, and done at different times.'[32] So the old system of washing was retained for large-scale linen – the 'great clothes' – and finer 'small linen', coloureds and cotton and flannel items were washed separately using soapwash.

In the élite household, soaking in lye had largely been replaced by soap-wash for general laundering by the second half of the eighteenth century.[33] Yet a century later it was still recommended by some manuals for washing baby linen, for cleaning purple silk and washing the contents of mattresses. The timescale of change usually accepted is that by 1800 the wealthy washed with bought soap, the middle classes with home-made soap, and working people with lye. The problem with this neat chronology, however, is that home-made soap seems to have been used mainly for scouring floors rather than clothes; and farmers' wives were still making lye from ashes in Warwickshire in the 1880s and in Suffolk in the 1910s.[34] It is a salutary lesson to see how quickly modern Western societies revert to the old universal ways of washing, whether it be the women of Italy deprived of soap during the Second World War and rediscovering the art of making lye, or the besieged women of Sarajevo batting their linen in the waters of the Danube.

THE BUCKWASH

How were these various techniques managed in practice? According to the writer of *The Laundrymaid*, bucking was archaic by 1877, when she recorded a visit to a house where it was still in use. The method she described used all four basic techniques – rubbing with a little soap, bucking with lye, boiling, and finally batting in the stream:

> The clothes were all sorted into three separate lots, and a large quantity of lye (made the day before from half a bushel of wood ashes) was standing by, ready for use. Three large tubs . . . with wooden taps in them, were placed upon low strong benches, and in these tubs the linen was laid, every article being taken one at a time, and spread broad and flat. The kitchen cloths and table cloths were in one tub, the towels and bed linen in another, and in the third, the shirts and other wearing clothes. A piece of yellow soap, about half a pound, was all that was to be used, and this was rubbed upon the collars and wristbands of the shirts, and upon grease spots in the table linen. As the things were laid in the tubs, some lye, a little warm, was from time to time put over them . . . till all were put into soak. This was done in the evening of the day before the bucking, and the things were then left in that state till the following morning, when the washing was proceeded with by pouring more warm lye over the clothes, and then drawing it off; this was repeated three or four times, having the lye each time hotter. The things were then taken, a few at a time, into washing-tubs, and washed in the lye in the usual way of hand-rubbing; they were then put into a boiler . . . and were boiled from half an hour to an hour, according to their quality, the strongest and dirtiest requiring . . . the longest time. After this they were put boiling hot into tubs or pails, and taken to be batted, swilled, and finished up at a brook about a hundred yards from the house, having a board set across it to hold up the water deep enough to dip the clothes in without catching up dirt from the bottom. . . . By the side of the brook was set a tub to blue in, and two washing stocks to bat the clothes upon.[35]

In the mid-nineteenth century, washing stocks and bats were so old-fashioned that the author described their use in detail:

> The clothes were first batted quite wet from the hot lye, holding the article in short folds, lightly by one end, and turning it over at every stroke from the bat . . .

then just dipped into the cold water and batted again; again dipped more freely in water, batted, rolled up, and squeezed upon the block; then well rinsed and blued; they were then ready to be dried.

The writer was impressed not only by the cleanliness of the clothes but also by the way a large amount of linen was processed in a short time:

I looked and listened in surprise, for I had never before seen so great an undertaking in the washing way. The family was a very large one, and, besides the household linen, there were eight men and four women servants in the house to be washed for. At first I could hardly believe it possible to be done by two persons only in two days, which I was assured would be the case. . . .

This should perhaps be described as the English way of washing, for the Scots and Irish were famous for their preference for treading the tubs of lye with their feet instead of rubbing with their hands. Either way, lye had a severely deleterious effect on the skin when it was exposed to it for a length of time, and laundrymaids' extremities must have become very sore and chapped.

Sketch of a woman batting linen on a washing stock. These were made of ash, and sloped away from the laundress so the water or lye would drain away from her. The bat was also made from ash. (From The Laundrymaid, *p. 56)*

THE SOAP-WASH

In 1877 when this account was published, bucking had been replaced by washing with soapsuds in most country house laundries. The writer of *The Laundrymaid* gave a description of the soap-wash which forms the basis of the following account.[36] Soaking and boiling were still an integral part of the process, but rubbing had long replaced batting and soap played a more important role than lye.

The account assumed two laundrymaids worked together, in a household consisting of man and wife and two children. The man's list of body clothing to be washed had 53 pieces, the woman's 61 and the children's 72; there were also 82 pieces of household linen, making a total wash of 268 pieces. These were first sorted into fourteen piles as follows:

1.   Coloured wool stockings
2.   Silk pocket handkerchiefs, white handkerchiefs
3.   Neckerchiefs, collars and frills, night caps, muslins, white gowns and white frocks
4.   Flannel waistcoats, flannel petticoats, white wool stockings
5.   Coloured gowns and frocks
6.   Shirts
7.   Petticoats
8.   Shifts
9.   Cotton stockings, drawers, pinafores, cotton waistcoats
10.   Fine tablecloths, fine dinner napkins
11.   Fine sheets, pillowcases and chamber towels
12.   Coarse tablecloths, glass and knife cloths
13.   Coarse sheets and coarse pillowcases
14.   Kitchen cloths, dusters, coarse towels.

The dirtiest of these were put to soak overnight. The next morning, pile 1 was washed first, separately, by one maid, while the other washed pile 2 separately. Then the two laundrymaids worked through the remaining twelve piles in the order given above, each pile being hand-rubbed twice, once by each maid, once on the right side and once inside out.

The Laundrymaid suggested the time which each pile should take, the amount of soap used and the various points at which suds could be changed. The timings for the two maids came to twenty-two and a half work hours in all, spread over two days.

As articles came from the second rubbing, they were wrung by hand. Keeping them in the twist, all the piles except the first and the last three were scalded with boiling water for half an hour each. The last three lots were boiled in the copper for half an hour in a mixture of two-thirds soap lather and one-third lye. The clothes, still twisted, could be put into the boiler in bags (to keep the scum off them), in hot but not boiling water; the water was then brought up to the boil and kept there. Care was needed not to use too much soap and not to overboil, both of which would 'set' the clothes – discolour them to a dull greyish hue which could be removed only by a strong bleach. As they were finished they were rinsed first in warm water and then in cold, wrung and hung out to dry. The final rinse could be blued. When dry, the wash was re-sorted, this time into ten piles, according to the method of finishing.

Needing starching, damping and ironing:
1.   Neckerchiefs, muslins and collars
2.   White gown and white frocks
3.   Coloured gowns and frocks
4.   Shirts

Damping, folding and mangling:
5.   Cotton stockings, shifts, pinafores, sheets, pillowcases, chamber towels, table linen, glass, knife, kitchen cloths

Ironing:
6.   Flannel and woollen clothing

Damping, folding and ironing:
7.   Petticoats, shifts
8.   Cotton waistcoats
9.   Nightcaps, drawers
10.   Handkerchiefs

Then followed a highly complex timetable of starching, drying and damping the piles, in an order which resulted in all the piles being ready for finishing at the correct time. Pile 5 was mangled, then the rest of the piles were ironed in order. The whole finishing process took almost another twenty work hours, of which the ironing took almost twelve and the mangling two and a half hours.

This system was theoretical, of course, yet basically the same system was described by a laundrymaid working at Shugborough in the 1930s. The methods were identical and the order of wash (family body linen, household linen, servant linen) was pretty much universal, the application of both common sense and domestic hierarchy.

THE POWDER SOAP-WASH

The system above used 6 lb of ordinary laundry soap. In 1877 the new powder soaps could change timings radically – a wash previously taking twenty hours would take four.[37] For these a third and entirely new system was needed.

The washing was divided into four piles according to fineness. The dirtiest parts of each item were rubbed with a soap tablet. Then a lather was made with the powder and all the clothes except flannels put in it to soak overnight. The next morning the copper was filled and lit, powder added as directed on the packet. The soaked clothes were wrung out, put into the copper and boiled for twenty to thirty minutes. As each item was taken out of the boiler, it was dipped in a pail of cold water, wrung, rinsed and blued. For flannels the powder was mixed into a cooler water. They were soaked for a short time and squeezed through the lather gently.

The wash-house at Shugborough, photographed in the 1970s, showing the wooden washing trays with fitted taps and the larger tubs for sheets, blankets and tablecloths. Wash-house floors were carefully tiled or flagged to drain to a single point, either in the centre or in one corner; a slope of 1 inch in a yard was recommended. (Cliff Guttridge, Staffordshire Arts and Museum Service)

When wet, *The Laundrymaid* warned, the clothes would not look as well as if washed by the old method, but they would improve greatly when dried. As an additional benefit, the water from the copper could be used later for cleaning tins, copper, brass and paintwork.

The Laundrymaid summarised: 'I cannot refrain from expressing my entire approval of this method over the original, not so much on account of the saving in time as the saving in soap and labour.'[38] Unfortunately for theory, these early soap powders tended to rot fabrics quickly. For this reason, the older system of using soap jelly remained popular for many years after.

FINISHING

The success or otherwise of the laundry depended not so much on machines but on the skill and know-how of the laundress. This was especially true of the finishing processes – starching, folding, mangling and ironing. It was the skill devoted to this stage of the work which set the country house launderers apart.

Blueing

In order to enhance the appearance of white linen, it was common to add a blue tint. There were several sources of laundry blue. The oldest was indigo, obtained from the plant *indigofera tinctoria*. In the seventeenth and eighteenth centuries it was marketed in several forms, called 'thumb', 'cake' or 'ball' blue. Because the Dutch held a monopoly on indigo from their colonies, the alternative ultramarine blue became more widely used, made from a naturally occurring silicate, later made artificially. It was considered to be both superior and, at 1*d* an ounce, cheaper than indigo. Ultramarine was also called 'Paris blue' or 'stone blue' and appears regularly in eighteenth-century disbursement books. Laundresses put it into a bag made from a small piece of flannel and squeezed it into the water. This is the blue which eventually became marketed by Reckitt and Sons.

There were other types of laundry blue, such as Prussian blue, a modern chemical invention based on iron, the textile dye aniline blue, and vedasse, a paste made from a decoction of woad twigs, and used in Holland and France.[39] Finally, an economical housekeeper could manage without any of these; by saving and soaking the blue paper wrappings of sugar loaves, she could make a strong blue water. The same blue paper was used to wrap linen to keep it from yellowing.

The Shugborough wash-house has two boilers, one for boiling whites and one, on the right, for heating water for the trays which are fitted to the opposite wall. Unlike a brewing copper, laundry boilers were usually made of cast iron rather than copper and had a rounded bottom suited to ladling out, rather than a tap. The third and central fire-box could boil a kettle to make starch or tea. (Cliff Guttridge, Staffordshire Arts and Museum Service)

Bleaching

Much time and effort was put into the pursuit of whiteness. Many of the early materials used in washing – urine and the poorer-quality laundry soap – had the effect of yellowing linen, as did the frequent use of soda and storing linen for a long time without use. For this last reason it was good practice to wash stored linen at least once a year so that it could be bleached.[40]

The traditional way in which linen was bleached was to spread it out on a lawn or field. As the linen dried in the sun and wind, it was kept damp by sprinkling with clean soft water with a watering can, or by throwing buckets of dilute lye over it, but in this case the linen had to be rinsed again before the final drying. This might go on for two or three days or longer and was the process used both domestically and by professional 'whitsters' who specialised in bleaching linen, both new and used.[41] Some of these were travelling bleachers who would call at country houses on a regular basis.

Every large country house needed a bleaching green or drying ground, 'a grassy corner . . . well open to the sun and . . . sheltered from high winds . . . the attentions of wandering poultry . . . and the incursions of pigs, puppies and calves – they not only soil the clothes, but will tear, and sometimes even eat them'[42] (see p. 161 for further descriptions of drying greens). The linen was laid out on the grass – kept fairly long, not close-shorn – as straight and even as possible, small items such as collars and cuffs on an old clean sheet. It was not put out while still boiling hot, for this would scorch the grass. It was turned periodically and when judged white and dry enough, the clothes were sprinkled a final time, rolled tightly and left for a few hours, before mangling or ironing.

Whitening on grass in this way was by far the most common method of bleaching before the nineteenth century and was still preferred by house laundrymaids in the 1930s.[43] The grass acted as an oxidising agent from the oxygen given off during photosynthesis, and the natural springiness of grass allowed air to circulate underneath, which was why fairly long grass was preferred. Midwinter sun was reckoned to be best and frosty air accelerated the bleaching process, especially a night frost. Flannels were not left out in the frost as this would felt them or even cause them to crack and flannels would also yellow in strong sunlight. Bleaching in this way required patience; the professional bleaching of new linen could take up to six months.

Other bleaching agents were used, especially in the nineteenth century when the pursuit of whiteness became something of an obsession. General whitening was helped by soaking in washing soda and lime was used as a bleach from the eighteenth century onwards: ½ lb of chloride of lime was mixed with two gallons of boiling water, left two or three days and bottled for use. Javelle water (sodium hypochlorite – a mixture of chloride of lime, sodium carbonate and water) was used on white linen and cotton; and pearlash, a concentrated form of potash was used both as a bleach and to reduce the amount of soap needed; it was used in a bag hung in the boiling wash.[44] Borax was used in the same way in the nineteenth century and in Holland whey or buttermilk was used in the last rinse to give a fine bluish whiteness.[45]

Drying

Ideally, bleaching was an integral part of drying outside. If an adequate grassy area was not available, clothes could also be laid out carefully on bushes. Best, because not too spiky, were clipped privet hedges, though at Berwick Hall near Shrewsbury there was a long tradition of drying delicate things on the holly hedge specially planted outside the wash-house. Clothes would dry quicker, however, on a clothes-line, made of either hemp or wire.

Quarter session records show that stealing clothes from lines or grass was an extremely common form of theft in the nineteenth century, but it obviously had a longer history. In the 1770s Susanna Whatman instructed her laundrymaid 'not to leave the linen in the drying ground at night, as it has been stolen'.[46] Carting washing was also risky. In January 1733 the Duchess of Kendall lost linen of 'considerable Value' when her washing, sent regularly by cart to her country house in Twickenham, was seized by highwaymen who loaded the bundles onto a spare horse brought for the purpose.[47]

Starching

Starching has been a feature of the laundering process since the sixteenth century and not until the end of the nineteenth century did the fashion for highly starched linen begin to decline in England. Starching was traditionally called the 'dry wash' or 'dry laundry', and even in early households was carried out much more frequently than the true wash – perhaps every day.

Throughout history, starch has been extracted for laundry use from all sorts of plants, the most important being wheat, potatoes and rice. During the late eighteenth century the most common source of starch was wheat, a practice which was condemned as being wasteful of a food staple by William Pitt, who recommended using arum and bluebell bulbs instead.[48] The finest starch, especially for fine body linen, was made from rice, though both potato and flour starches were good enough for furnishing fabrics. Potato starch was easy to make at home and nineteenth-century manuals still included instructions. Inventories show that ready-made starch powder was stocked by mercers by the seventeenth century; in the nineteenth century the best quality was a make called 'Glenfield'.

There were many tips regarding starching which laundrymaids passed on: a piece of loaf sugar could be added to make the starch clearer, and a small piece of wax, mutton fat or suet mixed into the starch made it less sticky on the clothes. Stirring the starch mixture with a wax candle would have the same effect; and a tablespoonful of turpentine or 'a good sprinkling of salt' added to ½ gallon of starch would add a beautiful gloss to the linen.[49]

Before starching, it was important to wash the linen, making sure that all old starch was removed, as old and new starch did not combine properly and as a result the fabric 'blistered.' Removing old starch required steeping for several hours in warm water to soften the starch; alternatively a few minutes standing in water mixed with a little malt extract would convert the starch to sugar which would quickly wash out. The linen was then dried completely before being rinsed out in starch.

BOILING-WATER STARCH

1 tablespoonful of good rice starch

3 tablespoonfuls of cold water

a small piece of tallow or white wax

A small teaspoonful of borax

Boiling water

Mix the starch to a smooth paste with the cold water; dissolve the borax separately with a little boiling water; add the tallow to the starch, then the borax, stir well; add the boiling water which will make the whole mixture turn to a stiff jelly. Add a good half pint of cold water to dilute. The borax adds gloss.

Old recipes say that starch needed to be boiled for at least fifteen minutes; tinned pans were apt to burn so old bell-metal pots were best. In starching a tablecloth, the ends are best put into the starch first, then the body. Fringes can be dipped into clean water after starching, as these should be left soft.

COLD-WATER STARCHING FOR STIFF COLLARS

'1 tablespoonful, or 1 oz of the best rice starch

Half a pint, or a small breakfast cup of cold water

A quarter teaspoonful of turpentine

1 teaspoonful of borax

Mix the starch with a little cold water, then add the turpentine; dissolve the borax separately in hot water then add to the starch. The turpentine makes the iron run smoothly, but too much yellows the linen.

Dip the the collars and cuffs, two or three at a time, into the starch, and rub them thoroughly, then wring out and rub them between the hands to enable the grains of starch to pass into the inner folds of the linen. Then stretch them out evenly on a clean towel, roll up tightly, and leave for a time, until the towel absorbs some of the moisture, when they will become easier to iron.'

(After Rankin, *The Art and Practice of Laundry Work*, p. 109)

Starch was applied in two ways. Hot-water starch, also called clear starch, was used for general purposes such as underclothes and household linen. Cold-water starch was used on areas needing to be very stiff and polished or 'glossed', such as collars, dress shirt fronts and cuffs. In cold-water starching the starch granules were uncooked and therefore entered more freely into the fabric. Glossing was functional as well as giving a good appearance: it made the fabric much more resistant to dirt. The process sounds simple but in practice it was easy to get it wrong – uneven dampening, for example, resulted in an uneven polish and too wet a collar or shirt front would come up in a 'blister' when ironed. After starching the linen was dried, then dampened again and rolled to make sure moisture was spread evenly before mangling or ironing.

Mangling

Mangling was the means by which damp-dried linen was smoothed by even pressure applied by a heavy weight, without the application of heat. It was very different from wringing water out of wet washing. Until the second half of the nineteenth century the two processes were completely separate – wringing was done by twisting in the hands and mangling by a box mangle. Later, a single machine – the upright mangle – was able to do both jobs. Since mangling was such a feature of the country house laundry, a separate section has been set aside for it in the next chapter.

Dampening and Squaring

Linen, and to a lesser extent, cotton is impossible to iron well if it is not adequately damp, so dampening clothes was a usual part of the routine. All the edges were dampened first, then the seams and double parts, then the garment was spread out and water sprinkled over the whole. Then it was rolled up tightly and left for half an hour for the dampness to 'regulate'. The French method of ironing differed from the English in that the linen was ironed wet, straight from

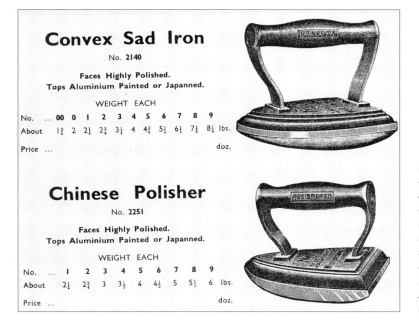

Extract from the 1937 trade catalogue by J. and J. Siddons, showing two versions of the curved-sole polisher or glossing iron. These were used with a rocking movement on a hard unpadded board to polish stiff collars or shirt-fronts and replaced much older mushroom-shaped glass polishers which were used cold. (P. Sambrook)

being wrung out. This resulted in a much glossier finish but needed hotter, heavier irons and a lot more time and labour.

One of the most important parts of the finishing process for household linen was pulling it back into shape before ironing or mangling. Without this 'squaring' or 'drawing' of the warp and weft it was impossible to get the corners square and the edges straight. With large cloths or sheets, it was impracticable to do this single-handed. One late nineteenth-century manual described the process:

> The operation requires two performers, who hold the cloth loosely by the four corners, the hems next to them. Lean back, so as to stretch it at the selvedges. Take in the next few inches of the hem, and stretch again, and so on, till you have the whole gathered into a kind of loose rope, which is now to be pulled smartly several times. Now bring the selvedges exactly to the middle, letting the two outer folds hang down. It will now be in four folds. Again take it by the corners and pull bias-ways, the two right-hands of the pullers first, and then the two left-hands. It may now be rolled tightly up and left till you are ready to mangle it or iron it.[50]

Ironing and Folding

In general, ironing was done in the direction of the selvedge, on the right side to give a gloss and on the wrong side to bring out patterns. Starched items were ironed with a very hot iron so as to cook the starch, and a small piece of wax tied in a piece of rag was kept handy to rub on the sole of the iron to prevent it becoming sticky with starch. Woollen underwear was ironed on the wrong side to make the surface smoother to the skin. Blankets were never ironed, but mangled, shaken vigorously and then rubbed with a piece of flannel to raise the pile.

There was a correct order for ironing garment parts. First to be ironed were the double thickness parts on the wrong side, then double thickness parts on the right side; insertions and tucks; edgings, small parts, and finally large parts. For example, in ironing servants' caps, the double-thickness frill of the caps was first lightly ironed while holding the body of the cap wrapped up in the left hand to keep it damp; next the body was ironed and finally the frill was finished with an Italian iron. For a gown, the waistband was ironed first, then the body, then the sleeves, last the skirt.

Except for double damask, tablecloths were ironed only on the right side. In the past, damask was never ironed, but dried flat and mangled to bring up the

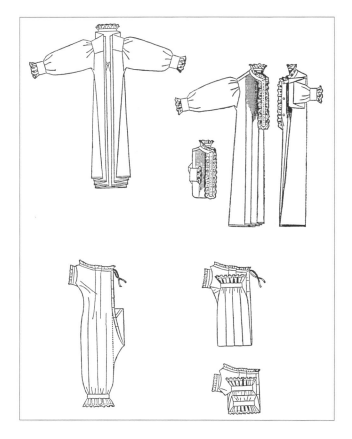

Diagrams to explain the method of folding lace-edged nightshirts and combinations. (From Jack, Art of Laundry Work, *pp. 44–7)*

sheen and pattern; in the sixteenth and seventeenth centuries and earlier, when it was fashionable to show a square or rectangular fold on the cloth, it was then very carefully folded and screwed down tightly in a linen press. Fringes were never ironed, but knocked hard on the edge of the table to separate them and then finished with a brush or comb.

Judging the right temperature for each fabric could only be learned by practice. Linen needed a hotter iron than cotton, muslins a cooler. Muslin was usually ironed twice, and was pulled out crosswise between ironing. Tablecloths were best ironed straight from the line at the correct dampness; for this reason cloths which had become too dry were put back into the wash, rather than simply dampened.

Folding clothes correctly during ironing could make all the difference to the finished appearance; folding for mangling was even more important, not only in the appearance but in time saved in not having to iron the article afterwards.

FOLDING AND IRONING A TABLECLOTH INTO A SCREEN-FOLD

For a cloth of any size you need two people:

Fold the cloth selvedge to selvedge with the right side inside, pulling the selvedge quite straight. Fold again in the same direction; to fix the centre crease line, beat it once against the table. Pull the cloth into shape so that the hems and selvedges are even. Hold up the cloth between you by the fold, with the selvedges hanging downwards; take the outer selvedge and bring it up and over the fold to the other side; beat against the table again to fix the crease lines – this will give the screen fold which is the traditional fold for tablecloths.

   Place the cloth on the table with the two folds along the front edge; press, do not push; iron the hems lightly, always ironing in the direction of the selvedge; then lift the top fold and spread out. Iron all of the surface opened to you, going over the fold and ironing the hems; lift up the fold still on the table to meet the top fold; iron the last piece and the hems. This will iron the whole of the right side of the cloth and all the hems. Turn cloth over so you are back at the beginning and repeat once. Fold cloth in half, leaving the name or mark at the top. Press the crease. When aired roll from the fold halfway, when it bulges, turn over and complete the roll. Tie with ribbon.

(After Cassells, *Household Guide*, vol. 5)

Every item had its own fold – tablecloths were screen-folded into four, napkins were screen-folded into three both lengthwise and widthwise, unless they were needed for fancy folds. Underclothes were particularly difficult to fold as they were heavily gathered.

STAIN REMOVAL

Stain removal was done before washing either by the lady's maid or the laundress, according to whether the article was body linen or household. Either way, it was a necessary skill using mainly very simple, easily available domestic cleansers. The only materials which had to be bought were usually highly dangerous acid-based cleaners. Good household management prevented the more difficult stains such as iron mould or mildew and most others were removable given prompt action, patience and the avoidance of fixatives such as soap, soda or hot water.

Fruit Stain

First try pouring boiling water over it. Never use soap as this will fix the stain.

Wine stain

Never wash with soap before trying to remove this as washing will fix it. Wet with cold water, sprinkle with dry starch and rub into a paste. Leave to dry for an hour; if not gone when this is rubbed off, try salt and lemon juice rubbed on for a few minutes, then removed by pouring hot water through it.

Grease spot

Fold a soft clean towel under the stain and rub a rag dipped in turpentine in circular motion beginning at the edges. Or make a paste with French chalk[51] and water; apply to the wrong side. Leave to absorb the grease, then shake and heat with a warm iron.

Iron mould

Sprinkle liberally with lemon juice, then leave in strong sunshine. [This does not work well, so laundresses were instructed by nineteenth-century manuals to use salts of lemon, which could be used only on white things as it bleached colours.]

Ink

If not dried, sprinkle with salt and rub with a cut lemon. Or soak in sour milk or boiled milk, or even better, buttermilk; as the stain comes away into the milk renew the milk; or rub the stain with a tomato cut in half; or dip the stain into melted tallow from a candle; send to the laundress in this state and the spots will wash out.

Egg stain

Washing any linen stained with egg in boiling water will set the stain and make it almost permanent. Instead soak in cold water.

Mildew

Sprinkle with salt then rub well with lemon juice. If this fails, rub with soap, then scrape some French chalk over the soap and leave in the open air. Sprinkle water over it as it dries and keep repeating the process. Then wash as normal.

Blood

If wet, wash in cold water; if dry, steep in cold water with washing soda, then wash as usual. Bleach in the open. Hot water will fix it. Starch paste is also effective.

Candle Grease

Put brown paper above and below the stain and press with warm iron, changing the paper as the grease comes away.

CHAPTER 7

'Ingenious and Simple': the Material Culture of Laundering

The equipment needed for early washing systems was simple if cumbersome: bucking tubs and stands for them; smaller tubs to catch the lye draining from the bucking tubs; washing bats; and some means of heating the lye. If space was short, all this could be stored in an outhouse and moved outside in good weather, so purpose-built wash-houses were not essential. A good supply of water was, so the site of the laundering would be close to the pump, well or stream. Since washing was intermittent, the housekeeper could wait for suitable weather and it is likely that much of the steeping and bucking was done outside. Farmhouses and larger houses probably had a room for washing which could also be used for other purposes.

Probate inventories of the eighteenth and earlier centuries list household equipment, and it would be possible to use these to track the introduction of special rooms and equipment for laundering. Although the detailed work on this remains to be done, study of three published collections of inventories (from a rural area of mid-Essex, from Wellington in Shropshire, and Lichfield in Staffordshire) shows that neither wash-houses nor irons were present in ordinary households until the seventeenth century.[1]

Another point which is well illustrated by inventories is that washing and ironing had different locational patterns within the house. According to the inventories, the single most common place where washing equipment was kept was the brewhouse and it seems reasonable to suppose that fixed equipment for boiling liquor or worts could also be used heating water for laundry; brewing manuals often mentioned this practice, albeit with horror.[2] In Lichfield and Wellington, however, the most usual place to keep smoothing irons was the kitchen, but in some households it was the hall (or 'house place', as it was often called in this part of the country). In rural Essex, the hall was clearly the most usual place to keep the ironing equipment. This variability no doubt reflects the changing roles of the hall and kitchen; the irons were kept wherever the main cooking hearth was fitted and early on this was in the hall, later the kitchen; the timescale of this change varied regionally and with time and status.

The probate inventory evidence used above relates to smaller households; but the difference in location between washing and ironing was present in élite households, too. 'Scouring' (i.e. scrubbing) and bucking were probably done by a contract washerwoman working either in her own home or in a washing space provided by the house. If attached to the house she might be called a washmaid. Laundering (i.e. starching, shaping and smoothing intricate personal linen) was done in the living quarters by a female body servant or laundrymaid. The latter would set up a working area in an unused bedroom or nursery or lady's maids' room, fitted with facilities for starching – a charcoal stove or brazier, a wooden bowl and a bell-metal pot.[3] Sometimes such a room was actually called a 'starching place' as seen in one of Robert Smythson's plans for Slingsby Castle in Yorkshire, dated around 1599.[4] A sixteenth-century list of domestic offices provided at Hengrave Hall in Suffolk included a 'scouring room' as distinct from 'the Laundry and Linen room'.[5] As late as 1720 Richard Benthall had a starching room at Benthall Hall.[6] The two functions of scouring/bucking and laundering were thus distinct, in terms not only of the nature of the work but also of location, status and personnel.

Following this tradition, when more sophisticated laundry premises were built into the élite house it was the custom to separate the washing and ironing facilities into rooms which were often called 'wash-house' and 'laundry' or in Victorian parlance 'wet laundry' and 'dry laundry'. Though separate rooms, the tendency was increasingly to build them adjacent to each other. Natural light being an important feature of both, architects preferred to build them at corners of the service blocks so that two walls of outside windows could be provided.[7] Nineteenth-century manuals recommended that the dry laundry be built directly above the wet laundry (as at Berwick Hall in Shropshire and Shugborough in Staffordshire); in practice they were also often built next to each other (as at Kelmarsh in Northamptonshire, Beningbrough in North Yorkshire, Ormesby near Middlesbrough and Killerton in Devon).[8] Even houses which at first sight appear to have a single dual-purpose laundry have usually been altered. Attingham, in Shropshire, had a combined laundry in 1913, a single large room fitted with washing 'troughs' as well as ironing tables and a windlass for the airing frame.[9] An earlier sale inventory, however, dated 1827, shows separate a wash-house and dry laundry.[10]

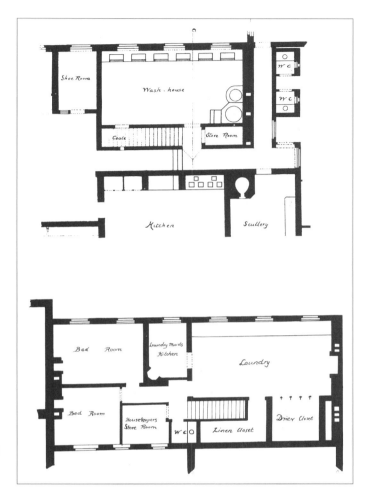

Layout of the ground-floor wash-house and first-floor laundry as planned in 1860 for the Bagot family at Blithfield Hall, Staffordshire. The wash-house incorporated a row of washing trays under the windows and two boilers. The laundry above was fitted with a drying closet heated by a stove on the ground floor. The laundrymaids lived on the job, their bedrooms and kitchen being next door. (Staffordshire Record Office)

Laundry complexes were usually built at a distance from the main living rooms, further away than the kitchen or butler's pantry. Unlike body servants, washmaids did not need to be within calling distance of the master or mistress, and did not need to be within range of wire bell-pull systems when they were introduced in the eighteenth century. So the unpleasant smells associated with early washing techniques could be placed at a distance and laundries could be built either within the main house or, increasingly as time went on, altogether separate. Thus Vanbrugh's design for Blenheim Palace in Oxfordshire (1715) placed a laundry with adjacent wash-house on the corner of the Kitchen Court furthest from the house; and William Kent's design for Holkham Hall in Norfolk (1730) positioned it in the south-east pavilion, within the Chapel Wing.[11]

The laundry was even more distant at Trentham, in a completely separate block of service buildings, adjacent to the brewhouse and the farmyard, well away from the main domestic offices which were grouped around another courtyard immediately to the rear of the family living quarters. The laundry was thus outside the security ring controlled by the main porter's lodge. This contrasts with the position of the laundries at Kingston Lacy and Shugborough, where the laundry was sited immediately opposite the kitchen. The Victorian architect Robert Kerr recommended a nearer site for small country houses, but a more distant site for larger households.[12] When the laundry was positioned in the stableyard, it was often connected to the main house by an underground tunnel – as at Kelmarsh, a laundry which is remarkably self-effacing, most of it being hidden away underground with only part of the top half being visible above ground level.

One of the finest restored country house laundries is at Kingston Lacy in Dorset. It stands at the side of the great house, on the right in this photograph, opposite the kitchen. The first floor of the double-storeyed building incorporated a drying loft. Viola Bankes remembered this fine laundry as it was in her childhood: 'There were two laundry rooms in a low building along one side of the courtyard with a semi-covered passage from the back door. We could look down on them from the backstairs or visit them, especially if our mother was away.' (From Bankes, Kingston Lacy Childhood, *p. 63) (Dudley Dodd, National Trust)*

Old letters – a scene at Knole, 1873 by Claude Andrew Calthrop (Mallett & Son Antiques Ltd/Bridgeman Art Library). The scene shows a lady reminiscing over breakfast in her room, while a smart maid makes her bed and an aged liveried footman burns torn up letters in the fire. Despite the grandeur of the room, one feels the servants have a comfortable relationship with their mistress.

John Sheepshanks and his maid, *by William Mulready (1786–1863) (Victoria & Albert Museum/Bridgeman Art Library). Although seated before a very grand fireplace, John Sheepshanks preferred to be waited on by a maid rather than a footman – or perhaps could only afford female service. Both this and the Stevens picture show a period before formal dress for housemaids was standardised into black.*

A Servant ironing *by Henry Morland, c. 1767 (Tate Gallery). This shows a personal body servant rather than laundry maid, comfortably seated to iron a pocket, sleeve or neckpiece. She is using a box iron made to a patent issued to Isaac Wilkinson of Denbighshire in 1738. This was an extrememly popular version of the box iron similar to that illustrated in a catalogue of 1937.*

A Lady's Maid soaping linen *by Henry Morland, c. 1767 (Holburne Museum & Crafts Study Centre/ Bridgeman Art Library). She holds a square of hard soap and is engaged in what Hannah Glasse referred to as 'little slop washes'.*

A comfortably furnished servant's bedroom at Lanhydrock (National Trust Photographic Library / Andreas von Einsiedel).

An Aspiring Connoisseur *by Alfred Ernie Stevens (1823–1906)(Whitford & Hughes/ Bridgeman Art Library). Like many paintings of servants, this has an equivocal feel to it. Despite the whimsical title, the expression on the maid's face is touched by doubt rather than envy. She cannot have been engaged in serious cleaning as she is not dressed in her morning dress and coarse apron and it is unlikely she would be simultaneously brushing and dusting.*

A photograph of Elizabeth Butcher, a housemaid at Petworth in 1881 (Kevis Collection). She is dressed in a smart dress of braided velevet and an elegant hat to match.

The Livery Room at Lanhydrock (National Trust Photographic Library / Andreas von Einsiedel). This shows footmen and coachmen's dress livery, which in the later 19th century would be issued only on special occasions.

The country house pattern of service survived well into the 20th century, even in some wealthy town houses, as shown by the household of the industrialist Frank Green (seated centre) outside his home, the Treasurer's House, York, in the late 1920s. The Treasurer's House was orginally built for the treasurer of York Minster and in 1930 was given by Frank Green to the National Trust.

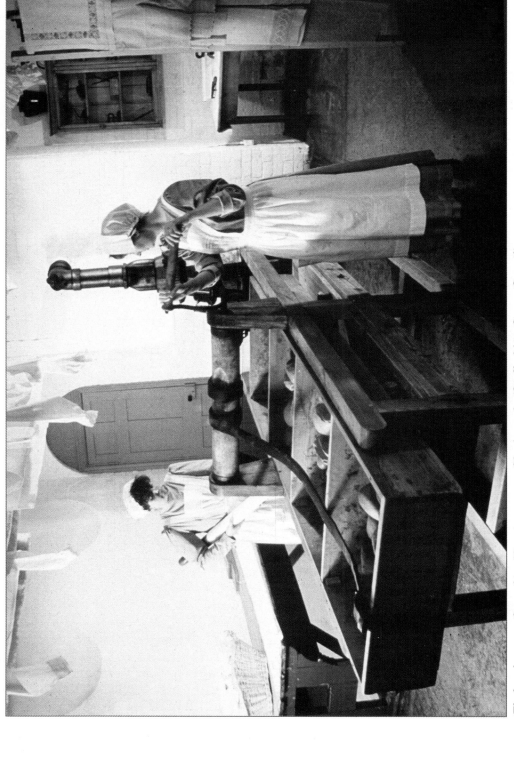

The laundry room of a working Victorian estate at Shugborough. (Staffordshire County Council).

The Brushing Room at Penrhyn Castle. (National Trust Photographic Library/Andreas von Einsiedel). This is extremely spacious and well-equipped for brushing suits, hats and boots. More often the brushing room was a tiny room with few comforts.

THE WASH-HOUSE

A few country houses – Traquair near Peebles, for example – still have records of their outdoor washing 'beach' where washing was batted; and rivers such as the Tay have place names associated with the outdoor washing and bleaching of linen. But large houses with an indoor water supply developed their own built-in premises, recreating in a more convenient form the advantages of a running stream. The laundry 'scrub' at Ormesby near Middlesbrough used this intermediate style of washing. The long stone trough which wrapped continuously around two walls of the room provided a stand for small tubs for steeping or soaping, as well as a surface for batting or scrubbing which could be quickly sluiced down. On a smaller scale is the little wash-house attached to a cottage at Ashbury in Warwickshire, now owned by the National Trust; here

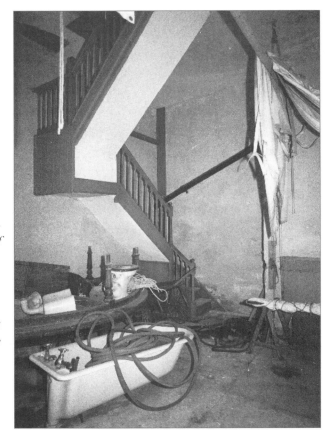

Once laundries became unused, they fell prey to the universal need for a dumping ground for all sorts of odds and ends. This view from the National Trust's archive collection shows the wash-house at Kingston Lacy, as it was in 1982, before restoration to its present state. The stairs led up to the drying loft. Viola Bankes had very different memories of it: 'All the washing of the family's and servants' linen was done, all day and every day, by the two Irish laundrymaids. The sheets, washed without chemicals and carried in huge heavy baskets to be hung out of sight behind the stables, would emerge beautifully soft and fresh.' (From Bankes, Kingston Lacy Childhood, p. 63) (Dudley Dodd, National Trust.)

there is a small shallow brick trough. There is a clear relationship between this type of trough and the later shallow fireclay sink, often called a slop stone, which was so common in nineteenth- and early twentieth-century back kitchens.

Many old wash-houses in country houses must have been fitted with stone scrubs to be used with 'portable, old round tubs', but Ormesby is a rare survival.[13] The more usual later eighteenth- and nineteenth-century wet laundry was fitted with a row of rectangular laundry 'trays', wooden sink-like fittings similar to the traditional nineteenth-century free-standing laundry trough, each tray measuring approximately 3 feet × 2 feet × 18 inches, the width at the bottom being 6 inches less than at the top. They are usually made of pine, the pieces closely dovetailed and with no nails showing inside. Kerr called this row of sinks a 'dresser' and thought it should be fitted immediately under the windows.[14] The row was needed for use by different laundrymaids and for different rinsing waters. Since they tended to leak if not used regularly, they were sometimes later lined with lead or copper or sometimes replaced altogether by brown ceramic sinks (as at Erddig) or by white porcelain (as at Hill of Tarvit in Fife), both retaining the shape of the original trays.

The washing trays were usually connected by lead pipes to a boiler for the hot-water supply, and directly to the cold-water supply, both controlled by brass taps over the trays. Underneath was an open drain. The floor in front of the trays was often covered with a wooden slatted platform to lift the laundrymaids' feet off the cold and wet floor. In the nineteenth century laundrymaids wore clogs rather than pattens, which were thought dangerous.

All wet laundries had a 'copper' or more accurately an iron boiler. Most country house wash-houses had two – one to be used for heating water for the trays and one for boiling linen. A few wash-houses (Trentham for example) had such a huge throughput that they were fitted with three. Sometimes boilers were filled with water by hand from a nearby cistern (as at Shugborough) or from a nearby pump (as at Erddig). Each boiler had an individual furnace fire and ash pit underneath and were usually connected to a common flue, at the base of which was usually some sort of small open fire for making toast or boiling kettles for making starch. Like a brewing copper, the laundry boiler was 'hung' so as to allow heat to wrap around the sides of the boiler in an anticlockwise 'wheel-draught'. It was therefore important to fill the boiler at least three-quarters full with water and to have an adequate but not too fierce a fire underneath. The hot-water boiler at Killerton in Devon was fitted with wooden panelling above, which channelled steam upwards into a ventilating outlet. Laundry furnaces were used as a means of rubbish disposal – cinders and all sorts of waste bits of wood could be burnt on them to eke out the coal.

Cleaning a laundry boiler after boiling clothes was a real chore as they usually had no tap. While it was still warm the water had to be baled out by hand, leaving a small amount in the bottom; this was used with a scrubbing brush to remove scum marks. The remaining water then had to be mopped up and the boiler thoroughly dried with a cloth to prevent rusting.[15] If the laundry was perpetually damp, the inside of the boiler was rubbed over with a piece of mutton fat to prevent rust. When the boiler was needed again all that was necessary was to fill it with water and washing soda; this combined with the grease and made it soluble.

To accommodate larger pieces of washing like blankets, the wash-house would also be fitted with one or two free-standing tubs, circular and coopered, later replaced by rectangular tubs held together by iron bars. The warmth of laundries

---

EXTRACTS FROM THE INVENTORY OF TRENTHAM, STAFFORDSHIRE, 1826

Laundry

3 window blinds
1 long deal table
2 large and 2 small tables
2 clothes horses – 5 folding ditto
7 chairs with rush bottoms – 4 stools
1 mangle – 2 winding jacks
9 clothes baskets – 7 old ditto
1 ironing stove – 3 Italian irons
15 large flat irons – 6 small ditto
3 tin candlesticks – 1 tin bonnet
1 copper tea kettle – 1 toasting fork
1 green steel fender and fire irons – 1
   footman
1 swing glass – 2 japanned tea boards
1 wooden knife box – 5 knives and forks
2 large and 2 small ironing blankets
4 ironing stands – 1 blanket brush
1 towel roller – 3 mangling clothes

Wash-house

7 wash tubs – one wrinsing tub
3 pails – 3 piggins – 3 iron furnaces
1 draining horse – 1 clothes horse
3 brass saucepans – 1 iron ditto
2 3-quart cans – 4 old candlesticks
1 horn lantern – 2 coal shovels
2 hair sieves – 1 wooden spoon
1 japanned coal box – 1 force pump

SRO Sutherland Ms, D593/R/7/106)

often created problems with infestations and at Coleorton in Leicestershire the laundress kept a dog to control the rats which used to pop up into the empty tubs through the plug hole. The dog was particularly encouraged since the tubs were also used by the laundrymaids as baths.[16]

Wash-houses needed a good water supply, preferably soft rainwater, which was believed to be less damaging to both clothes and hands, and gave a better colour to the wash. It was stored in cisterns, in older wash-houses made of wood perhaps lined with lead or zinc, later of slate or brick coated with hydraulic cement. Like Killerton and Ormesby, many houses collected rainwater off the roof as a supplementary soft supply. Before electricity was installed, water had to be hand-pumped from the supply, this being a regular twice-daily routine for the odd man, or in the case of the laundry at Coleorton, the laundrymaid herself. At Ormesby the state of the water supply could be seen at a glance from a gauge mounted on the wall. In the country house, conserving water was a way of life.[17]

Wash-houses were also supplied with a number of small-scale utensils. Unlike the commercially-made ribbed board, the traditional country house washboards were substantial, plain, thick boards made by the estate carpenters. They could be used either by rubbing the linen onto them by hand or with a scrubbing brush.

An early version of a laundry drying closet built at Kingston Lacy. It has wooden rails and front panels and is heated by a small stove situated to the left of the closet. (Dudley Dodd, National Trust)

The traditional willow clothes basket (or 'flaskett' in an inventory from The Vyne, in Hampshire) was locally made and varied in details, but basically changed very little over a long period. Most big houses also had at least one larger basket on wheels which was fitted with a calico liner, which could be trundled along the corridors into the house to collect and deliver laundry to the housekeeper and lady's maid. Some, like Ormesby, had a chute for soiled linen from the servants' landing to the wash-house below.

DRYING GREENS, LOFTS AND CLOSETS

Whenever possible linen was dried outside, in a drying or bleaching green or 'bleachery', as at Kinross House, built by Sir William Bruce in the 1660s and '80s; here the 'bletcherie' was combined with the 'Women's Bass Court', a partly grassed area outside the women's part of the house but away from the male Kitchen Bass Court.[18] In the country house of the eighteenth century and later, the tendency was to hide 'the summer green' more discreetly in a walled area at the back of the house, partly because of the increasingly private nature of much of the linen. On her visit to Newby Hall in the West Riding, Celia Fiennes noted a 'Landry Close with frames for drying of cloths, wall'd in . . . '. This was behind the flower garden at the back of the house.[19] Walled drying greens near to the laundry survive at Castle Ward in County Down, Calke in Derbyshire and Dunham Massey in Cheshire. Another position for the walled drying green was near the outer part of the kitchen garden, in what were called the 'slips'. A good example of this survives at Berrington in Herefordshire: the walls are of the same height as the kitchen garden, completely enclosing a rectangular grassed area, with a gravel path down the centre and only a single wooden door for access. Inside the walls, metal stays for clothes lines were fixed about 6 feet apart and stepped opposite each other so that a whole series of lines could cross the green. The lines were usually of hempen rope, though sometimes they were made of thin copper wire. The hemp lines needed careful maintenance – removal after use, and a periodic boiling with soap and soda.[20] At Berrington, attached to one wall is a wooden covered shelter to store the line props.

Special provision had to be made for indoor winter drying. In an old-fashioned house this might be a loft fitted with a ventilated louvred lantern in the roof, a drying stove, pulleys with racks or lines. Drying lofts exist at Kingston Lacy and at Dyrham Park where one appears on the plans of the wash-house dated 1700.[21] At Coleshill in Berkshire, the laundry drying loft was extended by removing a floor sometime in the

Left: Thomas Bradford's 'Tower' laundry stove, made in the late nineteenth century. Now in the laundry at Shugborough, it was originally supplied to a laundry in Wolverhampton. It has spaces for over forty flat irons and four curved-bottom polishers. Above: Thomas Bradford's distinctive star and crescent logo. (Staffordshire Arts and Museum Service)

nineteenth century, when the amount of linen to be serviced was increasing. Later the floor was put back when the laundry was converted into a house.[22]

In the mid-nineteenth century drying closets were an innovation which quickly became almost universal in large private laundries. These originated from a simple idea which still survives at Kelmarsh, of building a tall narrow recess alongside the laundry fire into which wooden racks could be pushed. Increasing the number of racks and fitting them with wheels which ran on tracks resulted in the sliding hot-closet, an early home-made version of which exists at Kingston Lacy. Later commercially made closets have survived at Erddig, Killerton and Berrington as well as in many other households.

THE LAUNDRY

The ironing room or dry laundry needed a fireplace with some sort of grate for heating both irons and water for starch. An inventory of the laundry at The Vyne in 1754 included 'a range', probably an ordinary open barred range of the day. Later laundries were fitted with special stoves, much preferred since they were designed to keep the iron clean from soot and smoke. A second inventory from The Vyne shows that they had installed a laundry stove by 1842. Simple ones could be home-made of brick with a small iron fireplace, like the one at the top of the laundry steps at Erddig. From around the 1860s more elaborate stoves were marketed by manufacturers such as Thomas Bradford of Salford, in a variety of shapes.

Irons were ledged on the stove according to how hot they needed to be and according to size. Most stoves had special places for round-bottomed polishing irons. For obvious reasons, laundry stoves were not usually black-leaded, but rubbed vigorously and occasionally given a thin coat of limewash which preserved the stove and made it look clean.[23]

One or two walls of the ironing room were usually built up with ironing boards – stout pine tables set against the wall and under the windows for good light. It was important not to have these tables set too high, for the ironer needed to be able to lean her full weight over the iron. The tables were padded with old blankets covered with strong linen or calico sheeting pulled tight and fixed with brass pins or tied to the legs with tapes. Both Beningbrough and Ormesby have good sets of built-in tables. A sizeable stretch of tabling was needed to deal with the large items, but small, shaped sleeve, skirt and shirt boards were also required, again padded with blanket and sheet pieces. Polishing boards for shirt fronts were not padded, as a hard surface was needed for this. These boards were used propped up on the table at one end and a chair or stand at the other.

In the early eighteenth century flat irons were still fairly expensive items not present in large quantities in country house laundries. In May 1723 the household at Little Crosby in Lancashire bought 'smoothing irons, two very large and good, £1' and on Nicholas Blundell's death in 1737 the kitchen possessed three smoothing irons complete with their 'cradles'.[24] By 1754, The Vyne had six and by the nineteenth century flat irons had become much more numerous, with many varied sizes. The laundry at The Vyne shows an increase from six to seventeen flat irons and an inventory of Trentham in 1827 shows fifteen large ones and six small. The irons were, of course, provided by the house but each maid would tend to use her particular set which she marked. She needed two, or preferably three, of each sized used, one or two for heating while the third was being used. At Coleorton in the 1930s, two laundrymaids had a dozen ten-pounders and eight eight-pounders and several smaller irons.[25]

The box or 'lock' irons which were heated by pairs of removable 'bolts' of iron and which appear in ones or twos in many eighteenth-century inventories are rarely

INVENTORIES OF THE DRY LAUNDRY AT THE VYNE, BASINGSTOKE

1754

A range two shovels a pair of tongs and a fire iron, a hanging iron, six flat irons, two box irons, four heaters, two clothes horses, a large deal table, three small tables three stools three flaskets [baskets], three chairs, two hair lines and a mangle for linnen.

1842

An ironing stove and pipes	Deal table
2 oak tables	9 flasketts
2 " "	Deal table
A mangle	6 wood trays
Oak cupboard	Arm chair
A bench	Two four fold clothes horses
Six chairs	A clothes line
Three stools	17 flat irons

INVENTORY OF THE WASH-HOUSE AT THE VYNE, 1842

The fitting up of the lead lined tubs	1 square wash tub
A 30 gallon washing copper with lead curb etc.	6 stools
[a lip to prevent boiling over]	a flaskett
An iron furnace as fixed	Lye drip
A large wash tub	A bench
Three wash tubs	A washing machine
7 wash tubs	

(From The Vyne)

mentioned in later country house inventories. As at The Vyne in 1842, they seem to have fallen out of favour. Useful for intricate pleats and laces they were the classic tools of the old body servant, but were less suitable for the huge amounts of linen and cotton going through the Victorian laundry. As one manual explained: 'When only one is ironing they are valuable, but for a number they are out of the question.'[26]

Each laundrymaid needed a firm iron stand of some sort to rest the iron on, often hand-made, and a tough iron holder, made by the girl herself, of several thicknesses of cotton squares with a piece of chamois leather in the middle to give added protection for her hand. She also needed a bowl for water, a piece of candle or beeswax for rubbing on the sole of the iron, and a couple of clean rags for damping or rubbing the linen as she ironed.

In the Trentham inventory of 1827 there were three Italian irons. To explain these we need to refer back to the earlier history of goffering, the origins of which go back probably to the sixteenth century when highly starched ruffs became fashionable. Ruffs were made of cambric lawn or fine holland and the larger ones were supported on a wire framework and sometimes dyed yellow with saffron. They were professionally made and bought ready-stiffened, and probably usually sent out again for professional refurbishment, with only the very wealthiest households employing a skilled starcher capable of doing this work.[27] Ruffs were shaped using starch and a poking stick – a straight metal stick which was heated in a charcoal brazier. It was made of iron or brass, often highly decorated and expensive. While it was being stiffened, the ruff itself was supported on a set stand.[28] There are references for the date of the introduction of heated poking sticks to England as being around 1584, and a date of 1564 for the introduction of the art of starching from Holland; this was when Elizabeth I set up a travelling coach and engaged the Dutch wife of her coachman to furbish it and to teach other laundresses her skills.[29] Another reference from 1592 mentions blue starch.[30]

Ruffs went out of fashion in England in the 1620s, though legal and religious professions kept up the tradition. Neck styles during the Commonwealth became much plainer, of course, but goffering returned in importance with the Restoration, though in a much freer form than before and using a greater variety of irons. What were now called fluting irons were similar to the old poking sticks, used commonly on the continent, but rarer in England, where goffering tongs seem to have been more popular. These were in widespread and long-standing use, especially throughout the Victorian period; they resembled the hair curling tong in form but had between two and five parallel cylindrical 'blades'. In the 1890s small ones were used for the frills on petticoats and larger ones, heated to a higher temperature, for sheets and pillowcases. Goffering tongs were heated by putting them in contact with the hot sole of a flat iron or on top of the stove.

The most common goffering tool in country house laundries was what became known in Victorian England as the 'Italian' iron or 'tally' iron. This was almost a development from the poking stick or fluting iron and consisted of an iron (called a 'loggerhead') which was heated in the fire and slotted horizontally into a metal sheath on a stand.[31] Used by pressing the linen over the cylinder with both thumbs, it produced fatter frills than the tongs and could be employed, for example, to flute the front edge of servants' caps, but also to iron awkward shapes such as sleeve gathers or to smooth narrow fabric such as ribbons, especially if made of a piled fabric such as velvet and if already made up into bows.[32] The

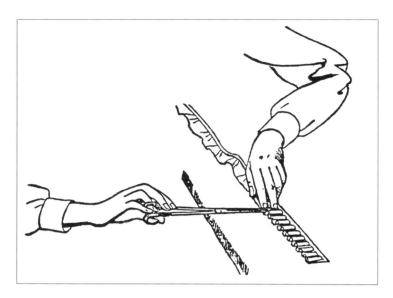

Goffering frills with tongs. Once in place the tongs were moved through a half turn. With practice, goffering could be done quite quickly but was hard on the wrist. (From Jack, Art of Laundry Work, *p. 35)*

'tally' iron was a versatile piece of equipment, which would account for it being so common both in terms of surviving examples and references in inventories of laundries. It came in a wide variety of designs and qualities.[33]

By the nineteenth century there were many varied goffering and smoothing irons and stands on the market, some for general use and some for highly specialised jobs such as ironing lace and hats, even irons with a dimpled base for making patterns on starched linen. Country house inventories rarely include these specialist irons. In general, it seems that Victorian country house laundrymaids used only basic tools – a selection of flat irons of different sizes, a couple of Italian irons, a pair of goffering tongs and a polishing iron with a curved base for glossing shirt fronts and collars. The tendency was to rely on manual dexterity and experience with simple tools rather than an array of complicated gadgets; even where country house laundries display examples of the more esoteric ironing gadgets, they have often been recently donated. Simplicity was the choice of the laundress, for this showed off her skill and even when laundresses were given gadgets they often did not use them, as with the protective 'shoe' for the flat iron which was in the laundry at Pilgrims' Hall but which no one used.[34]

Fashion played a part, of course. By the end of the nineteenth century it was no longer fashionable to finish the frills on pillowcases with goffering tongs. Instead, laundrymaids used the heel of an ordinary flat iron to 'crimp' them closely while holding the frill in tiny pleats with the fingers of the left hand – which sometimes got burnt as a result – one of those processes which looks deceptively easy when an expert does it but which takes long practice to perfect.

Most country house laundries were fitted with a windlass, chain and rack, sometimes a single one (as at Ormesby), sometimes two huge racks filling most of the ceiling area (as at Beningbrough) and sometimes two poles set vertically (as at Kingston Lacy). These were used mainly for airing linen which had come from the mangle or ironer, though some laundries, like Kelmarsh, had a system of pulleys and lines across the ceiling which was mainly for indoor drying. Laundry inventories also include clothes 'maids', or 'horses', sometimes referred to as 'winter hedges', also for airing clothes, the larger ones for sheets and tablecloths. Another design for airing clothes was the radial clothes horse, a metal stand which was fixed to the wall. Airing was an important process since so much of the linen and cotton had to be ironed when damp or even wet and starched items needed 'cooking' after ironing to 'set' the starch.

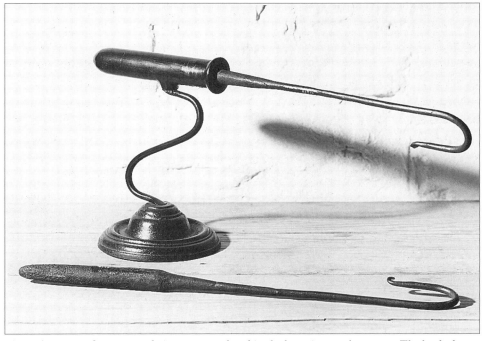

An Italian iron of a common design mass-produced in the late nineteenth century. The hooked irons were heated in the fire or on the top of a laundry stove, and were supplied in pairs so that one could be heating while the other was in use in the stand. (Staffordshire Arts and Museum Service)

THE BOX MANGLE

If the ironing room was large enough, a box mangle would stand against one wall, with a clearance of at least 4 feet at either end; if not it would stand in a nearby room or even in a separate outhouse. As we have seen, handwork and dexterity played a more important part in laundry methods than machines. Mangling was one area within the laundry, however, where a machine was important and no piece of equipment is more evocative of country house domesticity.

One of the most difficult jobs in the laundry was smoothing large lengths of linen tablecloths and sheets, the hand ironing of which would have taken hours. Yet it was in the very nature of the country house as a focus for status hospitality that large numbers of these were required, at both family and servant level. So any machine which helped in the turn-around of a quality finished article was useful. Before the nineteenth century, most household linen was not ironed at all, but smoothed while damp in a box mangle, then folded, aired and pressed in a linen press with the screw down.[35]

The box mangle's origins can be seen in the simple 'mangle board', known from medieval times and still in use within living memory in parts of Europe. The damp linen was rolled around a wooden cylinder and a flat oblong wooden board placed over the top; the operator simply pressed down with her weight on the board, at the same time moving both it and the roller from side to side; thus a combination of downward pressure and sideways movement smoothed the linen as it rolled and unrolled. This is mangling or calendering – not the process of expelling water from wet washing, which is called wringing. This simple process required a deceptive expertise; to be successful the linen had to be at exactly the right degree of dampness, it had to be folded and rolled onto the cylinder with great care and the downward pressure had to be correctly adjusted.

A large-scale version of the mangle board – a plank rolling on a flat bed – was in use in Scandinavia by the sixteenth century.[36] By the seventeenth century commercial fullers and dyers were using a similar machine in England, the plank having been replaced by a box containing heavy weights – stones for example; this became known as a 'pressure box'.

In England such boxes seem to have made the jump from trade to large-scale domestic premises during the late seventeenth century; in this new context they were called simply 'mangles'. Perhaps their adoption in the large domestic rural household relates originally to the fact that such households retained the tradition

Before mangles became common, mangle boards were used with a roller to smooth damp-dry linen and were given in pairs as highly decorative presents. This example is in the collection at Shugborough and is one of a pair passed down through the generations of a Staffordshire family, though Scandinavian in origin. (Staffordshire Arts and Museum Service)

of growing flax and processing their own linen. In many households, the line between linen finishing and linen maintenance must have been hazy.

These early mangles could be bought from a specialist maker and assembled in the laundry or made by the household joiner or carpenter.[37] They used human muscle to push and pull the box over the rollers. This simplest version survived on the continent; a push-type mangle can still be seen in the house laundry at Duivenvoorde Castle, Holland, for example, and one was in use in northern Norway within living memory, pulled and pushed by two children.[38] This type was superseded in Britain relatively early by other versions.

The next step up from the push-type mangle incorporated a wooden roller fitted into the top of the framework, above the box. Round this was wound a rope, or in some cases a leather strap, attached at either end to the box; by winding the roller with a handle, the box was moved sideways. This was no more complicated than a windlass on a well and was a simple improvement which could be made by a carpenter. If the strap broke, nothing more difficult was needed than a call at the saddler's.[39] Strap/rope mangles were undoubtedly the main type in use throughout Britain in the eighteenth century and were even included in the

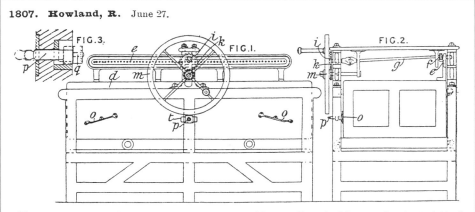

1807. Howland, R. June 27.

Mangling-machines. — Relates to box-mangles and has for its objects to make them run more steadily with less power, to render them better adapted to be driven by steam power, and to provide means for lifting the mangle box when required. A straight rack *e*, Figs. 1 and 2, is fixed to the box *d* and is engaged by a pinion *f* mounted on a shaft *g* connected by a universal joint to a short shaft upon which is a spur-wheel *i* in gear with a smaller wheel *k* upon the shaft of the fly wheel *m* which is driven by hand or power. By this construction the usual mangle wheel and chain are dispensed with. To raise the box it is provided with inclined planes *o* under which a roller *q*, Fig. 3, can be pushed by a slide *p*. A doubly-inclined plane *t* on the box *d* pushes the slide *p* back into place as it passes it.

Illustration of a patent for an improved box mangle by R. Howland, 1807, incorporating a horizontal rack which dispensed with a chain or strap and enabled the box to run more smoothly and to lift automatically when it reached the end of its run. (Extract from the abridgements, Patent Office)

estimate sketchbooks of such notable furniture designers as Gillows of Lancaster.[40] An early strap-type mangle at Aston Hall was made by a manufacturer who also made invalid chairs.

During the late eighteenth and early nineteenth centuries, however, the new availability of iron goods was brought to bear on box mangle design, a process which is illustrated by patent records.[41] One of the drawbacks with the strap/rope box was the effort needed to reverse its direction at the end of its run; several patents were taken out on inventions aimed to solve this problem. They usually involved a gearing system of some sort, automatically changing the direction of movement of the box without the operator having to change the direction of turning. Strangely, by far the most commonly surviving pattern, often called the 'Baker's Patent', does not appear at all in the records of the Patent Office. Recorded in a contemporary treatise on metal manufactures as being invented by Mr Baker of Fore Street, Cripplegate, London, it incorporated a circular cogged wheel and a large flywheel which eased the motion of the heavy box.[42] An important element in the Baker mangle, however, was the lever system fitted to the top of the cogged wheel and this was the subject of a patent dated 1823, belonging to William Warcup; so perhaps Baker bought up Warcup's design. By 1832, these improved reversing machines were recommended by J.C. Loudon as being the best;[43] and by the 1850s Baker & Co. were trading from Jamaica Row, Smithfield, Birmingham.[44]

References to these 'patent mangles' can be found in numerous country house inventories in the early decades of the nineteenth century. A sale inventory taken of the contents of Attingham Hall in 1827 includes a description of 'An excellent 7–feet hardwood-bed Baker's patent Mangle, with iron fly wheel, rollers etc.'. This must have replaced their old strap mangle which gave them trouble in 1818; the description was picked out in italics, so it must have been considered an important feature.[45]

The box mangle developed still further as large-scale premises such as orphanages and workhouses created a demand for more industrial-scale equipment. The simple mechanism of the box mangle could easily be adapted to belt drives, powered by steam, waterwheel and even, later, electric motors.

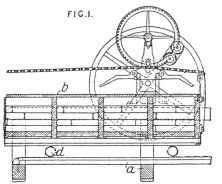

786. Chedgey, J. March 20.

Mangling and wringing machines. — Consists in the application of polished glass surfaces to mangles, &c. Fig. 1 shows the application to a mangle. The usual travelling box *b* is faced on its underside with a plate of polished glass, preferably cemented to a slab of slate or stone secured to the bottom of the box. The frame *a* is preferably built of stone or slate, and is similarly faced with glass. The cloth or other

FIG.1.

material is wound on rollers *d*, preferably formed of glass as described in Specification No. 1084, A.D, 1854, placed loosely between the box and frame *a*. As the box *b* is reciprocated to and fro, the cloth &c. is alternately unwound from and wound on the rollers.

Illustration of a patent for an improved box mangle by J. Chedgey, c. 1854. The innovation consisted of lining both the underneath of the box and the bed of the frame with polished glass. The description suggests the rollers should also be made of glass. (Extract from the abridgements, Patent Office)

The horizontal movement of the box was not the only feature subjected to innovation. At the end of its run, the box had to tip itself slightly upwards to allow the roller underneath to be removed. In early versions this was done by a knee prop – a stout piece of hardwood which was shoved under the box and pressed down with the knee. In the nineteenth century this was replaced by a metal lever or a bracket device. Another variable concerned the important matter of weights loaded into the box. This was always kept simple, using whatever came to hand. The box at Shugborough used large rounded stones from nearby Cannock Chase; and individuals have remembered paving stones used for the same purpose, blocks of cement, lumps of old iron and even, from Knowsley near Liverpool, heavy books. The bed of the mangle was also important to the finish achieved; in better-quality mangles this was made of mahogany and one patent lined both the flat bed and the underside of the box with polished glass. Later versions of the Baker's patent were built with a solid cast-iron frame and a hardwood box.[46]

The earliest patent for a box mangle is dated 1791, the last 1857. This constitutes the main period of innovation in their design, though not their manufacture or use. The box mangle continued in use in country house laundries to within living memory. Contrary to our throwaway habits of today, old mangles could be converted to 'patent mangles', a useful feature if the household was looking to reduce time and wage costs.[47] The necessary ironwork could be bought separately, by mail order; this was still available in 1892, priced just over £4.[48] Complete patent mangles could be bought from specialist laundry equipment manufacturers or suppliers either second-hand (priced £5 in 1863) or new (£7).[49] The two most famous of these were Twelvetrees, who specialised from an early date in commercial equipment, and Thomas Bradford of Salford, the premier supplier to household laundries of the second half of the nineteenth century. Another famous manufacturer was John Pickin, a smith who was established as a mangle-maker in Coleshill Street, Birmingham by 1829; in 1856 he was selling double-action patent mangles for £5, branching out to supply washing machines, knife cleaners, butter churns, perambulators and general iron goods. The business appears in trade directories until 1890.[50]

Box mangles needed a fair amount of space but could be set up in attics or spare bedrooms as they did not need a drained floor, though the floor had to be strong enough to carry the weight. Their usual site, however, was in the dry laundry. They could be used also as a wet wringer, in which case they needed to be situated in or near the wash-house with its drains,[51] but box mangles made clumsy wringers and were rarely used in this way.

DEVELOPMENT OF THE BOX MANGLE

Seventeenth century	Push-type box.
Eighteenth century	Rope-/strap-driven box.
Patent dated 1791	Ferguson Hardie – horizontal gearing.
Patent dated 1792	Thomas Hayes – horizontal gearing.
1797	George Jee – method of moving box by turning handle one way.
Patent dated 1807	Chester Gould – 2 tier flat-bed mangle.
Patent dated 1817	William Owen – 'Portable table or box mangle upon a new and improved principle for the getting up and smoothing of linen, cotton and other articles'.
Patent dated 1823	William Warcup – with swing-lever type system for turning it at the top of the cogged wheel.
Patent dated 1831	John Lee Stevens & Peter Waycott – horizontal gearing
1830s	Baker's patent – circular cogged wheel and flywheel.
Patent dated 1857	J. Chedgey – box faced on the underside with polished glass. Frame built of stone or slate and faced with glass.
Patent dated 1857	R. Howland – design to make mangles 'run more steadily with less power, to render them better adapted to be driven by steam power, and to provide means for lifting the box mangle when required'.

A sizeable table was needed for loading the box mangle rollers. If a sheet were to be mangled on its own, it was folded into four and laid out on the table, then rolled onto the roller, pulling it all the time so it was a tight, even fit; then it was wrapped around with a mangle cloth. This was made of unbleached and dressed linen woven to the width of the box. Smaller items could be mangled inside sheets or tablecloths, in which case the mangle cloth itself was laid out on the table, then the sheet laid on top and the smaller pieces on top of the sheet, taking care to get a standard thickness of cloth. The whole 'sandwich' was then rolled onto the roller so the mangle cloth was on the outside.[52] This was then slipped under the box in such a way as to part unroll when the box was moved backwards and forwards. Each roller would be mangled for a few turns.

When being mangled, the fibres of the linen would not only be pressed but would rub against each other; if the linen had been starched this would produce a smooth stiff finish, good enough for many ordinary household items. According to one laundry manual the old rope-mangle, though cumbersome and laborious to use, polished the linen 'as nothing does now, or so it seems to those who remember it'.[53] After mangling, the pieces could be taken off the roller and either folded or stored as a cylinder. Only best-quality sheets would need to be hand finished with a hot iron. Best table linen was mangled twice, taken off the roller after the first time and put back on the reverse way, or mangled once damp and again after airing to give a final polish. In this case the linen was slipped off the roller and stored in the roll.[54]

In the 1770s at Turkey Court in Kent, Susanna Whatman, with her great practical interest in the minutiae of her housekeeping, gave instructions that her housekeeper should look into the laundry on mangling day to see that the mangle was being used correctly and if this were not possible she should examine the linen when it came from the laundry.[55] An inspection of the mangling cloths was also recommended as a check on the wear and tear on the linen:

> The difference between proper mangling and carelessness makes as much difference in the look as between fine linen and coarse, and as table linen is worn round in turns, it may be a considerable time before any mischief is perceived in the Parlor. The general attention to a mangle is to see that it runs even, is carefully wiped of any dust or gritty matter, and that oil is properly supplied to the wheels, which will wear away and spoil without this attention.[56]

Box mangles were still described in a laundry manual published in the 1920s, when they were highly recommended as being one of the most efficient methods of mangling but hardly suitable for ordinary households due to their size.[57] By 1934 they had no place in a manual of modern laundry practice.[58]

The feature which made the box mangle so durable and popular was the fact that it could be made as simple or as complex as needed and there was little to go wrong. It did its job supremely well given a degree of understanding and manual skill.[59] This was provided by the laundress loading the rollers, but operating the mangle required nothing more than obedience to the laundress's instructions – hence this was often a job for children. One woman recalls how as a child she used to enjoy this responsibility, remembering especially the sound of the stones rattling in the box as she turned the handle.[60] For another young girl who turned the mangle bought by her father to enable her mother to work at home, the Baker's Patent became an instrument of maltreatment.[61]

In a country house context, turning the box mangle was usually done by the odd man; at Berrington Hall, this was written into his official list of duties for

Tuesday afternoons.[62] At Turkey Court, the odd man turned the mangle, but if he were busy, the maids were to turn it, one at each side – this sounds as if the mangle had two handles, presumably to lessen the labour.[63]

Box mangles were extremely adaptable. The country house was probably always the major market for them, but they were by no means restricted to this area. From memories of visitors to the laundry at Shugborough during the 1980s they have been recorded in a wide range of contexts. They were used in communal private laundries; typical was the one remembered from Birmingham where a communal wash-house which served twelve terraced houses was fitted with a box mangle, the use of which was included in the rent. They were also used in public wash-houses, as at Oldham where one is remembered from the 1920s when its use cost 4*d*. Sometimes an enterprising shopkeeper or publican would fit one in a back room and hire it out for extra income; and individual commercial cottage laundries would invest in a box mangle, charging for mangling by the piece. Sometimes whole areas or villages specialised in household laundering, as with 'Soapsud Island' in South Acton, West London, and the village of Pensby on the Wirral, where many housewives took in washing from the 'shipping gentry' of Liverpool; in this case groups of housewives bought a mangle. Some housewives might be simply clothes manglers, taking in clean linen to smooth rather than

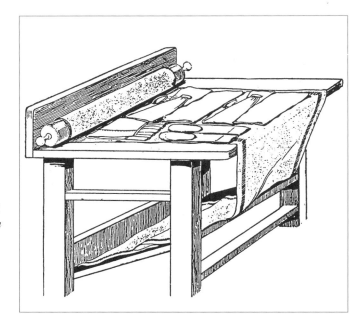

A German design for a mangle table, aimed at reducing the space needed for loading the rollers of a box mangle. The more usual mangle table was twice the length with no back board or sloping shelf underneath.
(P. Sambrook)

MANGLE CLOTHS

Mangle cloths measured around 76 inches × 32 inches and could be either plain or decorated with red or blue borders carrying designs of box mangles and single-colour patterns depicting laundry scenes woven into the centre.

They were specially woven to size so that thick hems would not cause creases in the linen and they were made of pale brown unbleached holland cloth, which could be dressed to add gloss.

Susanna Whatman, Mistress of Turkey Court in Kent, Gave Careful Instructions to Her Household:

‘ . . . be very careful in mangling that the mangle is wiped free from soil, that the linen is rolled quite smooth and that the mangling cloths are even. The cloths should hardly ever be washed, because they are long in acquiring that shining polish which makes the linen look so well. They should be of pale brown Holland manufactured on purpose, to be had at the mangle makers.’

Mrs Whatman was to have cause for complaint, however. In 1784 she had to buy new mangle cloths:

‘The former ones did not last more than ten years because they were ill-used. Mrs Mellish had not had new ones for thirty years.’

She went on to note:

‘Ours are of the wrong sort, and we must have the brown in future, as the common Irish does not at all answer for the look of the linen.’

But later, in 1799:

‘We have again had new mangling cloths, and that without my being consulted, and they are again of common linen. I have spoke very seriously about it, that nothing of the kind may happen in future.’

(Hardyment, *Susanna Whatman*, pp. 47–9)

doing the whole washing and ironing job; in Denmark such women were called *rullekone* (roller wives). A box mangle was also an indispensable part of the equipment of laundries in prisons, orphanages, convents, workhouses and hospitals; in the City General Hospital in Newcastle-under-Lyme a box mangle was used until the 1950s.

Perhaps the most amazing feature of the box mangle was its wide geographic occurrence. From the visitors’ book kept in the laundry at Shugborough, it has been recorded in places ranging from Ireland to the Russian steppes, from Canada to Australia, from isolated Norwegian fjords to the back streets of Paris. The last recollection of one in use was from the 1970s in a Copenhagen apartment block.

No doubt part of this popularity has been the economic role performed by the mangle. A box mangle could be a substitute for a pension or unemployment or disablement benefit. In a world where male employment was often dangerous and women were widowed young, a mangle could provide the means of survival. In Australian mining communities the mates of a miner killed at work would club together to buy his widow a box mangle; this also happened in the Llanberis quarries and among Black Country steel workers. Even in rural areas a box mangle could perform the same function, as witness a blind mangler in a Kent village whose only other source of income was sitting in front of his cottage begging. For any woman who could not go out to work but who needed extra income, a box mangle was a tremendous boon.

At the end of their lives, box mangles have been converted into useful furniture – doors, beds, tables, even a passable dresser. One was used as the centrepiece of a wartime wedding reception, held in an Essex country house laundry which was a good deal warmer than the draughty house which had been taken over as a billet by army officers; the wedding presents, including a glorious Worcester dinner service, were set out on the mangle.

THE UPRIGHT MANGLE

According to J.H. Walsh, the writer of a manual of domestic economy in the 1850s, the one serious drawback of the box mangle was the space required by both it and the table used to load the rollers.[64] On the continent laundries sometimes had a special mangle table, designed to take up less space than the ordinary table which needed to be at least 7 feet long to accommodate the usual sized mangle-cloth. Similarly, attempts were made to reduce the size and bulk of box mangles: Kent's 'Portable Table mangle', for example, used fixed rollers, one of which was ratcheted to move a flat bed; the framework could be clamped to an ordinary table and folded away in a box when not in use.[65] But for smaller households something still more compact was needed.

The development of box mangles was coming to an end by 1855, a year when there were thirteen patents recorded for upright mangles and washing machines but none for box mangles. But uprights did not simply follow box mangles chronologically; inventors had been working on upright mangles since the eighteenth century. Indeed the earliest patent for any mangle, Hugh Oxenham's of 1774, was for an upright machine. So inventors were playing around with upright mangles before and during the time they were trying to improve box mangles, but

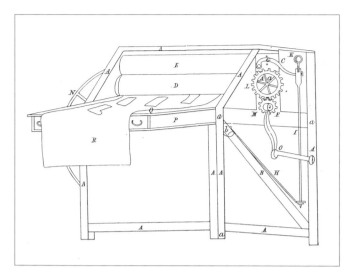

Illustration from a patent specification for an upright mangle by William Geldart and John Servant, 1817, No. 4161. The drawing shows the mangle cloth (R) pulled out over the table-like shelf at the front, with small items about to be fed around the second roller (D). It appears to be a two-rollered mangle, though a third roller might be hidden by the shelf. (Patent Office)

for some reason uprights did not take off commercially until the 1850s, while box mangles were a success over a much longer period. This probably had something to do with technical difficulties with uprights but must also speak volumes about the utilitarianism of box mangles. In practice, many country house laundries operating during the second half of the nineteenth century had both box and upright machines, the one for smoothing large items and the other for smaller pieces; and, of course, the uprights had the advantage that they could be fitted into the wash-house and therefore could also be used as a wet wringer. By the 1880s catalogues were advertising wringing machines which could double as smoothers.

Some of the early designers tried to arrive at a transitional machine, halfway between the box and upright; and at least one early patent had all the features of an upright machine but was set flat on the ground. The early uprights all had three rollers, and still used mangle cloths, which were pinned at one end to the central roller, enabling the clothes to be wrapped around it. Using the mangle as a wet wringer required only two rollers, as wet washing was simply passed through the rollers; in later machines one of the rollers could usually be disengaged. It was also found that a double-roller machine mangled dry linen perfectly adequately for most purposes, simply by passing the clothes through the rollers several times, so most later machines dispensed with the third roller altogether and therefore became much lighter in the frame.[66]

One very popular school manual admitted that mangling with an upright machine 'requires great care and attention in order not to stretch the articles nor

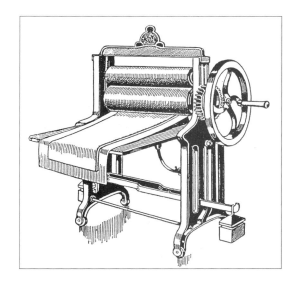

A late nineteenth-century upright mangle, looking superficially very like Geldart and Servant's much earlier patent, though the mechanism for applying pressure to the rollers differs. Again it seems to be a two-rollered machine. The mangle cloth was pinned to the second roller and stretched out so that the folded linen could be spread on it and the whole wrapped around the roller. In some early models the wide front shelf was actually made into a let-down table, as in an early mangle by Bernard and Joy now in the collections of the National Museum of Wales. To enable the laundress to unload the linen, the rollers were simply reversed. In this model the pressure on the rollers was provided by a system of weights rather than the more usual screw mechanism of later mangles. (From Rankin, Art and Practice of Laundry Work, *p. 38)*

strain them unduly'.[67] Using a box mangle was easier, since there was more time and space to arrange the clothes inside the mangle cloth. Mangling generally became less important as a result of improvements made in irons and the increasing use of commercial laundries. As a skilled operation it came to be greatly undervalued; Mrs Beeton hardly mentioned the process.[68]

THE WASHING MACHINE

Before the nineteenth century, wringing water from washing was usually done by hand or by twisting with a hook. Public washing grounds like Moorfields in London were fitted with rows of hooked posts for this purpose.[69] Commercial linen-makers used hooks and it is very probable that households who part-made their own linen adopted the same method for use in the laundry. The record in the diary of Robert Hooke, dated 1677 and usually cited as the first reference to a washing 'machine', used this same method; it described 'Sir John Hoskins's way of rinsing fine linen in a whip-cord bag, fastened at one end and strained by a wheel & cylinder at the other . . . whereby the finest linen is washt wrung and not hurt.'[70] This is hardly what we would describe as a 'machine', yet this word was used in country house inventories of the eighteenth and early nineteenth centuries, which sometimes referred to 'scrubbing engines' or 'washing machines'.[71] Unlike Hoskins's machine, almost certainly these were simply agitators, perhaps some sort of dolly peg used with a tub. Dollies occasionally appeared in eighteenth-century inventories by name; they were used primarily to wash blankets or sheets.

Although given a good start given by the Great Exhibition in 1851, it was the 1860s before washing machines as we would recognise them began to be sold in some number. These early machines were wooden-bodied, hand operated and, unlike box mangles, showed a wide variety of forms, though based on two main principles – the rubbing board and the mechanised dolly. Most of them incorporated wringers. One contemporary writer commented that 'washing machines, of every form and description, are among the inventions of the age, and to be found in most large laundries'.[72] Yet the extent to which they were adopted by the country house laundry remains a little unclear. It is a worrying feature of most reconstructed laundries that they attract donations of washing machines which have nothing to do with the country house context and which, if displayed indiscriminately, survive only to confuse.

One of the major manufacturers of early washing machines was Thomas Bradford; his distinctive motif is to be found on innumerable washing machines in museums and reconstructed laundries, as well as on box mangles, ironing stoves, crimping and goffering machines, linen presses, cinder sifters and butter churns dating from the second half of the nineteenth century. Born in Chelford, Cheshire in 1825, like most of the men who became household names in fitting out domestic premises, he was apprenticed as an ironmonger. He founded Thomas Bradford and Company, laundry and dairy engineers, based in Salford, and later set up a steam laundry in London. His 'Victress Vowel' series of washing machines was undoubtedly the most popular of its day.

It was the custom of catalogues of this date to include lists of purchasers and testimonials from delighted customers and Bradford was no exception; one of his catalogues contained a copy of an order from Chatsworth in Derbyshire: 'Sir, will you please send here, as soon as possible, for the Duke of Devonshire, one of your Washing and Wringing Machines, the same size as the one you sent to Holker Hall about a year ago.'[73] The ultimate accolade came from no less a customer than the Emperor Napoleon III, whose Empress bought a Victress Vowel in the 1860s at the Paris Exhibition: 'After minutely examining, personally working, and for half-an-hour witnessing the operation of a "Vowel" washing machine purchased by the Empress Eugénie for the Tuileries [I am] well pleased with the machine. It is ingenious, simple and very easy to work.'[74]

One of the features of the Victress Vowel series was that it was produced in a number of different sizes to suit different workloads. The most popular was the

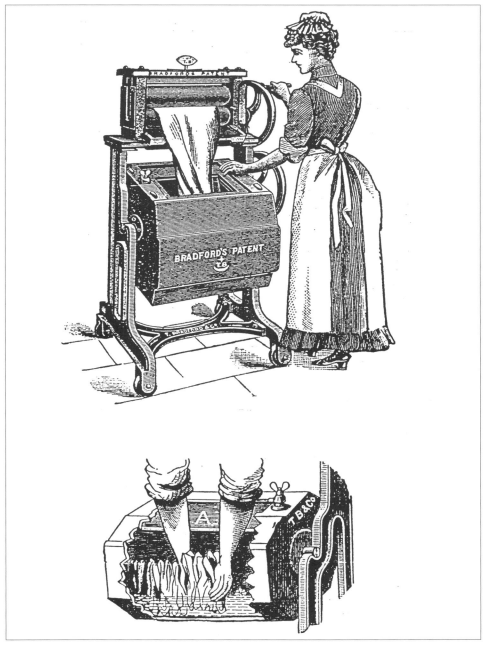

Illustration of Thomas Bradford's Victress Vowel series of washing machine. When the lower handle was turned, the whole of the body of the washer turned over, rather in the manner of a butter churn. The washing system was ingenious; the linen had to be loaded in the way shown in the lower diagram and the 'churn' filled with only a little water (as also shown). When rotated, the linen items were rubbed violently against each other. (From Rankin, Art and Practice of Laundry Work, *p. 34)*

'E' model, designed for family use and costing 8 guineas in 1862. The Vowel 'O' was larger, designed for hotels, schools and mansions and the Vowel 'U' for large hotels, hospitals and workhouses. For this last, Bradford advised specialist installation and operative training and eventually it was in this direction that the firm developed, rather than staying in the domestic market. In the catalogue of the Royal Jubilee Exhibition in Manchester in 1887, Bradford's stand consisted almost entirely of commercial laundry and swimming-bath machinery – finishing machines, steam driers and disinfecting equipment.[75]

Customer lists in catalogues showed that some country houses did purchase hand-powered washing machines; but these represented only a fraction of the thousands of houses in the country. For many house laundries economies of time and savings in labour costs were probably not commensurate with the expense or bother of one of

Early model Thor washing machine in the Staffordshire Museum collections at Shugborough. The clothes were put into the copper drum which rotated inside the outer copper box, a common design for earlier hand-driven washing machines. In this case, the power was supplied by a small electric motor bolted onto the frame underneath – ideally sited to receive splashes from above. This machine was supplied shortly before 1920 to Freeford Manor near Lichfield, by the Thor Hurley Machine Company of Chicago. An identical machine survives in the Berrington laundry. (Staffordshire Arts and Museum Service)

these early machines. They were hardly status symbols, neither were they particularly efficient. They were unpopular with laundrymaids because they were still dependent on hand operation and most of them were very heavy to operate when full. Small-scale two-rollered wringers, which could be fixed to the side of a washing tray or tub, were much more common in country house laundries than washing machines. A favourite was Bradford's 'Acorn' wringer with India rubber rollers, marketed from 1862 and a great improvement on button-crushing wooden rollers.

When electric-powered machines came onto the market, the situation changed. Bearing in mind the drudgery and discomfort, laundering could have been commercialised out of the realm of housework, as had been linen-making and soap-boiling before.[76] That it was not was due to the adoption of efficient washing machines in the home. Generally, this happened late in Britain, largely because of the late development of the electricity power network. In the larger households, however, individual generating plants were common from the beginning of the twentieth century, but in most houses the priorities were lighting and refrigeration.[77] Nevertheless, the specification for the new laundry at Sledmere House in Yorkshire in 1913 contained a powered washing machine, box mangle, upright wringer and drier. Around the same time, similar equipment was fitted at Carberry Tower, Midlothian, with the addition of a 'hydro-extractor' or spin-drier. Yet these households were exceptional; simultaneously, other country houses were fitting conventional hand-driven machinery.[78]

When washing machines were bought by the country house, they were operated usually by the odd man or gardener and though they undoubtedly relieved some of the laundress's labour, they saved very little washing time and no saving at all of time spent on finishing. Like the dolly, they were used at first mainly for heavy jobs such as washing blankets, rather than for general linen. In many houses it was not until the 1930s that efficient electric machines large enough to cope with the throughput of an estate were installed and even then they might be obtained somewhat reluctantly.[79] At Clumber Park in Nottinghamshire, a large commercial machine capable of washing thirty sheets at a time was bought second-hand from a commercial laundry, the result of pressure from a reluctant laundress who was being persuaded to take on the job by a desperate employer.[80]

The most popular domestic-scale electric machine for general country house purposes seems to have been the large copper-built machine made by the Canadian company Thor, who later claimed to have sold the first ever electric washing machines in 1906.[81] One of these machines was used for years in the laundry at Freeford Manor in Staffordshire and another can be seen in the laundry at Berrington.

CHAPTER 8

'We feel Much Happier Washing at Home': Laundry Management

So far we have given little attention to the employment systems adopted by the country house for its servants. In this respect, housemaids and footmen were relatively straightforward; they were full-time and paid a salary which before the mid-nineteenth century was paid annually, after a year's work. Later they were paid quarterly and later still monthly. In addition they were entitled to board and lodging when the family was in residence. In country house jargon this was called being 'at housekeeping'. When the family was away, the remaining household was put 'on board wages', a cash sum which covered the cost of feeding themselves. This sounds simple, but in practice the way in which the household organised this varied widely. In general, the withdrawal of meals when the family left the house included other agreed allowances – beer, sugar, butter, jam. Yet many households continued to supply these even when on board wages; for example, many households allowed small beer but not strong ale in such circumstances, though the wealthiest supplied strong ale all the time.[1] The way servants organised their food on board wages also varied; sometimes they pooled their wages and paid a kitchenmaid to cater for them; sometimes they fed themselves.

Laundrymaids, however, were more variable in their employment. Even within a single house, management systems changed over time. Essentially, the choice was between contracting out and laundering at home, but variations of these options were worked out to suit individual households.

CONTRACT WASHING

When the great wash was periodic it made sense not to employ a washerwoman full-time. So throughout the medieval period and right up until the eighteenth century, many élite households contracted their washing to outside washerwomen, even if the location and facilities for the wash were provided somewhere in the house. At least, that is the theory; so little research has been done on the early management of washing that we really know very little. Domestic accounts from Selby Abbey in Yorkshire suggest a change from the weekly washing of kitchen and dining linen by the monks themselves in the fourteenth century, to a contract laundress in the fifteenth.[2] A list of 121 living-in servants from Knole in Kent, dated from 1616 to 1624, also gives pause for thought.[3] Listed according to where they ate, it shows eleven women servants and a porter accommodated at a separate table within the hall, called 'the Landrymaids' table'. But what was meant by 'landrymaid'? The list includes two personal body servants, a dairy maid and a 'blackamore'. Presumably at least some of the others were laundrymaids but this does not necessarily mean they did heavy washing. They were probably dry launderers, that is starchers, washing and finishing small clothes, not washmaids; but we cannot be sure. Certainly, as we have seen, by the 1630s, Hertfordshire records from Hatfield and Gorhambury show the employment of both full-time laundrymaids and washmaids as well as extra day labour for specific times.[4]

As with the footman and the butler, the line between washmaid and laundrymaid was probably hazy, as it was between laundrymaid and chambermaid, and chambermaid and lady's maid. In 1704, at Swinton Hall in Yorkshire, a new chambermaid was required who, among other duties, would 'make and mend' the family's fine linen clothes and 'wash & smooth all the fine linens & muslins & dress our heads'.[5] Hannah Glasse's manual of 1760 instructed the chambermaid in stain removal, starching linen and washing stockings and other 'small clothes'.

What seems to be clear, however, is that throughout the seventeenth and eighteenth centuries, increasing amounts of linen and rising expectations of cleanliness led to a general improvement in laundry facilities. Many of the laundries surviving today were originally built in the mid-eighteenth century, perhaps following the example set by the royal palace laundries which were built early in the century. By the 1750s many houses had wet laundries and laundry yards, though at first dry laundering was still done in the living quarters by body servants. As the wash became more frequent, more regular day workers and permanent laundrymaids were employed.

The use of contract washerwomen survived, however, especially in towns. Bills for washing appear very commonly in both personal accounts and household disbursements books of London houses. For example, George Thomson, a

'Mrs Grosvenor, Landry Woman to the Queen [Charlotte]', a late eighteenth-century mezzotint. Obviously a body-servant and high-class laundress or starcher, she is squeezing a blue-bag into the rinsing water, apparently outdoors. (Colonial Williamsburg)

gentleman bachelor living in London in the 1730s and '40s, paid a washing bill once a month to his washerwoman, Mrs Marriot, the wife of his landlord.[6] The amounts varied between 5s and £1 8s; one larger bill included making up some shirts as well as washing and she often did mending for him. One month he paid £1 3s 6d to 'la blanchisseuse' or bleacher, who may or may not have been a different person. Thomson increasingly kept his accounts in French, so this may have referred to Mrs Marriot or a more specialist bleacher. He also paid 3s for having his leather breeches cleaned and for the purchase of washballs – presumably for Mrs Marriot's use. He was paying 2s 3d for two weeks' board for himself and two menservants; so washing was a substantial item in his budget.[7]

Thomson was a bachelor but even large wealthy households contracted out their washing while in London. In the summer of 1694, for example, the Leveson family rented a furnished house in London, for which they paid £3 a week rent, plus £1 10s for 'one week's use of linen' and a further £1 for a week's washing; thus linen and its care was only 10s short of the main rental.[8] London has a continuous history of areas where contract washing was carried on, from the old public washing and bleaching grounds such as Moorfields, Lambeth Marsh, Hampstead and Southwark to the nineteenth-century 'Soapsud Island', as South Acton was called. During the hundred years following 1870, this last area developed a huge laundry industry, originally based in small terraced houses, each with a wash-house, ironing and mangling rooms built on the back and with perhaps eight or ten people living in the rest of the house.[9] At its peak around 1900, there were at least 200 laundries in South Acton, employing over 3,000 people. Some of these were industrial-scale 'power' laundries, but many were still tiny premises whose only drying area was the front railings. Other large towns had similar areas where laundering was a major source of employment.

Some families kept to the contract system even in the country, using rural washerwomen or 'cottage laundries'. One woman was used by Pilgrims' Hall in Essex until 1944, when she was bombed out. Every week a four-wheeled dog cart was loaded with hampers of dirty washing from the hall and taken down to the washerwoman, the incredibly named Mrs Drain, returning loaded with crisp clean linen.[10] Dog carts, designed with a low enclosed body to carry sporting dogs to the shoot, were ideally suited to transporting linen around and were widely used for this purpose.

The cottage laundress might employ one or two other women part-time or simply use her own family as help. By the beginning of the twentieth century, cottage washerwomen were used more and more by the local big houses which were returning to the contracting-out system as the domestic service industry began to wind down. The standard of their work was generally very high, since they used only hand methods, sometimes subcontracting out large items like sheets to a power laundry.

The first steam-powered laundries were built in England in 1825. These were far from successful as they tore the linen to shreds and the commercial industry had to wait till later in the nineteenth century, by which time many of the problems of large-scale linen-handling had been resolved by textile manufacturers. One laundry which led the field in early power laundries was the Royal Laundry established in Kew Foot Road, Richmond. Called the Prince Albert Modern Laundry, it was built in 1849 at the suggestion of Prince Albert. A railway was built to connect it to London and it was manned by a staff of thirty-four Royal Engineers, needed to cope with the frequent breakdowns.[11] It handled over 700,000 items and its towering laundry chimney became a local landmark; its box mangle had a polished slate bed and was fitted with a gearing system for steam power.

The successful, later power laundries offered several levels of service: in 'rough' or 'dry work' or 'bag wash', laundry was sent in bundles and washed in bundles, then collected rough-dried and finished at home. In 'wet work' the linen was washed in a net with other people's washing and returned damp. 'Family work' meant the whole wash was laundered and ironed by machine, not by hand; this was suitable for plain working clothes which needed neither blueing nor starching. 'Handwork' was high-class laundering, the only type of work which came near to matching the service expected by a country house. The training offered by a high quality commercial laundry who specialised in hand work was highly prized; at one such laundry in Alnwick in the 1920s an apprenticeship cost £100.

Large-scale commercial laundries were never popular with the country house, however, which preferred a personal relationship with a self-employed washerwoman. The larger laundries could not afford to give individual attention,

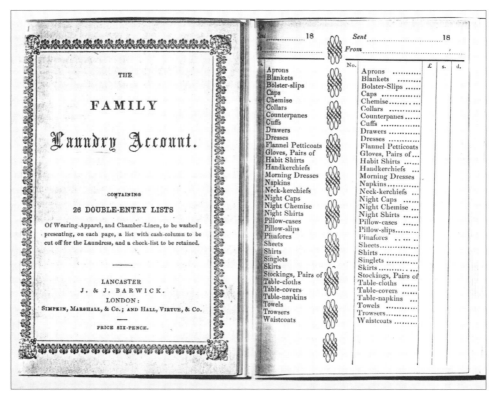

A family laundry account book, printed in 1851. The left-hand column of each page was retained by the sender, the right-hand side cut off down the fancy border and given to the laundress who could return it as a bill. (P. Sambrook)

so they shrank flannels, smashed buttons, used too much soda, and generally wore out clothes quickly.

Another problem with all types of contract laundries was the whole business of keeping track of the laundry. To this end housekeepers could buy laundry books, each page printed with a double list of items, one being a check list for the house and the other to be cut off and given to the laundress. The books contained twenty to thirty pages and cost perhaps 6d. Nevertheless there were still many complaints of lost linen.

The main reason for the unwillingness of some country houses to put out their washing, however, was the ever-present threat of disease being spread by laundered clothes. Early commercial laundries boiled clothes for at least one hour, which wore the clothes out. The invention of carbolic acid and other disinfectant soaps helped, resulting in the spread of the so-called 'model laundries'. Even country cottage laundresses had to face the hygiene issue. Mrs Orman Cooper, for example, who wrote an article on home laundering for the *Girl's Own Paper* in 1899, returned to home laundering after scarlet fever had been brought to her house in a basket of clean linen from Mrs Fowler, her washerwoman in the village. Mrs Cooper blamed the other customers not Mrs Fowler: 'People will not take the trouble to soak handkerchiefs in Sanitas water before sending them to the laundress; and we feel much happier washing our soiled linen at home.'[12]

...ayments for day labour in the laundry at ...rentham Hall, Staffordshire. Salary lists for ...e same year, 1841, show that the Leveson- ...owers employed one full-time laundrymaid at ...rentham, plus four others on the London ...tablishment; so these payments probably ...late to extra day labour during the annual ...ring-cleaning. (Staffordshire Record Office, ...593/2/22/1)

General view of the laundry at Berwick Hall, Shropshire, photographed in September, 1998. This is possibly the best surviving original country house laundry, in a house which is still privately owned. (Cliff Guttridge; courtesy of Mr and Mrs Angell-James)

HOUSE LAUNDRIES

Some houses seem to have had a continual record of swapping from home laundering to contractors. This was particularly common in houses like Attingham in Shropshire which was leased out for long periods. For others, it was unthinkable not to have a house laundry at their country residence, despite pressures to economise. In October 1823, a cost-cutting exercise was done at Tabley Hall, the Cheshire home of Sir J.F. Leicester, Lady Leicester and their three children.[13] In

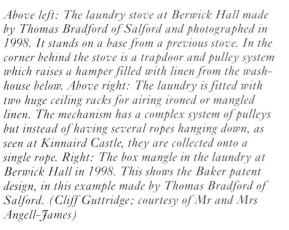

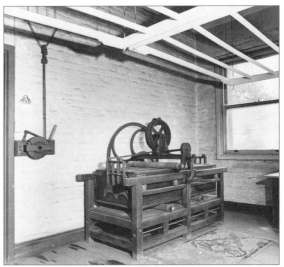

Above left: The laundry stove at Berwick Hall made by Thomas Bradford of Salford and photographed in 1998. It stands on a base from a previous stove. In the corner behind the stove is a trapdoor and pulley system which raises a hamper filled with linen from the wash-house below. Above right: The laundry is fitted with two huge ceiling racks for airing ironed or mangled linen. The mechanism has a complex system of pulleys but instead of having several ropes hanging down, as seen at Kinnaird Castle, they are collected onto a single rope. Right: The box mangle in the laundry at Berwick Hall in 1998. This shows the Baker patent design, in this example made by Thomas Bradford of Salford. (Cliff Guttridge; courtesy of Mr and Mrs Angell-James)

addition to the family, the house laundry at Tabley was providing a washing service for a housekeeper, a lady's maid, a nursemaid and a cook; other servants had to make their own washing arrangements at their own expense. The total annual cost of the house laundry (including the wages of two laundrymaids, board wages, coal, candles, soap, starch and blue, occasional extra washing help and the time of one man to help for two days a week) came to £144 9s. The estimated cost of sending it out to contract was £193 14s, a difference in favour of the house laundry of £49 4s 8d. Even so, alterations were made: the housekeeper, lady's maid, nursemaid and cook were no longer to have their washing done by the house, but were to be given a small cash allowance in lieu of washing; and the old mangle was to be updated to a patent mangle – by conversion not replacement. Given these improvements it was reckoned one laundrymaid with a casual helper could manage the wash; small savings were made in coal and soap and the second laundrymaid was dismissed.

Despite such economies, house laundries were described as 'hardly economical' in the 1870s, yet many survived until the early decades of the twentieth century.[14] The 1911 census showed a sharp decline in the numbers of private laundrymaids, yet some of the larger houses carried on laundering at home for decades, most of them adopting the 'bothy' management system described on p. 198.

Even in the house laundry, the employment conditions and methods of payment varied. The most usual was to employ full-time living-in maids, who were accepted in the community of the servants' hall; though if the laundry was sited outside the main house they were considered to be part of the outdoor staff not the indoor. Holkham, the Norfolk home of the Cokes, employed four laundrymaids throughout most of the nineteenth century. In 1819 these were paid £18 a year each; by 1871 the wage scale had become more hierarchical: £22, £16, and two at £10 each. At Petworth in West Sussex in 1872 the five laundrymaids were paid £25, £19, £17, £14 and £12.[15]

By the time a servant had risen to the point where she was head of a department in a large country house, she could count herself fairly comfortable. Early in the nineteenth century, 18 guineas a year was not bad pay for a working woman and a laundress might well increase this substantially by her board wages. However she managed it, Shugborough's laundress in the 1820s, Mary Halfpenny, accumulated £200 in savings which she invested in the Anson estates in the form of a personal loan to her employer, the 1st Earl of Lichfield. She left it on loan for over twenty years, receiving interest at 4 per cent per annum; it was finally repaid to her executors after her death.[16]

The largest country house laundries often employed a laundryman. In the nineteenth century Woburn Abbey had a laundryman who worked for thirty years at 18s a week and there are records of one at Hatfield in 1886.[17] Laundrymen were of two types: Charles (surname unknown) at Powis was an assistant to the salaried laundress; Frederick Lindrot, on the other hand, employed by the Leveson-Gowers at Trentham in the 1830s, was paid 10s a week to provide a laundry service and it seems probable that he subcontracted the work out to washerwomen.[18] He was paid expenses for his horse and cart and extra wages for periodic work such as carpet beating and curtain calendering, all of which totalled

£4 a month in addition to his wages. At this rate he had a turnover of around £74 a year. Woburn's laundryman was employed on a similar basis.

This arrangement seems to have changed at Trentham, for from 1840 there are records not of a laundryman but of a fairly complex system of salaried laundrymaids. There was one laundrymaid, Hannah Spilsby, who was permanently employed at Trentham on a salary of 12 guineas in 1840, rising to 14 guineas after two years. In addition there were five laundrymaids at the London establishment, living sometimes at Stafford House or Westhill, sometimes travelling with the family on their trips to Trentham. Of these London maids, four were within a hierarchical structure: the first, Mary Lavis was paid £21 a year, Mary Attwood £16, Ruth Barnett £14, and Ann Attwood £10 rising to £12. So Hannah Spilsby in Trentham fitted fairly low down into this hierachy. The fifth London maid, however, was personal laundrymaid to the Duchess of Sutherland. A Frenchwoman named Mme Rousseau, she was paid £37 a year and no doubt was a highly skilled dry laundress, working in a team of body servants to the Duchess which consisted of a French needlewoman, a lady's maid and a personal confectionery maid.[19] Of these, Mme Rousseau was the most senior in terms of wages. In fact Mme Rousseau was earning more even than Mme Harriet Galleazzie, the housekeeper at Stafford House, so she held a position of the highest status.[20]

As with other branches of domestic service the turnover of laundrymaids was high, though perhaps not as high as with housemaids. If they stayed for many years, they might receive a pension, though this was entirely dependent on the kindliness of the employer and the thoughtfulness of the senior servants. When an elderly laundrymaid came to retire in 1876 from Trentham, it was the housekeeper who wrote to the steward, George Loch, asking for a pension for her; Loch negotiated it with the Duke of Sutherland during a stay in Sussex at Uppark. The pension agreed with the Duke was 6s a week, by no means a paltry sum at a time when the salary of a first laundrymaid in work would have been around 10s a week. The Duke also suggested that when a vacancy occurred, the laundrymaid should go into the estate-funded almshouses.[21]

Houses which did not wish to involve themselves in such responsibilities preferred the flexibility of day work, employing staff to come in from the village, either on a casual basis when the need arose or regularly. Many settled for a compromise – one full-time laundress and several day workers to help her. Many day workers would have a much longer family tradition of domestic service behind them than the living-in maids.[22] One day worker (called here Mrs P.) was the third consecutive generation to work in the Shugborough laundry. Earning a few pence a week in the eighteenth century, rising to a few shillings a week in the 1920s, they might well bring a particular perspective to their service. Along with the young girls they were given the worst jobs and usually without the benefit of a proper breakfast, though in a laundry they could make toast in front of the stove or with a hot iron, and drink beer or tea. One of the tips given to Mrs P. by another day worker when she had to make her first blouse to wear in the Shugborough laundry was how to make it into a 'kedging blouse' – the loose blouse front hiding a secret pouch for the safe disposal of goods smuggled home.[23] This, too, was probably a long family tradition. It was not considered to be thieving, just an unofficial part of the 'perks' and only to be expected when some people had so little while others had so much.

At least one house appears to have paid their laundress by the piece. The elaborate laundry premises at Kingston Lacy in Dorset were built in the 1750s near to the back door of the house. Yet a washing book dated 1848–50 shows weekly amounts calculated not as wages but according to numbers of items laundered and varying from 8s to £2. The bill was paid retrospectively for between four and seven washes. This system of payment could cope not only with family absences (there are gaps in the book when no washing was paid for) but also with variation in quality of service (for a time, two payments were made each week to two people, one for family and table linen and another for servants' linen).[24] Here the laundresses had an ambivalent status, between living-in maids, day workers and contractors. For example, they were the only people from outside who were given an allowance of strong beer along with the live-in servants; other outsiders, including the carters and the man who came in once a week to help with the mangling, were given small beer only.[25] When the family left Kingston Lacy the laundry staff was expected to wash the linen which had been left, but thereafter the remaining servants did their own washing no more than once a fortnight. The soap was supplied – 8 lb for the household wash and 3 lb for the servants' wash.

There seems to have been variable arrangements about servants' own washing. As we saw with the footman Thomas, some had to organise this at their own expense. Some houses agreed to do the servants' washing in the laundry, but individuals had to do their own ironing. This was the arrangement in operation at Shugborough in the 1920s when servants could go into the ironing room whenever they were free on Thursdays and Fridays to recover their clean washing and do their ironing. Upper servants usually got 'washing provided' or 'washing money' in lieu. In 1886 the maids at Shugborough were paid washing money, between 16*s* and £1 each for eight weeks' washing.[26] Woburn seems to have operated yet another type of arrangement, the servants being allowed 1½ lb of soap a month, together with 5 oz of starch and 1 oz of stone blue.[27] In the 1770s

IRONING A STARCHED COLLAR

Place the collar on a table, rub thoroughly with a damp rag, and stretch the hems. As the cotton of the stitching shrinks more than the linen, it is necessary to pull it well to prevent creases. Then place the hand over the surface of the collar to disperse the fullness evenly, and pass a medium hot iron lightly but evenly over the wrong side, until all the surface has been slightly dried. Then turn over the collar, and remove any fullness from the right side with the damp rag. Iron slightly on the right side to set the linen, then press heavily. Then iron heavily on both sides alternately until quite dry, finishing on the right side.

POLISHING A COLLAR

This can be done with a flat iron, though a curved-bottomed glossing iron is better.

Place the collar right side up on a hard surface. Wet a rag in clean water and squeeze it out tightly. When the iron is hot enough, rub the surface of the collar with the rag evenly, taking care that the moisture does not penetrate into the underneath of the collar. Then press a very hot iron heavily (with two hands) slowly across the collar, pushing heavily on the stroke until it becomes glossy. A curved-bottomed glossing iron is used with a rocking action. The edges of the collar can be further polished with the upturned heel of the iron.

CURLING

Straight collars and cuffs may be 'curled' or turned into a circle to fit as follows: place the collar on a covered table, wrong side up, and pass a hot iron over its surface. Then take hold of the collar by the button-hole and pull it sharply after the iron, first from one end and then the other; the ends of the collar will curve until they meet. They must be thoroughly aired before putting away, as heat increases the stiffness.

Alternatively, double collars are better curled by shaping in the hand and then placing into a round collar box which will keep exactly the right shape. The box can then be placed in a cool oven or in front of the fire to air. The turned down corners of gentlemen's collar are folded by hand and never ironed in as this cracks the linen.

(After Cassells, *Household Guide*, vol. 5)

Susanna Whatman required her housemaid to wash her own things, including her dusters, early on Tuesday mornings, as well as help the laundrymaid wash maids' stockings and do her own ironing in the evening.[28]

It was usual for house guests, of course, to use the services of the laundry free during their stay. The incredibly rich Mrs de Wichfield, however, thought otherwise. In the 1930s the pampered guests at Blair Atholl were surprised to be presented at the end of their stay with bills for their personal laundry. Only the English left without paying them.[29]

The working hours of laundrymaids were notoriously long. An early start was advocated by all the manuals. By the 1920s Mrs P. walked over the Trent footbridge from the village, arriving at the Shugborough laundry at 7 o'clock in the morning; she left at 7 o'clock at night. When she arrived the living-in laundress would still be in bed, having been up earlier to light the laundry stoves and gone back to bed for a last nap. Mrs P counted herself lucky, for her grandmother had to start work at 4 o'clock in the morning. By earlier standards even this was late; it was not unheard of for laundrymaids to start preparations at 1 a.m.[30] In the 1770s at Turkey Court in Kent, Susanna Whatman left instructions: 'The night

The three-roomed laundry suite at Dunham Massey, near Manchester, incorporates a wash-house, ironing-room and separate mangling room, all of which have interesting detail. The ironing-room shown here has built-in tables along two walls with a stone quadrant sink under a corner cupboard. (John Bethell, National Trust)

Left: Water pump in the Dunham Massey wash-house. Right: Windlass to the clothes rack in the Dunham Massey laundry. (John Bethell, National Trust)

preceding [a wash] a light must be left burning all night for the maids to get up by . . . take care that it is put in a safe place and without risk of fire.'[31]

THE CHARITY LAUNDRY

Sometimes the country house combined necessity with charity. Young girls from orphanages or workhouses were most usually employed in working- or middle-class households, but even élite houses sometimes employed them as trainees.[32] This explains the position of the third laundrymaid at Shugborough in 1828, who received no salary but was provided with 'only cloathing'.[33]

Because laundering was considered suitable employment for women in distress, some houses funded charity laundries on a large scale. Lanhydrock in Cornwall, for example, sent its laundry to one of two local charitable institutions which were funded by the Robartes family.[34] A laundry in Worcestershire was run as a training school for girls from workhouses under the patronage of a local great house.[35] Operating between 1870 and 1925, all the girls – with an average age of about twelve

---

SMOOTHING LACE CURTAINS

'Do not iron lace curtains, rather pin them out flat on top of a large carpeted area – this can be done overnight:

'Cover the carpet with a clean old sheet or two, laid very straight, and then, having stretched a curtain, first in the length and then in the width – very gingerly, lest your fingers produce holes not contemplated in the original pattern – proceed to lay it out on the floor, one person at each edge, so that it is kept straight, and pinning it down at very short intervals. . . . Several curtains may, if necessary, be pinned over one another. They should, of course, be fairly damp when being pinned out. They will be dry by morning, when the pins may be removed, and the curtains will be found to look almost like new.'

(Purdon, *Laundry at Home*, p. 49)

– had come into the workhouse from broken homes: 'Father dead, mother deserted her'. They did the laundry for the big house as well as smaller neighbouring households. It was well run by the standards of the time – annually inspected and regularly visited by the chairmen of the poor law unions who supplied the girls. But it must have been a grim environment – long hours, hard work, strict discipline and spartan dormitory accommodation. The matron's book records misdemeanours:

> Five girls were so rude to Mrs Kitching that they were punished by having no pocket-money and no eggs for breakfast. They object to doing their work over again when not properly done. . . . Florence Ratcliffe's character not very satisfactory. She cannot get up in the morning. . . . Mary has to remain out of the laundry, she is so naughty.

There was a also problem with the boiler-man, Trumper, the only man on the premises:

> 25th July, 1893: Trumper has been very troublesome this week in putting the girls up to mischief and sauciness. He is also a great deal too familiar with them, especially Ethel Anderson. . . .
>
> 28th July: Matron has had a serious talk to Ethel. She had, however, been very impudent to Mrs Kitching and was sent to bed in consequence. . . .

4th August: Trumper has been given notice to leave, chiefly on account of the girls.

Girls were sometimes recorded as 'untrainable' and sent back to the workhouse; one was recorded simply as 'ran away'. But many (including the recalcitrant Ethel) were placed successfully in country house service, as anything from second to fifth laundrymaids; those not up to the hard work in a laundry were placed as housemaids or kitchenmaids.

THE BOTHY LAUNDRY

One variant of the house laundry is recorded only in oral history. Unlike footmen, laundrymaids did not keep diaries or write their autobiographies, so for closer access to the quality of their working lives we are restricted to taped memories. The five laundrymaids whose interviews with the author contributed most to the following account came from ordinary working families. They changed jobs fairly frequently to be near to sisters, to look after elderly relatives, to get more money, job satisfaction or security, and they had close relatives who worked in different levels of domestic service. All five had worked at other less affluent levels and all five married; three left work to raise a family, one as a widow with three young children.

The record of their experiences was taken during several conversations with each. Mrs P. worked at Shugborough as a day worker, coming in every day from the local village where she spent all her life, her reminiscences focusing as far as possible on the year 1919.[36] Nesta worked at Shugborough in the 1920s and earlier at Chirk Castle, near Wrexham and at Lockerbie.[37] Ella worked as laundrymaid at Powis Castle in the mid-1920s, recalling a time in her life when she was very near the bottom of the employment pile, spending much of her time servicing senior maids.[38] Peggy worked at Clumber Park in Nottinghamshire in the 1930s, alongside her mother who herself was an experienced laundrymaid and came from a long line of domestic servants; later in the 1940s Peggy moved on to Maer Hall in Staffordshire.[39] Molly was trained at a girls' home in Lincoln and later went to work at Coleorton Hall in Leicestershire.[40] Though their recollections necessarily relate to a time late in the life of the domestic service industry, their working environments were still wealthy and well organised. But times were changing, as their evidence shows.

Four of the five laundrymaids spent most of their working lives in a 'cottage laundry'. This term is usually applied to an independent, commercial wash-house attached to a cottage, operated by a washerwoman who serviced her local community, which might or might not include the big house. In the early years of the twentieth century, however, the term was also used to describe a mongrel system developed by the country house to ease the controls resented by so many living-in servants. This was a period when full-board service was being replaced in many instances by day work; yet the old board system had advantages for young girls who needed to travel away from home for work. A compromise was worked out and widely adopted on many estates including both Powis and Chirk. It was sometimes also called a 'bothy laundry', a term adopted here to distinguish it from the strictly commercial cottage laundry.

The Powis laundry provides a good example of the bothy laundry system; the laundry and a four-bedroomed cottage were newly built in the 1920s about half a mile from the castle and four miles from the nearest village, on a fairly isolated site. It replaced the old house laundry which had been in the castle outbuildings. The laundry was without electricity so methods were traditional, based on handwork and simple but strict methods of quality control. Three laundrymaids lived in the cottage. They were all paid £1 a week board wages in lieu of board, considerably more than their salaries. The £1 was put into a kitty and given to the head maid, the laundress. In this case she was such a good housekeeper that not only did they live very well but they made a small profit every week which was shared among them. Nesta's experience at Chirk was similar – within the period of a year she saved more money from her board wages than she received from her annual salary of £12.

Within the Powis cottage, shopping, cleaning, lighting fires, cooking and so on was shared between the girls. The youngest maid, Ella, was only thirteen years old; yet she had to take on most of the burden of cooking for the others, a nerve-racking experience if the girl had not been prepared by her mother. She also did most of the dirty chores around the house. Shopping was not very onerous as supplies were brought to the cottage each week by a butcher and a grocer, each with a horse-drawn van, but one of the maids had to walk a mile each day to fetch milk.

Despite being given a degree of autonomy over their own lives, the ranking situation extended into the cottage where the laundress's position was pre-eminent. The two juniors rose at 6 o'clock to clean and light the kitchen range and make tea; the youngest maid in effect waited on the laundress – she took a cup of tea upstairs to her in bed and later at 7 o'clock took up warm water for her personal toilet. The second maid went into the laundry to scrub the floor while the youngest tidied the cottage and cooked the breakfast which was eaten sitting around a table in rank order; afterwards the youngest did the washing-up. All was finished by 9 o'clock when work started in the laundry. The long-established servant custom of having a main meal at midday was here abandoned, as they did their own cooking and all three were busy in the laundry during the day.

A slightly different version of the bothy system was recorded from Coleorton Hall, Leicestershire, in the 1930s. Molly had been abandoned by her mother as a baby, but received a good training at a home for girls in Lincoln, which did high-quality laundering for Lincoln Cathedral. She was around eighteen when she went to work as assistant to the Coleorton laundress, Sadie, who lived in a cottage on the estate with husband Albert and daughter Megan. Molly went to live with them in the cottage; she was paid 10s a week and given her keep in return for working full-time in the laundry and helping with housework, shopping and child care. The laundry washed for the main hall and the dower house, using a weekly routine similar to Shugborough's. Happily, the laundress and her husband provided the family environment which Molly had missed, fitting her out in second-hand clothing and including her in evening sing-songs with their friends.

It is clear that the bothy system had many advantages – it taught girls how to budget and look after a household, and it gave them greater freedom while still under the eye of a senior member of staff. This of course was particularly useful for young country girls who had to travel some distance away from the parental home to find work. The training was rigorous and highly valued.[41] The bothy laundries were much preferred by the girls themselves, even the younger ones for whom they represented a lot of hard general housework. Though hours were long, the timetable was more flexible than in the main house. The system was much missed by Nesta when she moved from Chirk to Shugborough to be near to her sister, for Shugborough clung to the old ways of the house laundry and full-board servants.

The bothy laundry system was also popular among employers. It gave greater privacy to the family and removed the sight of washing from the vicinity of the other servants and guests – at Powis the old drying yard was embarrassingly visible from the windows of the bachelor quarters of the castle. It also helped to encourage good servants to stay longer. As a result, bothy laundries seem to have been fairly widespread, for though Nesta worked in five households in her day, Shugborough was the only one to retain the house laundry.[42] Peggy never worked in a house laundry but could remember her mother telling her tales of the old house laundries in Norfolk where she worked as a girl, working over twelve hours a day.

The bothy system was not limited to laundries, of course. Its origins lay in the traditional practice of providing bothies to accommodate farm labourers and trainee gardeners; and at Chirk in the 1920s it was also used for six housemaids, part of a household of considerable size and wealth which employed fifty-four indoor staff.

THE FAMILY LAUNDRY

One trend among the larger, wealthier households contributed towards the spread of bothy laundries – the centralisation of laundries into a single 'family' laundry. The idea of sending washing from a family's London house to the country seat had been around for centuries, but it became more widespread after the development of a railway network. The trend was set by the royal laundry at Richmond, which handled washing from Buckingham Palace, Windsor Castle and even Osborne House on the Isle of Wight. Other households followed the example; by 1893, for instance, Chatsworth in Derbyshire had an up-to-date laundry driven by water turbine which laundered for the family's London house in Piccadilly, and for their houses at Chiswick, Hardwick Hall in Derbyshire, and Bolton Abbey in Yorkshire, as well as Chatsworth. Again, until the Second World War, the washing from Anglesey Abbey in Cambridgeshire was sent in hampers every week, along with the laundry from the family's London house, to their house at Ingerfield Green, where there was a large laundry employing four laundrymaids. This closed during the war and afterwards Lord Fairhaven's washing was parcelled up every Monday and posted to a laundry run by his shirt-makers in Jermyn Street.[43]

The development of the family laundry made viable a greater degree of investment in modern laundry equipment, especially heavy-duty washing machines for blankets. The laundry's proximity to the main house became less important, indeed a degree of distance was an advantage and with the distance and the use of washing machines came another trend. It now became worthwhile employing a laundryman to work the machines and to drive a pony and trap. In the bothy laundry at Powis the laundrymaids were aided by a full-time laundryman whose job was to look after the fuel, fill the boilers with water, work the winch on the rack, turn the box mangle and help with the washing of blankets. He also drove the horse and cart which delivered the washing to and from the laundry. Thus the change to bothy and family laundries resulted in greater employment of men in and around the laundry, a trend which was common to many processes which moved from the strictly domestic towards the commercial.

Sometimes this trend was an informal one. As the domestic service industry generally ran down and numbers of maids were reduced, the remaining maids had an even harder time than before. At Clumber in the 1930s, the workforce in the laundry was reduced to two – mother and daughter – even though the agent's family wash was added to the family's. A large-scale electric washing machine helped with the heavy wet work, but the amount of ironing still increased. Peggy's invalid father was roped in (unpaid) to help his wife and daughter with lighting fires, turning the box mangle and ironing straightforward household pieces, as well as making all the meals for the two women.

FREELANCING

Because they were slightly more independent than the old house laundries, bothy laundries sometimes moved into yet another phase of change. At Whittington near Lichfield, the buildings of the estate laundry survived virtually unchanged until 1992; the cottage and attached laundry were situated not within the main house but just outside the kitchen garden wall and very close to the village. In this case, the laundress was allowed to take in washing from villagers as long as it fitted in with the house routines. The practicalities and economics of these 'foreigners' were considered her business not the household's, a system which would hardly have been possible had the laundry been situated within the house itself. Supplementing laundry wages from external paying customers was thus a means of allowing the laundry to carry on when the output from the house was declining, postponing the dreadful day when the house would have to go public.

This trend towards 'freelancing' seems to have been fairly common. At Coleshill in Berkshire the laundry survived by taking in washing from the village, although later it was converted into living accommodation.[44] At Maer Hall in Staffordshire, Peggy worked as laundrymaid from 1945 until the 1960s, with the assistance of her husband. When the last of her employers died in 1963, the estate was sold and her laundry eventually converted into a house. But these changes took two to three years to resolve and in the meantime Peggy stayed on in the laundry, firstly to wash all the curtains in the big house ready for the sale and later to do other people's washing. Paying her own running costs, she built up a clientele of five or six local customers. Not knowing what the commercial rates were, she charged too little and found the going very difficult, so when the sale finally went through she was happy to retire.

A similar but extended story comes from Milland Place in Sussex in 1953.[45] Although accommodating a married couple rather than a group of women, the Milland bothy laundry shows how a woman could change by degrees from a

Laundry Cottage, Milland Place, Sussex, photographed in 1953. The laundry is the wooden structure at the side of the cottage. (Rural History Centre, University of Reading)

living-in servant to a self-employed independent laundress. Mrs Lewis became laundress to Lady Nanerene & Ferrard around 1900. A few years later she married the houseman but stayed on at work, in itself a radical change from the traditions of nineteenth-century domestic service. In 1920 she and her husband moved to a cottage on the estate, where a wooden extension was built to house a new laundry. The couple continued as employees of Milland Place, receiving a monthly wage, which by the 1930s was £12 10*s* between them, with rent, coal and lighting found by the estate. From that time Mrs Lewis began to take in additional laundry from other houses to supplement this wage, charging for this extra work by the piece. From 1939 onwards she ran the laundry entirely as a private business, paying 4*s* 6*d* a week rent for the premises. She retired in 1953, by which time she had nine regular customers. Many of these had been with her for a long time and delivered their washing by chauffeur-driven Rolls-Royce, for Mrs Lewis's quality of work was famous.

In 1953, Mrs Lewis still ran the business as if it were a house laundry, pooling all the customers' washing and keeping to the weekly routine. She washed

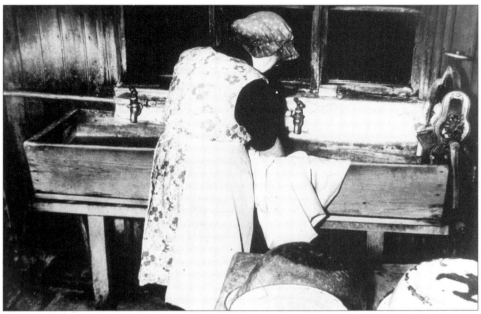

Mrs Lewis working at the wooden washing trays inside the laundry at Laundry Cottage, Milland Place, in 1953. (Rural History Centre, University of Reading)

Mrs Lewis operating her box mangle at Laundry Cottage, Milland Place, in 1953. (Rural History Centre, University of Reading)

coloureds on Saturdays; whites were soaked over the weekend and washed on Mondays; mangling and ironing took from Tuesday to Thursday; and Friday was taken up with cleaning the laundry and collection and delivery. Her methods, too, remained unchanged – local spring water was heated in the two boilers, washing was done by hand in the wooden trays and finishing was done using a box mangle and flat irons.

This continuity of technology reveals Mrs Lewis's misfortune. Her rent covered the hire of the box mangle and other equipment, but because her charges were low, she never accumulated sufficient financial resources to modernise; yet she was without the human resources which the country house traditionally afforded and which made hand labour bearable – assistance from other maids and the odd-job man or laundryman. Widowed early, Mrs Lewis was on her own. She was paid by the piece not by a salary, and had all the worry of maintaining sufficient customers to keep her business going and to meet her costs. Like Peggy, she undersold her services. Supplementing income by taking in extra custom as at Whittington was one thing, total independence was another. Simply by paying her and her husband an inadequate wage which was barely increased over time, the family pushed her into commercial insecurity and a life of the utmost drudgery.

STRUCTURE AND QUALITY CONTROL INSIDE THE LAUNDRY

The essence of the whole country house system was hierarchy. Yet hierarchy was not merely adopted by the servant world as a sort of mindless 'aping of their betters'; it was built into the fabric of their work situation. The laundries described by our five informants were each staffed by two or three laundrymaids working to a head maid usually referred to as a laundress. The maids were themselves ranked in number downwards in keeping with experience and age. Pay was ranked accordingly: at Powis in 1927 the second laundrymaid earned 8s 6d a week, the third 6s 6d; significantly, Ella did not know what the laundress earned.

In all types of country house laundries, the work as well as the staff was ranked. The better-quality linen was washed, ironed, polished and folded by the laundress or the first laundrymaid. The least experienced maid dealt only with the servants' linen, graduating eventually to the children's linen. There was nothing inherently snobbish about this; the coarser, cheaper-quality linen was plainer and easier to handle than the finer frilled pillow cases and petticoats of the family; the system was used as a practical means of training.

Even the irons were ranked. The laundress's favourite irons were marked with her name and restricted for her use solely; at Shugborough only the laundress was allowed to handle the glossing iron and to polish the shirt-fronts.[46] Each maid had her own tub and each iron had its own place on the stove – sensible systems for the smooth running of a busy workplace. Ironing day was extremely pressurised and no one wanted to waste time by having to search for the right implement.

In all the laundries described by our maids, rank was revealed by the working clothes worn, though in the 1920s and '30s this was true only when the maids were expecting a visit from one of the family. The lower maids wore stiffly starched and pleated bibbed aprons, while the laundress wore a plain but snowy-white waist apron. They still wore regulation cotton print dresses and were still expected to make them up themselves or at their own expense, though the material was given to them. Nesta was very fond of her dresses at Shugborough; they were made of very good quality red striped cotton – much better quality than she could afford herself. She had them made up by the village seamstress who fitted them with the ultimate in luxury – tiny buttons made of real pearl. At none of the bothy laundries were maids expected to wear caps, but they were still required in the house laundry at Shugborough, though now only outside the laundry; to be caught capless by the housekeeper or a member of the family was still a major breach of etiquette rewarded by a severe telling-off from the Countess of Lichfield herself. Servants still had to look like servants and not like family; when Nesta first went to Chirk she proudly sported the latest American bob, but since the girls of the family had recently had their hair bobbed Nesta had to agree to let hers grow out.

Every week was structured. At Shugborough and Chirk the whole routine began on Monday morning with the ordered washing, first fine linen, then personal cotton, table and dresser cloths and napkins, then servants' clothes and 'rubbers', and last the drawsheets – the grey calico cloths put down in front of the fireplaces while blackleading. All this took two days; Wednesday was mangling day and Thursday and Friday were ironing days; Saturday was taken up with delivery and sorting, as well as cleaning the laundry and wash-house. At Powis the routine was different, for Monday, Tuesday and Wednesday were ironing days; Thursdays the laundry and wash-house were scrubbed and the cottage cleaned from top to bottom. Friday and Saturday were the main washing and drying days. At Clumber also, the turn-around day was Thursday, when dirty washing would arrive in hampers on trolleys, pushed by the odd man.

All the interviewees were clear as to the reason for such a rigid systemisation of workplace – the laundress's god was quality. That quantity was an issue we have

The laundry at Kinnaird Castle, Brechin, Scotland in 1898. The clothes horse carries items which are airing after mangling or ironing. To the extreme right of the laundry stove are the tracks of a hot closet. (Royal Commission on Ancient and Historical Monuments of Scotland, the Earl of Southesk)

already seen, yet busy times such as house parties were given extra resources in the form of help from casual labour. The real pressure on the laundress was to keep up the high standard of work and many of the seemingly petty restrictions were aimed in this direction. Thus there were rules about washing: satin was scrubbed with brushes, but linen and cotton were rubbed by hand. There was an order to hand-washing a garment: each piece was held with the selvedge running downwards, the right side on the outside; the fabric was rubbed between the hands, fabric to fabric, otherwise the skin would become raw. It was important to rub 'the straight way of the stuff, and with the threads'; this applied especially to linen which would never come clean if rubbed on the bias. Blankets were pressed against the side of the tub or a rubbing board. Flannels were squeezed rather than rubbed, drawing them up and down in the water through the hands. The dirtiest parts of garments were attacked first, then small pieces like sleeves, and finally the main part of the garment, all the time giving particular attention to the seams, which could harbour fleas. Once this was done, the whole garment was turned inside out and rubbed again. The blueing of linen was not allowed by the Shugborough laundress. 'If I couldn't get my washing white without using blue, I wasn't worth being called a laundress', was Nesta's comment.

Every item had a 'proper' way to be pegged – at the strongest point, with the selvedge always running downwards. Buttons and tapes were protected by careful folding; stripes were pegged vertically so colours did not run; pleats were dried pinned in. Heavy linen tablecloths were never hung by the corners but doubled over the line, the side facing the wind left shorter than the other to keep it open to the wind. Chemises and combinations were pegged either by the bottom or the shoulders. Delicate items like nets were hung on the line over a towel. Waistcoats were pegged by the bottom of the back lining, trousers by the back of the waistband. Small items like collars and cuff were strung together on a piece of tape. All body linen was dried inside out; and multiple items were pegged in batches, for instance all the hand towels from the kitchens together, so that it was easier to keep track of things.

It was standard practice to fold items so that the family monogram ended up on the top left-hand corner, making for easy identification when visitors' linen was mixed up with family's. Folds were designed so that items could be unfolded quickly and with a minimum of risk to the starched and snowy perfection. The screen-folds of tablecloths were ironed into a grid to assist the footman in the precise laying out of the table. Napkins were put into screen-folds and garments were folded so that all buttons and closures ended up inside.

Skill in folding was especially important in family laundries, where finished laundry had to be packed into hampers. The Powis Castle laundry did the washing for the family's London house, occupied by the Viscount Clive with a young family which needed lots of clean nappies. Fresh country air was considered vastly superior for these and so the weekly wash, dirty nappies and all, were dispatched from London by train to Welshpool, there to be collected by Charles and the horse and cart each Friday. A week later and the clean laundry was packed into wicker hampers and returned to Welshpool station. The puffed sleeves of the babywear were packed with tissue, and folded clothes were placed within each hamper according to a strict order and all wrapped individually in calico bags or tissue paper – itself carefully ironed.

Checking was rigorous and served to strengthen hierarchical controls, for the workload was such that total checking by the laundress herself was impossible. Spot checking might be acceptable in a commercial laundry – the laundress simply took a shirt at random and hurled it across the room; if it stayed folded it had been ironed correctly[47] – but in a house laundry this was inadequate, so each maid checked the work of the next maid down in the hierarchy. Mistakes were corrected by repetition; the slightest inaccuracy with a pleat, the tiniest suggestion of a triangle at the end of a fold and the item was ruthlessly shaken out across the table and put back to the rinsing stage. Perhaps to hasten the learning process, the presence of triangular creases were said to bring bad luck. Nesta had difficulty in remembering her right from her left – crucial in ironing monogrammed napkins – so she made up a rhyme which she used to chant quietly to herself. All the maids were subjected to the favourite invective of the country house laundress – 'We'll have no cottage ironing here, thank you.' But all seem to have been anxious to learn; as Nesta put it: 'The better you did it, the more pleased with yourself you were.'

Individual skill was at a premium, but many of the jobs within the laundry required teamwork, another key word in the servant world. At Shugborough the best table linen was mangled and then fully ironed by hand; it was impossible to do this single-handed. Periodically the Powis laundry was sent the huge net curtains from the London house, grubby with London dust. They needed three laundrymaids to each curtain, for each was surrounded by frills which had to be goffered – in this case using a pair of tongs. These were used with a twisting action of the wrist combined with a strong downward pressure – an action which over time was highly stressful to the wrist – and the slowest had to keep up the pace set by the laundress.

Long hours shared over a hot iron were eased by companionable talk – at Powis there were frequent tales of the hardships endured in service in the laundress's youth when servants knew their place and were expected 'to grovel'. At four of the five laundries singing was a favourite pastime. The Powis laundress loved singing Irish songs and at Shugborough Nesta's Welsh father had brought her up to sing tenor along with him. Thus there were frequent complaints about Shugborough's laundrymaids who could be heard singing away at 6 o'clock in the morning. Shugborough's laundry was old-fashioned enough to wash blankets by hand, a few at a time so that all were washed once in a year; and the back-breaking job of shaking them into shape was transformed into a joke enjoyed by all three maids as they built up a three-part rhythm to the tunes of popular songs or favourite hymns. Even Nesta's well-earned midday break was often spent resting on her bed singing. Nesta was, in fact, a human alarm clock; being fairly good at getting up in the mornings she was given the job of waking all the other servants by banging on their doors. She herself made sure she was awake in time by

A Working 'Batman'

Institutions sometimes show an amazing ability to hang on to archaic techniques. The Royal Navy used mangle boards as late as the 1920s; here their use is described by H.L.B. Bolton, of Deddington in Oxfordshire, who sent to *The Countryman* his reminiscences of fourteen years on the lower deck.

'Duck suits were wrapped around the roller as taut as possible and laid on the spotlessly scrubbed mess table. Then, one hand grasping the handle of the bat and the other pressing hard about midway, the bat was given a sharp push and the roller was rolled under pressure between bat and table. Some half-dozen rolls sufficed for ordinary wear, but on a station where tropical kit was worn the bluejacket's 'tiddly' or shore-going whites came in for special treatment. They were made of drill and usually specially cut for him, with edging and collar of blue jean. The suit was turned inside out, and leaves torn from a glossy magazine were place carefully in direct contact with the whole of the outside of the suit. 'Jumper' and trousers were then folded, and each piece was rolled as much as a dozen times. The gloss was transfered from paper to suit, which had a finish almost up to the standard of linen from a Chinese laundry.'

(Ann Cripps, *The Countryman Rescuing the Past*, p. 162.)

The naval mangle bat was home-made, as recalled in the same book by another sailor.

'When a ship was newly commissioned, each mess was issued with a set of mess traps, but this did not include bat or roller. So the senior hand would scrounge a piece of hardwood, preferably oak or teak, from which he would carve the bat with his pocket-knife or 'pusser's dirk'. It was shaped like a cricket bat, about 3 ft long, 3 in to 4 in wide and 1 in thick, and was sanded and scrubbed to ivory smoothness. The roller was a 2 ft section cut from the loom of a broken oar, again sanded and scrubbed; it was also used as a rolling pin for pastry in days when all food was prepared by members of the mess and only cooked by the ship's cook.'

E.W. Taylor of Didcot: (Cripps, *Rescuing the Past*, pp. 161–2)

coming to a private agreement with one of the stablemen who threw gravel at her window – until the housekeeper found out and provided her with a much more respectable alarm clock.

Country house laundresses did not try to keep their skills to themselves. They seemed happy to teach younger girls and occasionally even gave formal lessons to girls from the local school; at Craven Arms in Shropshire, once a week the whole girls' class walked to Stokesay Castle to be instructed by the laundress.[48]

Nesta MacDonald, a laundrymaid at Shugborough in the 1920s and '30s. She is pictured here with her bicycle on the canal towpath near to the house. (Staffordshire Arts and Museum Service)

By modern standards, of course, discipline was strict even in the 1920s. The girls were not encouraged to think things out for themselves or to try new methods even when these seemed to ease their labour. The favourite adage was 'There's a right way and a wrong way of doing everything and the right way is usually quicker in the long run.' But the rules were very clearly laid out and on the whole resulted in little backbiting or favouritism, though this judgement may well be affected by hindsight. The girls' response seemed positive – you were told the regulations when you went there and if you were prepared to limit your lifestyle to fit, you could be very happy. Work was hard but companionable; every day was rounded off with a pleasant half-hour around the cottage or servants' hall fire drinking cocoa or tea and sharing the jokes of the day. By the 1920s, even at Shugborough some of the old ties were loosening. Every Sunday was free, although the maids were still expected to attend church, walking down the drive and across the footbridge over the Trent in a 'crocodile'. However, Nesta was not only allowed but even encouraged to go out on Saturdays. She had to sort dirty linen on Saturday mornings; thereafter the rest of the day was hers and she often went out to visit friends, returning home by 9 o'clock. The maids were also allowed to attend the frequent dances in Rugeley or Penkridge; every such excursion required permission but this was forthcoming on the understanding that they would be home by midnight, would come in quietly and would be up as usual the next morning. They were usually accompanied by the menservants, part of the fun being the journey home through the otherwise silent Staffordshire lanes singing at the tops of their voices, the women riding the men's bicycles and vice-versa. Most of the younger maids had their own bicycles, which were cleaned and oiled by the handyman. For Nesta, as for Ella at Powis, and thousands of other women who found themselves in similar rural isolation, the bicycle can hardly be overstated as a means of liberation.

CONCLUSION

Far from being low-status possessions, fine quality domestic linen was highly prized as heirlooms and as part of trousseaux. For women who were allowed to own in their own right so few things of value, it was endowed with a significance which was almost religious, a material embodiment of the spiritual and enduring quality of family. This was reflected in the care taken over it. Even when out of use and stored, linen was regularly counted and reorganised.[49] One nineteenth-century manual described this attitude retrospectively:

> Two or three generations back a well-kept and well-stocked linen-press was ranked with old silver and old furniture as a sign of the refinement and respectability of the owner; and a housekeeper who could be content . . . to use it promiscuously, and to keep it in an ordinary drawer or cupboard . . . had no perception of the sacredness which belonged to household mysteries.[50]

Quarterly washing was similarly significant. As pointed out by de Bonneville, it 'incarnated, like spring house-cleaning, a cyclic vision of time', a life structured around the seasons.[51] The periodic turn out of linen and furniture has a strong element of the religious about it, just as the religious year has elements of a pagan respect for the natural seasons. De Bonneville also pointed out that choosing the date for the seasonal wash would not have been easy. Many days were eliminated by sacred duties: washing should not be done on Fridays (the day of Christ's death) nor on any of a multitude of other annual dates in the Church's calendar.[52] Other features associated with laundering had almost a communal ritual quality;

THE HAND-DRESSING OF FLAX.

Flax went through a complex series of hand processes before a viable thread could be made. These were aimed at rotting the outer husk-like covering and separating the fibre from this and the woody inner core:

1. The flax stems were pulled by hand, never cut.

2. The fibres were then tied in bundles and either 'stooked' in a field to dry or, in fine weather, spread out on the grass and left for two or three days.

3. If the seeds were needed for next year's sowing, they were next removed by 'rippling', drawing through a coarse-toothed comb set vertically into a board or bench.

4. The fibres were then ready for 'retting' – the rotting of the outer husk of the fibres. This was accomplished either by 'dew retting' or 'water retting'. In 'dew retting' bundles of fibres were spread out flat in a field, all pointing the same way and the bottoms slightly overlapping. The retting was accomplished by the action of mould. Sometimes this was accelerated by sprinkling with water. The fibres were 'tedded' – turned over – several times during the time taken for retting – anything from two or four weeks to three months. By this time the colour of the stem changed from browny-yellow to dark grey. 'Water retting' could be done in standing ponds, flowing streams or specially-built tanks. The bundles of fibres were weighted down in the water with stones or planks.

5. When the outer part of the fibres were easily separated by running between finger and thumb, the flax was dried by spreading over a field, then re-tied into bundles and stooked until they became a pale creamy colour.

6. The next process was 'breaking' – beating the stems to break up the decayed woody straw from the inner fibres, using a wooden mallet.

7. The straw was then removed from the fibres by 'scutching', a sort of violent combing with a bat and board.

8. The fibres were then 'hackled', combed with progressively finer combs, to smooth and align the fibres and separate the finer fibres from the shorter coarser fibres called 'tow'.

The thread was then ready for spinning, reeling into hanks, bleaching or dyeing as yarn, weaving and the final bleaching of lengths of cloth.

(After Baines, *Linen*)

spreading clothes out on the grass underscored the abundance of the household and therefore the social status of the owner.

The fact that much of the linen had been made in the household also added to its meaning. Flax and hemp growing required long, dedicated hours of skilled work. Even hand-weeding had to be well organised in order not to damage the fragile plant; it was done by women, who used even the direction of the wind to support the stems.[53] Bleaching yarn and whitening cloth used the power of sun, wind and grass, not machines. The women who were employed for such jobs may have been casual day labour, but they knew their own craft. Each of the separate phases needed time, patience, judgement and manual dexterity. The time-consuming techniques used in bleaching new yarn and cloth – the souring in bran water, the bucking in lye, the grassing, the scouring of the woven cloth and the final beetling of the cloth to give a smooth lustrous surface – all these were prototypes for the methods used in the seasonal wash itself.[54] Descriptions of processes used in the finishing of linen are almost identical to accounts of the buckwash. As washers of linen, women might well have learnt their skills from making it.

Linen processing was seasonal, so buckwashing was also seasonal. It would not have seemed 'dirty' to accumulate linen, just the 'natural' order of things, part of the seasonal round of domestic chores. The more delicate and expensively laced and ruffled body linen derived from a different tradition and was cared for by different people in a different routine.

The ritual quality of washing should not blind us to the sheer hard work involved, especially in handling linen. The buckwash and the batting were no sinecure, but the abandonment of the buckwash and the adoption of processes more suited to cotton and other goods meant a good deal more hand-rubbing at the tub. A farm labourer's wife in the 1860s thought 'farm labour isn't so hard as the washtub'.[55] Even in this century, a young girl in a convent laundry had a hard time: 'By the end of a working day I was standing first on one leg, then on another, trying to rest each in turn. On washing days I would be soaked through and through, from neck to feet, for the tubs were high (at least to me). Water trickled all down me from my hands to my armpits, from my so-called water-proof apron down to . . . my boots.'[56]

The laundrymaid in a house laundry might not suffer the physical brutality inflicted on a girl in a working-class laundry, but the heavy lifting was endless and exhausting. Laundrymaids needed to be hard-working, skilled and strong, points of some importance when setting them on.[57] The image conjured up by Nesta might be very attractive – clean, robust and cheerful – but for every one like her there were probably others like Mrs Waters, another laundrymaid in another country house, a tough, brawny woman who wore a man's cap and smoked a pipe as she clumped downstairs from her room to the wash-house in a pair of heavy, hobnailed boots.[58]

It is true that laundrymaids differed from other living-in servants in the degree of attachment to the country house. As we have seen, this varied widely both over time and with individual circumstances. The development of different systems of management and living accommodation was characteristic of laundering in ways which were impossible for other forms of cleaning which had to be performed *in situ*. Laundering offered unusual opportunities for the lateral extension of services and for economies of scale between different households within the same family.[59]

This 'independence' of laundrymaids might well have offered a challenge to the structured and close-knit community of the country house. In this respect Girouard's description of them as 'the Achilles heel' of the domestic household might be justified. Often working nearer to the stable block than to the housekeeper, laundrymaids also had the reputation of being heavy drinkers – mainly because they were heavy workers. Until the nineteenth century their drink was beer and ale, later large quantities of tea. Traditional paternalistic attitudes could accept this: beer was food as well as drink and anyone involved with hard labour needed plenty of it; the harder the work, the more beer was needed.[60] But it was still a rather unladylike quality and perhaps contributed to their reputation for sexual licence. Whether this last was in any way earned is impossible to judge. In one house the drying room was the venue for secret dances and at another the laundry was described as 'nothing but a brothel'.[61] In both these instances the main perpetrators were other staff, including upper servants, who used the more remote and private laundry as a convenient venue which was one step towards more neutral territory than the main house offered. It does not necessarily indicate that laundrymaids were freer with their favours than other maids.

That this 'independence' caused managers some concern can be seen on the ground, however. In Barry's rebuilt Trentham of the 1840s the laundrymaids' sleeping accommodation was high up in the belvedere tower, well away from their laundry in the stable block. At Pakenham Hall in Ireland an underground passage from the laundry to the drying ground was built in the 1840s to prevent the laundrymaids meeting the grooms.[62] Many ground-floor wash-houses have either high-set windows or opaque glass as a barrier between laundrymaids and stablemen. Retired laundrymaids maintain this was aimed at making it impossible for grooms to see ladies' underwear going through the wash, rather than to stop socialising, but the opaque windows in the first-floor laundry at Berwick Hall could only be aimed at stopping laundrymaids from looking out over the stable yard.

Some households maintained a stringent hold over their households. At Barry's Trentham the domestic yard and stables were situated within the security 'fence' surrounding the main site. The rear access to this was controlled by a lodge-keeper who was instructed to record activities regardless of extenuating circumstances. His duties included logging in and paying some of the day labourers, but also he was to report anyone going in and out between 11 o'clock at night and morning working hours, anyone who ought to sleep inside the gates but was absent, and anyone who was drunk or who smoked tobacco within the gates. His record book shows he followed orders: 'Wooley junior entered the lodge gates at 9 o'clock accompanied by the laundrymaid. I went and ordered him out of the gates at half-past 10 o'clock at night' and again 'Osborne the postillion, came in at the lodge gate 55 minutes past two o'clock in the morning. . . . Osborne, postillion, was without the gate all night.'[63] Other nights he recorded serious instances of poultry stealing, illustrating perhaps the real reason behind the system, for Trentham was situated at the edge of a growing industrial conurbation and the site needed security from unwelcome attentions from outside. The recording of the comings and goings of servants was perhaps a secondary function, but was nevertheless thought necessary.

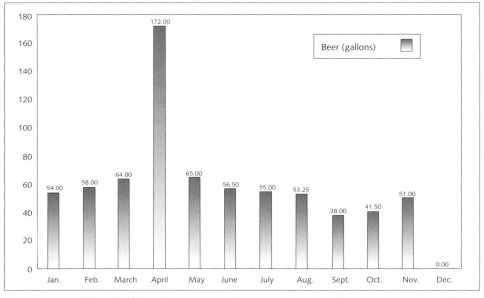

Consumption of household beer by laundrymaids at Trentham Hall, 1848, showing the effect of spring-cleaning. This probably reflects an increase in both work rate and the numbers of casuals employed. The beer was made on the premises by a full-time brewer-cum-baker. (Staffordshire Record Office, D593/R/11/7)

CHAPTER 9

'Clear from Spot or Blemish': the Meanings of Cleaning

Throughout the seventeenth and eighteenth centuries the élite household became progressively more highly structured. Rooms were given individual functions and servants became more specialised. Along with this went an increasingly elaborate system of domestic record-keeping. Later, in the nineteenth century, a highly structured household became even more important as boundary definitions elsewhere were under attack from social mobility and new wealth from industry and trade.[1] The order and structure of 'little things' became part of the Victorian domestic philosophy. The management of objects involved in everyday living established 'bonds of appropriateness' on which was built the whole order of society. It inculcated habits 'without which man would tend to the savage state'.[2] Within the household the boundaries of different orders were clearly defined by an intricate system of markers, some of which took a physical form. Others were much more subtle, encoded in esoteric language or visualisation.

The most obvious of the boundary markers was the baize door – a physical barrier between the backstairs and the front of the house which was carefully soundproofed.[3] The space on either side of this barrier was further subdivided. The front of the house was divided into family rooms for day-to-day living and 'public' or 'state' rooms for formal entertaining; between these two there was often one doorway on each landing which created as clear a separation as the door to the backstairs. Further subdivisions within the front of the house separated off the nursery (varying in size according to family life cycle) and the bachelor rooms for single visitors (depending on whether it was a sporting household). The back portion of the house was divided into specialised spaces which were subject to an even more complex network of relationships.

STATUS

Retired servants often say that the feature they found difficult to accept was not the structuring of work but the impossibility of escape from the ranking system which went with it. The paternalist philosophy of the traditional country house contrived to control body and soul, operating through a hierarchical system which expressed itself in all sorts of ways. Physical definition was most obvious in the eating place for dinner and supper. Meals such as tea were often eaten in the place of work, but main meals were segregated according to status. Senior servants ate in the steward's room, where they were waited on by a steward's room boy and where they ate better food and stronger drink than the junior staff who ate in the servants' hall and were provided with beer and ale. The outdoor staff – stablemen and gardeners – ate in their mess-rooms. Part-timers and casual workers ate either in the stable mess-room or brought their own food to consume in their place of work. This hierarchical system operated when the family was in residence, but might change when the household was put on board wages. Then the Trentham household, for example, tended to split along gender lines, into groups of maidservants who ate together, and menservants who stayed together in the servants' hall.[4]

When the full household was in residence, the seating at the servants' hall table was also ranked – men on one side, maids on the other, each in rank order, with the butler and housekeeper at the ends.[5] Where there was a separate steward's table, the head of the servants' hall table was the coachman or an under-butler. At Anglesey Abbey early in the twentieth century, the hall chairs were all painted different colours so that everyone would know their place.[6]

Status markers were also seen during family prayers at which daily attendance was compulsory. Markers were subtle and in the 1920s were remembered as such by William Lanceley – not just that the family, butler, housekeeper, cook and lady's maids sat on chairs while the rest of the servants sat on benches, but that the benches were from the servants' hall and had to be carried through each day. Thus the ordinary servants were made to feel not quite as entitled to be there as everyone else, and only one step removed from the sweep's boy who was not even allowed to attend.[7] At Cragside in Northumberland in 1920, the communal nature of family prayer was abnegated by the way these were conducted, with a line of family and a line of servants kneeling along opposite sides of the room, their backs towards each other.[8]

Blinkered adherence to ranking systems between different groups of servants could result in real distress. Mrs Queenie Cox, interviewed in her old age by

Frank Victor Dawes in the 1970s, had worked as a fourteen-year-old housemaid in a house where her elder sister was nursemaid. The two girls were not allowed any contact: 'If I saw my sister out with the children she was not allowed to speak to me, or me to her. Nurses were on a higher level, you see.'[9]

Individual work groups had internal systems of rank, as we saw with the laundrymaids. Similarly, within the context of the rest of the domestic staff the head housemaid was a person of some standing, reckoned to be a senior member of staff and taking her meals with the other seniors. She had her own bedroom, next to the dormitories where the more junior housemaids slept. Behaviour patterns within the group reflected these differences; when the Shugborough housekeeper and a group of housemaids moved about the corridors they walked in rank order, the lowliest last but having to scuttle to the front of the line to open the doors for the housekeeper.

The hierarchy of goods in the country houses was also well developed. The distinctions between weaves of linen – damask, diaper and huckaback, fine linen and coarse linen – was a marker not only of functional suitability but also of social status. This extended to every piece of furniture in the servant bedrooms – washstand, type of bed, carpeting and curtains. Even the clothes which servants wore were part of the elaborate code: a waist apron indicated a higher rank than a full bibbed pinafore and no apron at all an even higher rank. For the family, livery might be an indicator of high status, but to the wearer it was a stigma to be risen above. The attributes of servants were depersonalised by uniforms. Maids' washing dresses were often colour-coded according to department.[10] Hair was hidden and fashionable hairstyles were not allowed as this would blur social boundaries. Even names might be changed.

Underlying all the ranking systems of the country house was of course the nature of work. As Leonore Davidoff has pointed out, those who were closest to activities which were defiling or arduous were hidden furthest away from high status areas.[11] Housemaids' work – the removal of the detritus of other people's lives – was low status, but as this could not be placed physically in the low status parts of the house maids were trained to do it invisibly. The ultimate removers of defilement, laundrymaids, were allowed inside the main house only to collect and deliver laundry and often that was done for them. It was not acceptable to see laundrymaids coming into the house for this purpose, so access had to be discreet, even to the point of being through an underground passage.[12]

The mark of good housekeeping was inconspicuousness. In the 1760s Hannah Glasse advised the young housemaid not to 'make any noise, but learn to walk

The servants' hall at Erddig, near Wrexham. A long table with benches or chairs, side tables and clock were standard furniture for such rooms. The famous portraits of the servants of Erddig line the walls. (National Trust)

softly, and not disturb the Family'.[13] Victorian manuals agreed: 'It is bad management to allow such undertakings to interfere with the comfort of the home.'[14] Not without pathos after fifty-two years of 'invisibility', an old housemaid commented: 'It is very difficult to be a housemaid, to do your work well and never be seen, and gentlemen fifty years ago did not care to see her often.'[15] Physical invisibility indicated social invisibility; wealthy Victorian men particularly did not want to see the processes of tidying away dirt and so strong was this desire that many were described as 'hating' servants.[16] Divorced from the domestic sphere of life, it was beneath their notice, faintly ludicrous, and the proper concern of women and low-status men.[17] This was a very different attitude from that of Nicholas Blundell at Little Crosby in the 1720s. A throwback to an earlier age, Blundell concerned himself with the minutiae of household life, and who was happy to take his maidservants out skating.[18]

Domestic privacy – part physical, part conceptual – became another of the boundary markers. Before the eighteenth century, servants were regarded as extensions of family and senior managers came from only a slightly lower social level than the master. The notion of privacy was unimportant, so the enfilade of bedchambers leading directly from other chambers did not matter. As owners came to value protection from intrusion by servants of a lower class, the whole layout of the country house was modified. Corridors were built to allow discreet access to rooms; even tiny 'hidden' staircases were fitted into dressing-rooms to preserve the invisibility of housemaids.[19] In this context, domestic privacy for servants was not only unnecessary, it was even undesirable, an attack on social barriers, at least until individuals became sufficiently senior to have earned the shift from dormitory to private bedroom. Thus we can see that the denial of privacy and comfort inflicted on junior menservants in their basements and teenage housemaids in their attics was an expression of social differentiation.

The problem of privacy was especially difficult in the declining years of domestic service. The household was faced with two conflicting courses of action. To persist with the old paternalistic household meant putting up with resident servants whose entire life was subject to family control. Yet this meant more servants around the place, trespassing upon the family's privacy. Changing to day labour meant servants went home at night, leaving the family to themselves, yet taking with them into the outside world intimate household secrets. Such servants had to be trusted neither to pilfer nor gossip, both of which eroded family privacy.

Another mark of social distinction was cleanliness itself. Davidoff has argued that until the nineteenth century the boundaries between the wealthy and the lower classes were defined by the ownership of goods and not by cleanliness; until then everyone had been dirty and cleanliness became a boundary marker only with the increase of new forms of dirt and the pressures of new wealth.[20] Davidoff's timescale, however, is misleading in respect of personal hygiene and it is certainly inaccurate in respect of household cleanliness. Keith Thomas found ample evidence of cleanliness existing as a social marker long before the nineteenth century. Quoting a sixteenth-century source on personal hygiene, Thomas wrote: 'Cleanliness was a form of social distinction by which people staked out a claim to respect and preferential treatment. It was an attribute of higher social status.'[21] Again, the eighteenth century was a time when English society was noted for the importance it placed on having fine linen to wear, a feature which applied to both sexes and which was remarked upon by many foreign travellers.[22] In itself this was an indicator of contemporary notions of personal cleanliness as well as wealth.

FOLDING SHEETS READY FOR MANGLING

Sheets must be folded in half, selvedge to selvedge, right side outwards. Dampen hems generously with fingers, then sprinkle the rest. Turn over and sprinkle the other side of the fold. Stretch the selvedge. Take the two selvedges to meet the centre fold, then fold in half weft ways, keeping the name on the upper part. Place hems just below each other to avoid bulk. Leave to dampen.

When mangling with an upright mangle, feed the piece to the rollers and turn so the rollers just grip the front edge of the piece; then tighten the screw; with the left hand stretch the piece; tighten the screw more and turn the rollers while pulling the piece back with the left hand. Put through three times.

(From notes left by the late Rhoda Layman)

What did change in the nineteenth century was the idea of what constituted cleanliness. For the first time wealthy people took to bathing and washing themselves all over, whereas previously baths were regarded as suitable only for the sick and the infirm.[23] For normal respectable individuals the washing of hands and face was believed to be sufficient, as long as clothes, especially men's shirts, were changed frequently. [24]

So if cleanliness was a social marker, were country houses clean? The ownership of elaborate and fabulously expensive goods brought a widespread natural desire to see them looked after and presented well. These desires pre-dated the nineteenth century, as can be seen by the numbers of owners who rebuilt domestic offices in the eighteenth century. The rabbit warrens of service rooms were no doubt a demonstration of status in themselves but there was also an element of functional need. As William Hazlitt pointed out, cleanliness has long been associated with the ownership of material goods: 'The more any one finds himself clinging to material objects for existence or gratification, the more he will take a personal interest in them, and the more he will clean, repair, polish, scrub, scour, and tug at them without end, as if it were his own soul that he was keeping clear from spot or blemish.'[25]

Early writers on household management did not give detailed instructions on how to clean the house, but they did expect cleanliness. Thomas Tryon, for example, wrote in 1682: 'Most people take care that their furnitures are daily brushed and rubbed, and their very floors are washed.'[26] Foreign travellers such as François de la Rochefoucald (1784) commented on the cleanliness of eighteenth-century English households: 'In general, the English have many more servants than we have, but more than half of them are never seen – kitchen-maids, stable-men, maidservants in large numbers – all of them being required in view of the high standard of cleanliness. Every Saturday, for instance, it is customary to wash the whole house from attic to basement, outside and in.'[27] In 1772 another traveller commented upon the wooden floors in English houses which were 'washed and rubbed almost daily' giving 'a whitish appearance, and an air of freshness and cleanliness, which the finest inlaid floor has not always'.[28]

TO CLEAN FURNITURE

Fine furniture, whether walnut or mahogany, should be dusted and rubbed over every day. Once a week they need more time: first dust the furniture carefully; then rub any stains with a damp sponge, drying it off immediately; if stains are stubborn rub them with a piece of cork, taking care to follow the grain. Then apply your oil or wax paste, put on with a piece of soft wool fabric, using another piece of wool for taking off the paste. Then finish by rubbing with a piece of linen cloth . . . Pay especial care to cleaning all the paste from the edges of tables – this will rub off onto the clothes of diners.

Occasionally you may want to brighten the colour of tables, in which case wash them with a sponge dipped in hot, never boiling, beer, then dry quickly and apply oil or paste. This will bring up the wood slightly lighter and with a very high polish.

(After Anon., *The Footman's Directory*, pp. 37–9)

TO CLEAN MIRRORS

Take a piece of clean, soft sponge. Dip it into water, and squeeze it out again, then dip it into some pure alcohol. Rub it over the glass, then dust it over with some powder blue, or whitening sifted through muslin. Rub it lightly and quickly off again with a cloth. Then take a clean cloth, and rub it well again, and finish it by rubbing it with a silk handkerchief.

Do one side of a large mirror at a time for the smoke of the lamps or candles often leaves a kind of oiliness on the glass, which you will find extremely difficult to get off.

(After Anon., *The Footman's Directory*, pp. 42–3)

Well-scrubbed kitchens and dairies, spotless pans and crisp bedlinen were the result of complex reasoning concerned not only with social manners but also with beliefs about religion and health. For example, an integral part of early concepts of cleanliness was the 'miasma' theory, the idea that disease was spread by bad smells – by the smell itself, not the cause of the smell. As Keith Thomas has pointed out, it was believed that mixing bad smells was particularly dangerous. In the late seventeenth century, 'there was much concern to separate the different smells of cooking, young children and bodily waste'.[29] Is this perhaps part of the explanation for the proliferation of domestic offices, for the banishment of nurseries to the top floor and laundries to the estate cottage? The logical conclusion to such thinking is embodied in the adage so beloved of writers of Victorian domestic manuals – 'A place for everything and everything in its place'; this itself strikes echoes in Mary Douglas's famous 1970s definition of dirt as 'matter out of place'.[30]

The country house was a place where cleanliness was high on the list of priorities at least from the eighteenth century; and as we have seen, even before this, household accounts show regular purchases of materials for domestic cleaning. Yet there must be qualifications to this verdict. Caroline Davidson thought that much of the appearance of cleanliness was probably superficial.[31] This must have been particularly true in kitchens and sculleries before the commercial production of soda. The lack of cleaning substances which would cut through grease must have been a real problem, which was not solved until the early decades of the nineteenth century.

How far the country house was responsible for the spread of improved standards of cleanliness into other social contexts is difficult to assess at this distance. Anecdotal evidence is conflicting – the journal of Jane Carlyle showed her servants to be so slovenly that she had to deal with a plague of bedbugs herself; whereas the later reminiscences of retired laundrymaids point to a heightened sense of the importance of cleanliness and 'correctness' in their own household linen. The 'emulation' concept in relation to domestic material goods is generally a difficult area and one which academics have debated at length.[32] There is evidence to show that in some respects the middle-ranking household was more forward-looking in relation to material culture than the élite household and it is at least a tenable thesis that innovation in cooking facilities in the late eighteenth century came out of the commercial rather than the élite sector, especially roadside inns which required a fast turnover of food. Perhaps the size and institutional nature of the élite household held it back. Yet emulation was certainly a force in the country house world. In the early nineteenth century, the Sutherlands' land agent James Loch had a powerful influence on the attitudes and actions of the agents of neighbouring smaller country estates such as the Fitzherberts and the Ansons. Might not this process also work in respect of domestic management? Troubles with servants must have occupied many after-dinner conversations of the élite, but the existence of a parallel system of social networking by servants between the great houses as revealed in the diaries of footmen reveals a different channel for the spread of information – servant to servant as well as family to family. Whether such networking contributed to the spread of new ideas or reinforced old ones is a different matter.

Most élite households had individual idiosyncrasies in their domestic regimes, yet overall their household structures were remarkably uniform. This is amazing, given the absence of schools of domestic management in this country before the end of the nineteenth century, and the failure to unionise domestic service.

The laundry block at Berrington Hall. This forms the northern side of the main court. (Derek Evans, National Trust)

Left: The laundry washing trays at Berrington Hall. Right: The drying closet at Berrington Hall. The four sliding racks are grouped into two, between which stands a furnace which heats the pipes inside the racks. The whole system was made by Thomas Bradford of Salford. (Derek Evans, National Trust)

Can we attribute this uniformity to the influence of prescriptive manuals, or was there some other force at work? A highly structured, conservative management built on well-known and widely adopted traditional lines was of immense benefit to servants who wished to move around. It enabled them to fit into different households quickly, to 'know their place' immediately; in effect to drop in and out of households and, in the case of menservants, domestic service as a whole. There is an intriguing relationship here which requires detailed exploration elsewhere. Was it employers or employees who built and maintained the hierarchical structures which were so all-embracing? What was their common origin and to whose benefit did they operate?

GENDER

As we have seen, the gender balance of workers in the élite household changed radically over time. This trend continued throughout the nineteenth century when it became increasingly acceptable, though not fashionable, to use female parlourmaids as 'front' servants. This change served to set even further apart those wealthy households which continued to employ footmen to serve dinner, porters to clean the front steps and laundrymen to organise their washing.

The change to women servants required a female manager. In the seventeenth and eighteenth centuries, a housekeeper in a great household was a sort of caretaker left by the family to look after the house in their absence and organise its seasonal cleaning – in other words another sort of 'invisible' servant, a senior housemaid. The management role which we associate with her post in the nineteenth century then belonged to a male, the house steward. The gradual rise of the housekeeper can be followed through inventories; not until 1792, for example, does a 'housekeeper's room' appear in the room list at Hardwick Hall.[33] In the wealthiest aristocratic families with multiple households, moreover, the old steward system survived long into the nineteenth century, a single house steward being retained as an overall manager over housekeepers in each of the houses.

As women became more central to the cleaning of the household a very real problem arose – that of having women, and in particular young girls, cooped up in close domestic proximity with men. In the medieval household this problem had been avoided by using day labourers and by making sure that what few women there were in the household were rigidly segregated from the men. In the eighteenth and nineteenth centuries, most houses retained some degree of gender segregation. Generally speaking women worked to female middle managers and men were supervised by men. So the physical area of the backstairs could be divided into men's and women's corridors, staircases, work places and living accommodation; sometimes there were even separate back-door entrances. This segregation broke down only in the kitchen where women cooks and kitchenmaids worked directly for male chefs. The only common area of cross-socialisation was the servants' hall and even here middle management attempted to formalise and even ritualise behaviour.

Clearly men were involved in housework, even in the Victorian laundry where work was differentiated according to gender. Box mangling required two people, one to prepare the rollers while the other turned the mangle. Country houses usually employed extra help to turn the box mangle, even when there were two or more laundrymaids. This could be the odd man or a person employed specially, but invariably it was a man. The rational explanation for this is that the box mangle was heavy to turn. Yet in other contexts box mangles were often operated by children. In practice, when set up correctly they were not heavy, but finely balanced. This is especially true of the patent mangle, which certainly required less strength than lifting heavy baskets of damp linen. Nor was turning the mangle a skilled job; loading the washing onto the rollers took dexterity and experience and this was always done by the laundress. It seems that the country house management did not expect women to cope with machines with moving parts. This also applied to the use of transport. When the laundry was sited away from the house and a horse and cart was needed to collect and deliver linen, a man was employed to do this.

Distinctions of gender went deeper. Linen and the possession of linen were associated with the female world and with feminine virtues of comfort, decency, patience, nurturing, health and hygiene. This was the image exploited by Edwardian advertisements for soap or starch. Yet the intimate nature of bed and body linen meant that it was also associated with the converse of these – dirt, sex, immorality and punishment.[34] The persons associated with combating such defilements themselves became socially defiled by their contact. This was the other image of the laundress, responsible for the banishment of her workplace further and further away from the house. The housemaid, who was also privy to the intimacies of country house life, had a similar problem. Face-to-face contact between the defiled and the undefiled was to be avoided at all costs. So the relationship was depersonalised in an effort to come to terms with what was felt, even unconsciously, to be their contaminating influence.[35]

The burden of maintaining more and more elaborate house furnishings was similarly gendered. The dusting and polishing of expensive and high-status furniture in the public rooms was done by footmen, not housemaids. Footmen carried coals to the dining-room, library, drawing-rooms, and also to the best bedrooms, but other bedrooms, staircases, corridors and the more distant interiors were serviced by housemaids, who also did the large-scale cleaning of all rooms, particularly the grate cleaning and floor scrubbing. Footmen washed glass, china, silver and looking-glasses, but scullery maids washed pots and pans in the kitchen.[36]

Such a consistent gendered differentiation of work in the élite household does support Lorna Weatherill's distinction between high- and low-status jobs as mentioned briefly in the introduction to this book. The picture is complex, however, as there are also elements of rationality in the distribution of work. Defensive cleaning was a response to the delicacy of furnishings and it made sense to delegate some jobs to trusted individuals. The choice of those individuals might be influenced by a genderised mindset or by other more practical exigencies. The routine care of pictures, for example, was probably in the domain of the housekeeper, the 'curator' of the house in the absence of the family, not the footmen or butler, who accompanied the family on their trips away.[37]

Diligence and Dissipation *or* The Modest Girl and the Wanton, *an engraving of a painting by James Northcote, 1796. Modern studies in women's history sometimes explore the idea of 'inversion' – the contemporary depiction of two warring images of women, the qualities of virtue and chastity opposing other female attributes of weakness and impurity. Laundresses were particularly open to such interpretations, of which this is a superb illustration. (Colonial Williamsburg)*

It is worth looking at the position of a footman a little more closely. Recognised by all historians of domestic service as a marker of status, he also had more subtle roles. For example, inside the household he presented the acceptable face of service, a sort of silent buffer zone protecting the master against face-to-face confrontation with other more menial servants, the purveyor of 'messages' to the uncontactable from an aristocracy which both depended on him and loathed him. Like most people between two worlds he was not particularly admired by either.

To mark both functions, deference-giver and contact zone, he had to don appropriately elaborate dress. Another part of his working life, however, was involved in housework, a throwback to the old traditions of feudal manservice; this required him to work in a different and lower-status part of the household 'stage' for which he donned different clothes. Such jobs did not take a long time individually, but, like housewife's chores, they mounted up. Again like the housewife's chores, footman's jobs suffered from being undervalued. In comparison with housemaids, he might be allocated to high-status work, but by the end of the nineteenth century the concept of 'separate spheres' of household activity was so established that a footman was simply a man doing women's work. The qualities of a good servant – hard work, obedience, respectfulness – were easy for women to relate to, but when this same ethic was applied to men they became the 'despised qualities of the menial or lackey'.[38] The uneasiness felt by men in such circumstances was often hidden beneath a manner which was both strained and supercilious, and intensely disliked by employers and other servants.

The nature of footmen's domestic work compounded the problem. By the nineteenth century, the more specialist and skilled jobs – like picture cleaning – had moved out of the remit of servants into that of tradesmen and restorers; spring-cleaning was in the hands of housekeepers, so footmen were left with routine cleaning for the comfort of the family, not the care of the furniture. Footmen's work was ephemeral, with no end product to give a lasting sense of achievement. The appearance of a gleaming table had to serve as 'rare and tangible proof' of his labour.[39] Eric Horne, looking back at a lifetime in gentlemen's service, remembered this aspect:

> It is useless to describe the thousand and one things that comprise a footman's duties, which, in every place he goes to, is different. It is like throwing a stone in a pond, rings are formed in the water, which eventually fade quite away. So that at the end of his day's work he can show nothing that he has done. He has made nothing, produced nothing, yet he has been constantly on the alert all day, not knowing where his next job will spring from.[40]

That footmen themselves felt this was an imprisonment is shown by another extract from Eric Horne's autobiography:

> Although we used to make what amusements we could amongst ourselves, I felt that I was gradually going into a net, and losing all liberty in life; the constraint

became almost unbearable, but what could I do? I had no trade in my hands. I knew nothing but a gentleman's service wherewith to get a living . . . a sort of man–woman existence, at the mercy of the gentry's whims and fancies; cooped up day and night, without variation.[41]

The description of 'a man–woman existence' is revealing. Not only did Horne feel trapped but he implied that this situation would have been acceptable for a woman, part of her normal lot in life, but for men it was damaging. It is perhaps relevant that the suicide rate for footmen was higher than average, while that for gamekeepers, an occupation clearly reserved for men, was very much lower.[42]

Ironically, the unease of menservants trapped by inappropriate work was in a way shared by many houseowners who came to feel that they were themselves in thrall to the 'terrible tyranny of servants'. Charles Dickens articulated this feeling: 'They keep us in a decent bondage, the ladies in a sort of terrorism' and later: 'It is we who are in the service of these 'treasures', not they in ours.'[43] The love–hate relationship with footmen exemplified this dual bondage and was one of the reasons why footmen came to be so vilified and why, in the nineteenth century, many households replaced footmen by maidservants who did their work cheaper and with better temper.

TECHNOLOGY AND SKILL

According to Davidson spring-cleaning came 'into vogue' in the nineteenth century, in line with rising standards of living and the greater availability of cleaning substances.[44] The fact that spring-cleaning was done at all implies a degree of cleanliness, yet today spring-cleaning is almost a forgotten discipline among housewives, who take offence at the thought that their house needs such rigorous cleaning at any time.

The case of the country house is special, however. Firstly, there is evidence that the tradition of spring-cleaning in this context is older than the nineteenth century and relates to the idea of a seasonal, almost ritual, purging of the house. What changed in the nineteenth century was the involvement of the mistress. In the Victorian household, spring-cleaning was usually done while the family were away; the whole domestic timetable was carefully planned to avoid disruption of a wealthy lifestyle. This contrasts strongly with the more involved eighteenth-century mistress of the Susanna Whatman mould, who would have found it difficult to delegate the organisation of spring-cleaning to servants. Secondly, as all housekeepers of country houses know today, the problem is often not under- but over-cleaning. Contents are so fragile that cleaning methods and routines have

To Clean a Hair Mattress

A mattress should normally be cleaned at least every two years – the ticking washed and the hair cleansed. Take out the hair and plunge it into a tub of lukewarm water in which a handful of washing soda has been dissolved. Move it up and down in the water, squeeze it as dry as possible, and put it into a basket on the top of another tub, or in the open air. After it has dripped for about an hour, spread it out on a sheet in the sun or in front of the fire. It dries very soon, and will be found as crimp and full of spring as when new. The ticking may then be re-filled, bound, and stitched down.

to be carefully designed to maintain a balance between cleanliness and deterioration. Today, seasonal cleaning still has a part to play in achieving this balance, though now it is carried out during the winter. Certainly the eighteenth-century Susanna Whatman understood defensive cleaning; hence the worries about laundrymaids helping housemaids and the strictures about not touching gilt picture frames. The protective measures of muffling the house in case-covers, drawing curtains across pictures, pinning papers over drapes, are much older in tradition than the nineteenth century. Long before this, country house staff and their employers were in an 'unstated partnership' designed both to maintain comfort and to preserve the household treasures for future generations.[45] The elaboration of the country house interior and the purchase of more and more luxury goods created more housework, but of a special kind, requiring special skills and organisation.

Historians of twentieth-century domestic technology tell us that early machines were not savers of time, and not simply because they were inefficient and therefore inherently time-wasting, but because they encouraged the ownership of more and more goods. It seems that new domestic technology created more housework, just as new roads create more traffic. In the context of the country house laundry, early innovation related to manual systems rather than mechanisation. Did these changes produce more work or less?

The old system of the buckwash was ideally suited to the cleaning of household and plain body linen. As our nineteenth-century observer admitted in *The Laundrymaid*, the buckwash might have been time-consuming but it did not involve long hours of hand-rubbing and could cope with large quantities of linen relatively quickly. But it did not clean cotton well, nor was it suited to more sophisticated dyed or printed fabrics. So the change to cotton which occurred

A view of the laundry and the mangling class at the Royal Bluecoat School, Wolverhampton, around 1890. The girls are mangling towels on upright machines, though part of the metal structure of a box mangle can be seen against the back wall, behind the laundress. (Staffordshire Arts and Museum Service)

throughout the eighteenth and nineteenth centuries resulted in the adoption of the more laborious hot soap-wash, if necessary alternating with buckwashing. One of the selling points of cotton was that it could be washed more easily and more frequently than linen, but this was only true if hot water, plentiful soap and the labour for hand-rubbing were available. So was created firstly the need for more hand-labour and subsequently the spur to develop large-scale laundries and manufactories of better laundry soap and, ultimately, soap powders.

Ironing shows a similar change. The early growth in ownership of linen of better quality and wider variety was accompanied by the development of a machine to help in its handling – the box mangle. It was well suited to the particular qualities of linen, smoothing and polishing with a minimum of effort. Laborious hand finishing was wasted on linen sheets which unless changed every day quickly came to resemble screwed-up tissue paper. But the box mangle was not suited to the presentation of complex personal body cottons which needed ironing, a skill which had been limited previously to body servants. As cotton goods replaced even household linen, the skill of mangling was replaced by the skill of ironing – much more time-consuming, much more laborious. Expectations of finish were raised, until the time arrived when even sheets were ironed, which would have been thought ludicrous before.

The old technologies of the buckwash and the box mangle were derived from the processing and making of linen; if a housekeeper could make linen, she could easily service it. Within the household, productive skills such as these could be seen publicly; they could be quantified, earning respect for a household which was large enough to depend on its own agricultural resources and to be able to make many of its own workaday materials. In the nineteenth century, when the linen-producing household became the cotton-consuming household, respect had to be earned in different ways, by the extraordinary elaboration of textile goods. To service this, techniques had to change, even if it meant the adoption of more time-consuming and laborious methods. The conclusion must be that housework was changed by the introduction of new goods and new systems of work, perhaps made more acceptable in the type of substances used, but the time taken was not necessarily reduced and the status earned not necessarily enhanced.

Another view of the laundry at the Royal Bluecoat School, Wolverhampton, probably taken shortly after the photograph on the previous page. Line-shafting has been installed to drive the box mangle, but at least one of the upright mangles is still in place, as are the iron stove, the spiral racks and the large overhead rack. The girls are being taught the two-handed press used for collars. (Staffordshire Arts and Museum Service)

It was the growing consumption of not only purely luxury goods like furnishings and art treasures but also of items providing for the decencies of life which helped create more and more housework. As the consumption and categorisation of goods developed to the point of fetishism, so the diversity of the servants' roles developed. Servants were themselves an indicator of wealth, the specialised, hierarchical and sometimes pointless nature of their existence attesting to the degree of consumption of goods in the household. They were also the monitors and managers of consumption, contributing their expertise to what Galbraith called 'the administration of wealth'.[46] They could also work as the agents and movers of consumption, requiring of their employers more and more goods and services to help them in their pursuit of their own form of status, choosing some directions at the expense of others. Finally, servants could also be the disseminators of consumption, footmen gossiping about acquisitions and retired laundrymaids taking home new standards of cleanliness which lasted a lifetime.[47]

Despite being the repository of all sorts of luxury furnishings, the country house attitude towards innovation in technology or work systems was uncertain. In the wealthiest households both innovation and archaism carried status. In the Trentham of the 1840s, the Sutherlands employed the most fashionable architect of his day, Charles Barry, renowned for his excellence in functional planning. Barry's domestic offices at Trentham were a tribute to rationality. There was a clearly discernible 'hot spot' comprising kitchen, sculleries and stillroom, all of which needed regular deliveries of large quantities of coal. On the opposite side of the yard was a 'cold spot' – dairies, confectionery and larder, all needing ice. Some distance away beyond the porter's lodge was a 'wet spot' – the laundries and brewhouse which needed quantities of coal and water. The equipment incorporated into Trentham was both modern and ingenious. The remodelled house was fitted with water closets, gas lighting, hot-air central heating in the living quarters and steam cookers in the kitchen.[48] Yet in the organisation of staff this same household harked back to a much earlier age, retaining as middle managers two archaic posts, groom of the chamber and usher of the hall, both of which originated in the medieval noble household.[49] In the person of Mme Rousseau, it also retained a highly skilled and highly paid personal body servant as 'starcher'. Barry's Trentham thus illustrates the complex nature of the country house involvement with innovation in the nineteenth century – its material culture might be modern but its management systems were medieval.

Perhaps the one single technology which made an immense difference to housemaids' work was the degree of internal plumbing. Mark Girouard summarised the history of plumbing in country houses as 'a two-steps forward one-step back story'.[50] The medieval privy or garderobe which polluted the moats and made the house stink; the sixteenth-century close-stool which depended entirely on servants to remove the pan; the short-lived fashion in the late seventeenth century for water closets (short-lived because without an S-bend they too stank); eighteenth-century earth closets which used sand or soil instead of water; and the final triumph of the late eighteenth-century water closet as sold by Joseph Bramah to the rich. In practice most houses were a mixture of more than one system until the end of the nineteenth century. In 1793 the Ansons spent £45 on two Bramah water closets for the use of the family; yet over a hundred years later, the servants were still using a suite of smelly pan closets which were built at the back of the service yard and which had to be cleansed by regular burning.[51] This ambivalence, part of the tension between spending and saving, was especially marked in the wealthiest households, where it is noticeable that most efforts to reduce wasteful expenditure related to servant comfort, while spending on family comfort continued unabated.

There was, of course, a logic behind the country house reluctance to install modern plumbing and bathrooms. What was the use of expensive drudgery-saving devices when the whole function of servants was to do the drudgery? There were comforts in archaism: 'The ritual of the hip bath on its mat in the bedroom, with the steaming jug of hot water and the neat, warm towels, and – with luck – a bright fire was one the older generation were reluctant to give up.'[52] Hip baths were still used in some houses in the 1940s, as one unimpressed visitor recalled:

Pitch dark when called by a dear old man who entered my bedroom and pulled back the heavy curtains. . . . Tenderly this old retainer brought into the room a red blanket which he spread before the empty fire-grate. Then he trundled a small tin hip-bath on to the red blanket. Then he brought a brass can of tepid water, enough to cover the bottom of the bath. The room must have been several degrees below zero. He might have been a ghost performing the customary function of a hundred years ago.[53]

The sense of security and the 'entrancing smell' engendered by age are redolent in Lilian Bond's poignant account of Tyneham before it was evacuated during the Second World War:

The essence of it may have been the wholesome smell of well-scrubbed floor boards left . . . uncovered here as in the passages and bedrooms. Other ingredients, such as lavender, old furniture and a certain shut-up dampness must have entered into it. . . . One whiff of it, if I could smell it again, would . . . take me back across the years and I should be a child again with Tyneham quiet and homely as I knew and loved it then. . . . I suppose that strangers might have been impressed by the general shabbiness of paint and furnishings. Carpets and curtains, chair covers and bed hangings had all served their turn for generations. Original colours may have been improved by age and wear, at any rate they had reached a stage where their several colours blended softly and harmoniously. The idea of Tyneham rooms decked out with spick and span upholstery . . . appears incongruous.[54]

Many country households pursued an anti-consumer-goods philosophy which contributed to the prolongation of manual work and drudgery and to lost opportunities in the transformation of housework.[55] It may have been the workforce itself which was responsible for this conservatism, fearful of de-skilling, of losing the status of experience and hard work which gave them their only hold over their employers. The point was illustrated in a testimonial included in an advert for the Syracuse clothes washer around 1906: 'Miss Ashwell had some difficulty to persuade the washer-woman to use the Machine at first, as she said "it was no way of working to wash like that", – i.e., there was no work in it, 'twas too easy – but now the woman much prefers it to the other way.'[56]

Until the rundown of the domestic service industry compelled employers to search for alternatives, cleaning methods in the country house relied on endless hard physical labour. Even the privileged children of the family remember this.[57] Yet the trained country house servant was also skilled, as contemporary manuals took pains to point out: 'It is with rubbing clothes as with washing paint and scrubbing floors. Workers who have not acquired the knack, splash about, fuss, and fatigue themselves, and make little progress; those who have skill go to work quietly, and with little apparent effort accomplish their desired purpose.'[58] Although this extract has a whiff of the deferential servant about it, the point made is nevertheless true. Despite the heavy manual nature of much household work the core of many servants' jobs was highly skilled. Like most skilled trades it created its own ranking systems based on expertise and age. Many writers have pointed to such systems as examples of the innate snobbishness of the backstairs world. There is no doubt that inter-servant relationships could take on a semblance of caricature but even within such a situation not all hierarchies were necessarily based on snobbishness and social prestige. In a work environment a

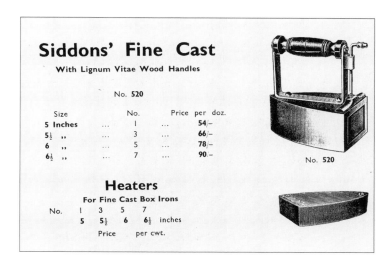

Extract from a trade catalogue by J. and J. Siddons of West Bromwich published in 1937, advertising a box iron of the same design as patented in 1738 by Isaac Wilkinson of Denbighshire. These were produced in quantity in the nineteenth century and became easily the most common form of box iron. The door at the back slid upwards to allow the heater to be placed inside; since only the heater was warmed by being put into a fire, the sole of the iron remained clean. (P. Sambrook)

ranking system could be based on valid considerations of skill, experience and the need for training.

Where quality of work and individual skill is at a premium, training and work disciplines become paramount. Many laundering techniques sound easy but are difficult in practice; the glossing and curling of collars, for example, required a dexterity which came only with practice. Girls were not born with these skills; far from being 'natural' and innate, they were learnt by practice. Early prescriptive writers took it for granted that this practice was provided in the girl's own home; one from the 1770s thought that 'all women are more or less acquainted with washing'.[59] Yet in the élite house laundry, a new girl worked a long time before she was trusted even to iron a white shirt, never mind reach the required speed of two minutes per shirt.[60] As a late Victorian laundry textbook explained: 'Ironing requires a great deal of practice, and it cannot be well done unless done with speed.'[61] These two quotations from manuals, dated 1773 and 1898, show the changing attitudes to laundering skills over time – the early one seeing them rooted in homely skills and the second trying to establish a groundwork of professionalism. Similarly the manuals point out the difference in perceived skill and status associated with the two processes of washing and ironing.

The acquisition of skill changed people's perception of themselves. If the laundrymaid regarded herself not as a mere appendage to an overgrown household, but as a worker within a highly skilled and identifiable occupation, questions of deference towards her employer took on a slightly different hue, just as working-class women's changing view of their domestic sphere affected their attitude to husbands.[62] Oral history tells us that the laundress felt a real pride in the quality of work and traditions of her trade. She also had a real awareness of her own worth, whether or not she felt herself to be exploited or occupied in work which was seen by others as low status. She was, after all, partly responsible for the appearance of important individual members of the family and more than one laundress recalled that this fact gave her status, both in her own eyes and those of other members of the household. She was in effect the inheritor of the highest traditions of skill inherent in the late medieval body servant.

Methods of training servants in their manual skills were thus important and traditional. Pain was part of the process; there was a strong element of 'I had to go through this so why shouldn't you'. The training of footmen was typical of country house employment. Waiting on servants was one method: 'I suppose I first learnt to be a servant by being a servant to the servants: the table in the servants' hall to lay, the staff cutlery to clean and the staff meals to put on the table.'[63] Footmen also learnt by watching other servants and occasionally trying out their skills on selected guests: 'You watched the other one and you were made to watch because you knew you would be doing it yourself sooner or later. And you were allowed to practise on a guest that wasn't quite so well turned out or who hadn't got such good clothes; you were allowed to try your luck with him.'[64]

As with young housemaids scrubbing endless stone corridors, new servants were deliberately given unpopular jobs to teach them discipline and fortitude. There was a fine line between this and outright physical abuse. Eric Horne, later butler to numerous members of the aristocracy, remembered the chores pushed onto him when starting his career as a young helper in the stables: 'I was not supposed to do any indoor work, but he [the footman] would make me clean the knives; he would lock me in the boot hole till I had cleaned them. One day I would not do something he wanted; he caught me, and held the part I sit on in front of the open kitchen fire, and then took me out in the yard and sat me down in the snow.'[65] This is perhaps an extreme example, but many young servants were subjected to physical and verbal abuse from their supervisors over long periods. Some seemed not to resent this: Alfred Taylor, a footman at St Fagan's, Cardiff, remembered, 'You didn't regret that because you had the training and it always stuck with you.'[66] If the senior servant was addicted to drink life could be particularly difficult. John James, a young single-handed footman under an experienced butler, was in this situation and remembered it only too well: 'I came in for a lot of cursing and swearing when my work was not done quick enough for his liking.'[67] On the other hand there were senior managers who advocated a more enlightened approach. The Italian house steward of the Sutherland household in the mid-nineteenth century, Senor Vantini, was criticised by the Duke and Duchess for being lax with the servants. In his defence he wrote: 'It has been said I am to [sic] good towards them, perhaps it may be so, but the reason is because I think that a man is brought to his duty more by kindness than by *rigueur*.'[68]

Constructive criticism was another method of training. Peter Russell was trained as under-butler at Kensington Palace by the butler, Bysouth, who watched him throughout dinner, then afterwards criticised him. 'I think I learnt fairly fast, as much to get away from his constant staring as out of anxiety to do the job properly.'[69] Sometimes the employer took a hand in this process. Russell remembered the Princess Marina's habit of keeping a notebook and slim silver pencil by her side at table. 'If anything went wrong, and this applied particularly if we had guests, she would make a note, and . . . we would be criticized for some breach of behaviour the following day.'

Even the discipline in the servants' hall was part of the general training of a domestic servant. In households without a separate steward's room table, it was usual during the main course of the meal for all the servants to eat in silence; then the head servants retired to the housekeeper's room for their sweet, and the 'babble would break out'. According to Eric Horne, this 'instilled discipline. Had conversation been allowed from the start the meal would have been prolonged. The idea was to get it over and get back to the job.'[70]

SERVANT RESPONSES

So how did servants respond to their situation? No doubt many accepted it with little conscious thought; this was their lot in life and they got on with the business of living, developing strategies for maintaining what Davidoff has called 'compensatory definitions of self-worth'.[71] Stressing their own skills and the difficulties of their job was one means of coming to terms with what potentially at least was a degrading relationship. The fact that the skill might be real does not preclude its use as a strategy of personal survival.

Another strategy was emphasising the virtues and possessions of the employing family – taking a pride in 'our people' or taking immense trouble over their high-status goods. The housekeeper at Shugborough happily wrapped herself in with the whole philosophy of the country house: 'It was just a world of its own. I never knew about the outside world. I devoted my whole life to it. I was so interested and I was so happy . . . I never bothered going out much after I was housekeeper.' The strength of proprietorial satisfaction and the pleasure some servants got from looking after beautiful things are easily underestimated in hindsight, but they are redolent in this extract from one butler's memoirs:

> Here am I today . . . lovely old silver dating back to 1610 to garnish my table with, wines as choice as ever man had in his charge . . . I see them every day and really they are as much mine as anyone's. I look after them, clean them, love them. To sit down and clean just one cup takes me quite an hour, and with the wireless softly playing I . . . rub and polish away thoroughly happy, knowing that the little dinner that is coming off will be all the better enjoyed if my silver is shining and my glass sparkling.[72]

Romanticisation of the past was a common strategy. John James, writing in the 1940s, looked back at a lifetime in service and found compensating features in the old days, when faithful servants were treated as part of the family, rewarded with the affection of the children they served and leading contented lives within a limited circle. In the introduction to the memoirs, Shaw Desmond described James as writing about his employers 'respectfully, almost adoringly' and James built this up into a sort of 'golden age myth', contrasting this comfortable picture with service as it became later in the 1930s and '40s, when servants were better educated and demanded independence and free time.[73]

The creation of a personal social world was another response to life in a closed, isolated community. The interchange of visits, the invitations to dances, the acquisition of musical and dancing skills, all these helped to make contact with other houses within the same world, to let off some of the pressure which inevitably built up in such a closed environment, at the same time as strengthening bonds within individual households and defining personal boundaries. The laundrymaids' singing performed much the same function, helping them to cope with heavy work and long hours.

Using the opportunities of service to their own advantage was a response common to most of the menservants' memoirs, especially in relation to travel. In the 1830s both the 23-year-old Thomas and William Tayler were interested in the world around them: 'If a person wishes to see life, I would advise them to be a gentleman's servant. They will see high life and low life, above stairs as well as life below. They will see and know more than any other class of people in the world.'[74] Later, at the end of the nineteenth century, the young John James also had a general curiosity about life while stuck in a very restricted corner of creation; indeed, this was his original motivation for entering service, 'being very ambitious to see the world, and my only means of doing this, as far as I could see, was by going into service.'[75]

In the 1830s William Tayler was more aware than his contemporary Thomas of the iniquities of service, especially in town: 'In London, men servants has to sleep down stairs underground, which is jeneraly very damp. Many men loose their lives by it or otherwise eat up with the rhumatics. One mite see fine blooming young men come from the country to take services, but after they have been in London one year, all the bloom is lost and a pale yellow sickley complexion in its stead.'[76] Eric Horne's later autobiography reveals a good deal more of this attitude. Although obviously fond of many of his masters Horne was aware of their foibles and of their unreasonable expectations, as well as critical of the treatment often meted out to servants.

Another response, of course, was the restlessness which was so typical of domestic service. The idea of the long-serving faithful retainer was not entirely a myth. Some houses, like Kingston Lacy and Erddig seem to have had a tradition of long-serving staff and some servants spent their whole lives in the service of

Part of the servant household at Shugborough photographed in the 1870s. The view was taken outside the kitchen and the servants' hall and shows some of the maids with gardeners, grooms and the blacksmith. The latter, the tall man to the left, tries to hold the stable guard dog, a huge mastiff with a white chest and a studded collar. (Staffordshire Arts and Museum Service)

one family. One such was Andrew Crozier, the son of a labourer and lodge-keeper who first started work for the Armstrongs at Cragside in 1881 as a ten-year-old page boy with a salary of £8; by 1891 he was footman and he later became butler to all four Lord Armstrongs, dying aged eighty-six in 1957.[77] Yet this was untypical of most servants, even of those working in country houses. As historians know only too well, chasing servants through the decadal records of the census is a barren task, for they rarely stayed in one place that long. Housemaids were perhaps more fortunate than others, for there were more of them and they could move between households in the same family to gain promotion.[78]

Servants seemed to cling to this mobility as the one form of independence which was left to them. Yet this independence was in reality limited. One of the features of footmen's and butler's autobiographies is the continual search for something better – inside their trade or out of it. For many men domestic service was a periodic experience, a safety net to fall back into when ventures outside – pub-keeping was a favourite one – failed.

For women, of course, the most desired escape was marriage, for until the end of the nineteenth century everyone took it for granted that a woman left her place when she married. The segregation into gendered work patterns and the attempts at controlling internal social contact which we saw at Westhill reveal the paradoxical nature of domestic service in this respect. Seen as a safe haven to which parents could dispatch their daughters for training and experience, the élite domestic household was in reality a marriage market every bit as important for the working-class girl as the London season was for her social superiors. Employment in the big house broadened horizons, presenting wider choices for marriage partners than ever country village society could. This must have contributed greatly to the restlessness, the continual searching for a better place with better prospects in relation to both work and an eligible marriage partner. Albert Thomas articulated this in the 1940s: 'I am sure that if you asked any girls what they were waiting for, 75 per cent would say "Mr Right".'[79]

This search for a sexual partner was not restricted to women. In the 1830s Thomas's diary at Westhill shows clearly enough that though he was ambitious to move up the servant hierarchy, and keen to learn from a sophisticated world very different from that which he had left behind in Cheshire, he was also assessing the women with whom he came into contact. Instead of settling down with Martha, his girlfriend from home, he took time to look around, expand his experience and enjoy himself. Obviously there must have been casualties in this general scenario – men who were disappointed, girls who were used and abused[80] – but demographers tell us that this feature of domestic service was of critical statistical importance. Not only did it mix people and their genes up, but, more importantly, economically it served to delay the age at which servants married. Before the widespread use of contraception, the age at which people married was the most important means by which populations controlled their birth rate. In this respect, the institution of service has been described as a 'crucial demographic mechanism' in pre-industrial north-west Europe, allowing the marriage age to be delayed and the birth rate lowered, as well as offering a long-term alternative to marriage for those who found themselves without a partner.[81]

Given these sorts of undercurrents and expectations, it is not surprising that many households fell victim to internal jealousies and petty rows. The root cause of Westhill's rows was certainly sexual jealousy, others may have been the product of group dynamics or perceived inequalities about money. Rows between servants appear in most autobiographies and even children noticed it. At Pilgrims' Hall 'there were traditional mild feuds, probably the same in all such houses, between stable and garden, garden and kitchen, kitchen and pantry, kitchen and nursery, nursery and schoolroom. One grew up with a vague awareness of these and cagily regulated one's doings so as not to be caught between two fires.'[82] Deeper-seated jealousies between individuals or factions are often revealed by letter books recording correspondence between family and servant.

CONCLUSION

This study of the work of servants in the country house has pursued three levels of 'reality'. The sandwich is made up of stereotypical images of each of our servant types, created by both contemporary and modern observers, the prescriptive image of servants in contemporary manuals, and the actuality of servant experience culled from memoirs and diaries. It is important to distinguish between these three and also to be aware of their limitations. The use of stereotypes, for example, has proved a useful tool – to the writer as well as, it is hoped, the reader. At such a distance in time, however, it is impossible to come to a conclusion as to their accuracy, and that was never the intention; rather the formalised depictions present specific issues by which to order questions about behaviour and skills. The existence of stereotypes says a good deal about servants, and even more about employers and their social context, but comparing the picture with the reality is comparing two different animals. To borrow from one of the most perspicacious historians of domestic service, Leonore Davidoff, writing in a different context – there is no answer because there can be no answer.[83]

Soap adverts sold an image to their customers which was not far removed from that articulated by the advice manuals: 'A laundry maid should be a strong, active, cleanly woman; one who has confidence in her own powers, who knows how to value time.' (From Anon, Laundrymaid, *p. 5) (P. Sambrook)*

What is clear, however, is that the reconstruction of country house domestic management requires a multiple approach. We need closely focused studies on individual houses or skills, as well as an awareness of the big picture, the whole story of domestic hierarchy. It is also clear that in exploring country house domesticity, a concentration on methods and skills rather than objects is helpful, especially if we wish to encompass change over time. We also need to explore work organisation and management systems, as well as the meanings and motivations revealed by material culture, written and oral reminiscences and the documentary record. Once we begin to look at country house domestic interiors from these viewpoints, we put the humanity back into the otherwise soulless expanses of basement and attic. Only with these tools can we begin to unveil the true complexity of the communities which made up the working end of the country house.

Examples of Butlers' Pantries, Housemaids' Closets and Laundries

These are selected interiors from National Trust properties in the United Kingdom and are open to the public during normal open times. For a fuller list, including NT interiors not open to the public, see Hardyment, *Behind the Scenes*, pp. 241–3.

The Argory, County Armagh – late nineteenth-century wet and dry laundries, dressing-rooms.

Beningbrough Hall, North Yorkshire – Victorian wet and dry laundries, box-mangle.

Berrington Hall, Hereford and Worcester – Victorian laundry, drying closet, walled drying ground.

Castle Ward, County Down – Victorian wet and dry laundry, dressing-rooms.

Castle Drogo, Devon – 1927 butler's pantry, bathroom.

Charlecote Park, Warwickshire – laundry coppers

Cragside House, Nortumberland – 1860s butler's pantry, electric dinner gong.

Dunham Massey, Cheshire – wet and dry laundries, mangle room with box mangle, butler's pantry, housemaids' closet, refurbished in Edwardian period.

Erdigg, Wrexham – wet and dry laundries, drying closet, box mangle, servant's bedroom, bathroom.

Felbrigg Hall, Norfolk – nineteenth-century dressing-room.

Hill of Tarvit, Fife – Edwardian wet and dry laundries, drying closet and box mangle, dressing-room, bathroom.

Killerton, Devon – Victorian wet and dry laundries, drying closet, box mangle.

Kingston Lacy, Dorset – nineteenth-century wet and dry laundries, drying closet, box mangle, loft.

Knole, Kent – seventeenth-century dressing-room.

Lanhydrock, Cornwall – late nineteenth-century livery room, linen lobby, housemaids' sluice room, dressing-room, bathroom, servant's bedroom.

Ormesby Hall, Middlesbrough – wet scrub and dry laundry, box mangle.

Shugborough, Staffordshire – Victorian wet and dry laundries, box mangle.

Speke Hall, Merseyside – Edwardian bathroom.

Tatton Park, Cheshire – nineteenth-century butler's pantry, basement railway, linen room, dressing room.

Uppark, West Sussex – butler's pantry reconstructed to its 1874 condition, lamproom, 1880s–90s.

NB the laundries at **Berwick Hall** and **Powis Castle** are **NOT** open to the public.

Notes

Place of publication is London unless otherwise stated

Chapter 1

1. For examples of servant autobiographies see bibliography. A book based on reminiscences is Frank Victor Dawes, *Not in Front of the Servants: a True Portrait of Upstairs, Downstairs Life,* (first published in 1973, Century in association with the National Trust, 1989).
2. For example, Christina Hardyment, *Behind the Scenes: Domestic Arrangements in Historic Houses* (National Trust, 1997), previously published as *Home Comforts: a history of Domestic Arrangements* (Viking in association with the National Trust, 1992).
3. For example, Adeline Hartcup, *Below Stairs in the Great Country Houses* (Sidgwick & Jackson, 1980).
4. For example, Merlin Waterson, *The Servants' Hall: a Domestic History of Erddig* (Routledge & Kegan Paul, 1980; new edition published by National Trust, 1990; reprinted by the National Trust in 1990).
5. Pamela Horn, *The Rise and Fall of the Victorian Servant* (first published 1975, Stroud, Alan Sutton Publishing, 1986); more recent and with a comprehensive book list is Jessica Gerard, *Country House Life: Family and Servants, 1815–1914* (Oxford, Blackwells, 1994).
6. Others have noted the lack of emphasis on work; see Edward Higgs, 'Domestic Servants and Households in Victorian England', in *Social History*, vol. 8, 2 (May, 1993), 201.
7. In a context wider than the country house, the components of work, technology, gender and status are the subject of a large academic research base within the historical studies of gender and the consumption of goods. A place to begin is John Brewer and Roy Porter (eds), *Consumption and the World of Goods* (Routledge, 1993).
8. Lorna Weatherill, *Consumer Behaviour and Material Culture in Britain, 1660–1760* (Routledge & Kegan Paul, 1988), pp. 8–9; see also Lorna Weatherill, 'The Meaning of Consumer Behaviour in late seventeenth-and early eighteenth-century England in Brewer and Porter, *Consumption*, pp. 206–27.
9. Brewer and Porter, *Consumption*, p. 2.
10. See instead Una Robertson, *The Illustrated History of the Housewife, 1650–1950*, (Stroud, Sutton Publishing, 1997); Christina Hardyment, *Mangle to Microwave* (Oxford, Polity Press, 1989); Caroline Davidson, *A Woman's Work is Never Done: a history of Housework in the British Isles, 1650–1950* (Chatto & Windus, 1982 and 1986).
11. For discussion of 'rationality' in housework see Leonore Davidoff, *Worlds Between: Historical Perspectives on Gender and Class* (Oxford, Polity Press, 1995), pp. 73–102.
12. Weatherill, *Consumer Behaviour*.
13. Amanda Vickery, 'Women and the World of Goods: a Lancashire consumer and her possessions, 1751–81' in Brewer and Porter, *Consumption*, pp. 274–301.
14. Brewer and Porter, *Consumption*, p. 5.
15. For discussion on the tension between 'profligacy' and 'parsimony' see Davidoff, *Worlds Between*, p. 91.
16. Helen Morris, *Portrait of a Chef: the Life of Alexis Soyer, sometime Chef of the Reform Club* (Cambridge, Cambridge University Press, 1938), pp. 34–5.
17. Ruth Schwartz Cowan, *More Work for Mother: the Ironies of household Technology from the Open Hearth to the Microwave* (New York, Basic Books, 1983).
18. Davidoff, *Worlds Between*, p. 74.
19. For functioning of the noble medieval household see Kate Mertes, *The English Noble Household, 1250–1600; Good Governance and Political Rule* (Oxford, Basil Blackwell, 1988).
20. Judy Wajcman, *Feminism Confronts Technology* (Oxford, Polity Press, 1991); see studies in Gertjan de Groot and Marlou Schrover (eds), *Women Workers and Technological Change in Europe in the Nineteenth and Twentieth Centuries* (Taylor & Francis, 1995).
21. Davidoff, *Worlds Between*.
22. Weatherill, 'Meaning of Consumer Behaviour', p. 214.
23. Higgs, 'Domestic Servants and Households', p. 202.
24. Leonore Davidoff, 'Mastered for Life: Servant and Wife in Victorian and Edwardian England', *Journal of Social History*, vol. VIII, 4 (1974), 413. This paper was reprinted in Davidoff, *Worlds Between*, pp. 18–40.
25. Claire Seymour, 'Indoor Domestic Servants under the Age of Fifteen in England and Wales, 1850–1914' (unpublished Ph.D. thesis, University of Keele, 1991).
26. Jessica Gerard, 'Invisible Servants: the Country House and the Local Community', *Bulletin of the Institute of Historical Research*, 57 (1984); Gerard, *Country House Life*.
27. A preliminary essay is Pamela Sambrook, 'Supplies and Suppliers to the Country House' in Pamela Sambrook and Peter Brears (eds), *The Country House Kitchen, 1650–1900: Skills and Equipment for Food Provisioning* (Stroud, Sutton Publishing in association with the National Trust, 1996, paperback 1997), pp. 197–209.

28. SRO, Sutherland MS, D593/R.

29. For discussion on working-class autobiography see David Vincent, *Bread, Knowledge and Freedom: a study of nineteenth-century working-class autobiography*, Europa Publications, 1981.

30. SRO, D4177/1–2, manuscript, 'A Daily Journal or Memorandum Book' by a footman in the service of 2nd Duke of Sutherland, 1838–9. The diary is attributed in the catalogue simply to 'Thomas'. For commentary on this diary see Kitty Fisher, 'Life Below Stairs' in *Staffordshire History*, vol. 3 (Autumn, 1985), 12.

31. Dorothy Wise, *The Diary of William Tayler, Footman, 1837* (originally published by St Marylebone Society Publications Group, 1962), extracts quoted in John Burnett (ed.), *Useful Toil: Autobiographies of Working People from the 1820s to the 1920s* (Allen Lane, 1974), p. 185.

32. Eric Horne, *What the Butler Winked At* (Werner Laurie, 1923).

33. William Lanceley, *From Hall Boy to House Steward* (Edward Arnold, 1925).

34. Albert Thomas, *Wait and See* (Michael Joseph, 1944); John James, *The Memoirs of a House Steward* (Bury Holt, 1949); Ernest King, *The Green Baize Door* (William Kimber, 1963); Peter Russell, *Butler Royal* (Hutchinson, 1982).

35. Dawes, *Not in Front of the Servants*; Samuel Mullins and Gareth Griffiths *Cap and Apron: an Oral History of Domestic Service in the Shires, 1880–1950*, Harborough Series no. 2, (Leicestershire Museums, Art Galleries and Records Service, 1986).

36. Useful specialist manuals: Anon., *The Laundrymaid, her Duties and How to Perform them* (Houlston's Industrial Library, no. 23, 1877); Anon., *The Footman's Directory and Butler's Remembrancer* (4th edn, 1825).

37. Higgs, 'Domestic Servants and Households', pp. 201–10.

38. For a discussion on the use of manuals see Michael Roberts, '"To bridle the falsehood of unconscionable workmen, and for her own satisfaction": what the Jacobean housewife needed to know about men's work, and why', *Labour History Review*, vol. 63, part 1, (1998), 4–30.

39. Lesley Lewis, *The Private Life of a Country House* (Newton Abbot, David & Charles, 1980 and reprinted by Sutton Publishing in association with the National Trust, 1997); Lilian Bond, *Tyneham: a lost heritage* (Wimborne, Dorset, Dovecote Press, 1956 and 1984).

Chapter 2

1. Dawes, *Not in Front of the Servants*, p. 64; Burnett, *Useful Toil*, p. 149; J. Jean Hecht, *The Domestic Servant Class in Eighteenth-century England* (Routledge & Kegan Paul, 1956), p. 54.

2. Isabella Beeton, *Beeton's Book of Household Management*, (1859–61, reprinted by Chancellor Press, 1989), p. 964.

3. E.S. Turner, *What the Butler Saw: two hundred and fifty years of the Servant Problem* (Michael Joseph, 1962), p. 213.

4. Lady Violet Greville, 'Men–Servants in England' in *The National Review*, vol. XVIII, (1892), pp. 812–20.

5. Charles Booth, *Life and Labour of the People in London*, vol. VIII 'Population Classified by Trades' (Macmillan, 1896), pp. 228–9.

6. SRO, Anson MS, D615/E(H)42.

7. Daniel Defoe, *The Insolence and Insufferable Behaviour of Servants in England . . .* (1724); Jonathan Swift, *Directions to Servants* (1745)

8. Dorothy Marshall, 'The Domestic Servants of the Eighteenth Century' in *Economica*, vol. IX, 25–7, (1929), p.17.

9. Hecht, *Domestic Servant Class*, p. 86.

10. Marshall, 'Domestic Servants', p. 24.

11. Hecht, 'Domestic Servant Class', p. 160.

12. Mrs Harris writing to her son, dated 10 May 1764, quoted in Marshall, 'Domestic Servants', p. 37; for a more detailed account of the movement to abolish vials see Hecht, *Domestic Servant Class*, pp. 163–8.

13. See Dawes, *Not in Front of the Servants*, p. 65; for a description of the running footman see Hecht, *Domestic Servant Class*, p. 55–7.

14. According to John James, the last running footman in private service in England was employed by the Duke of Queensberry, although as late as 1851 two running footmen were employed at the opening of an assize court in the north of England: James, *Memoirs*, p. 97.

15. Samuel and Sarah Adams, *The Complete Servant* (first published in 1825, facsimile edition by Southover Press, 1989), p. 143.

16. Hecht, *Domestic Servant Class*, p. 51.

17. John Trusler, *The Way to be Rich and Respectable* (1777), quoted in Hecht, *Domestic Servant Class*, p. 7.

18. Adams, *Complete Servant*, p. 16.

19. Hecht, *Domestic Servant Class*, p.2.

20. Households employing indoor menservants were taxed, on a per capita basis, from 1777 to 1937. See Horn, *Victorian Servant*, p. 9.

21. This was the context of a short story by George Eliot in which a stable groom was pressed into service as a footman. He came with a 'slight odour of the stable' and when removing the tea things from the drawing-room, he brushed the crumbs from the tablecloth 'with an accompanying hiss, such as he was wont to encourage himself with in rubbing down Mr Birdmain's horse'. George Eliot, 'Amos Barton' in *Scenes from Clerical Life* (1910, paperback edn by J.M. Dent, 1976), pp. 28–9.

22. Burnett, *Useful Toil*, p.149

23. SRO, D4177/1 and 2.

24. Thomas noted that the Strauss Band consisted of twenty-seven professional musicians, mainly Germans, who travelled around Europe, playing at royal courts.

25. Thomas would have been given a travelling allowance for this journey, estimated on the basis of the cost of the tickets plus 'travelling board allowance' to compensate for loss of meals. In 1860 the Anson family allowed travelling board wages of 5s for a whole day, if breakfast, dinner and supper had been missed; if just dinner, it was reduced to 2s 6d – SRO, Anson MS, D615/E(H)45.

26. Acting as escort to members of the family in the carriage was also a 'close duty'.

27. Horn, *Victorian Servant*, p. 97.

28. On one occasion Thomas admitted to his diary that he opened a message he was delivering to Lord Morpeth. According to Mrs Beeton, this was by no means an unusual habit, though not one to be encouraged; Beeton, *Household Management*, p. 969.

29. Mullins and Griffiths, *Cap and Apron*, p. 36.

30. Albert Thomas described the right way to sound a gong: 'I was always taught to commence very quietly, gradually raise the tone, give three strokes hard and then gradually reduce the tone until it dies away altogether'; Thomas, *Wait and See*, p. 165.

31. Lewis, *Private Life*, pp. 133–4.

32. Thrice a day for lunch, dressing time and dinner; see Diana Cooper, *The Rainbow Comes and Goes* (Rupert Hart-Davis, 1958, reprinted Century, 1984), pp. 34–6, quoted in Mark Girouard, *A Country House Companion*, (Century, 1987), p. 138.

33. For the various methods of serving food, see chapters by Peter Brears and Valerie Mars in C. Anne Wilson, (ed.), *Luncheon, Nuncheon and Other Meals: Eating with the Victorians*, (Stroud, Alan Sutton Publishing, 1994).

34. King, *Green Baize Door*, p. 35.

35. Lanceley, *Hall Boy*, p. 174.

36. Ibid., p. 175. An aiguillette (shoulder knot) was the footman's trademark.

37. King, *Green Baize Door*, p. 13.

38. Hecht, *Domestic Servant Class*, pp. 52–3.

39. Horne, *What the Butler Winked At*, p. 11.

40. The technical names for carriages appear in Thomas's diary without explanation; they were obviously familiar terms within the household. The family coach would have been a heavy formal vehicle with forward and backward seats, driven by a coachman sitting at the front outside the body of the vehicle. A 'phaeton' was a smaller, lighter convertible carriage driven from inside the vehicle. By 'phogang' Thomas probably meant a 'fourgon' a heavy, enclosed vehicle used for carrying luggage but fitted with a few seats for servants; they were usually sent on in advance of the main party. A 'chariot' was a formal four-wheeled vehicle fitted with forward-facing seats and driven by a coachman sitting on a front box. A 'briska' was a heavy, long-distance vehicle which could be converted into a sleeping carriage. The 'barouche' was a convertible vehicle with both forward- and backward-facing seats; the dicky was a single seat at the back of the barouche. The whole entourage needed twenty or more horses at any one time.

41. Dawes, *Not in Front of the Servants*, p. 26.

42. King, *Green Baize Door*, p. 37.

43. James, *House Steward*, p. 16.

44. Lanceley, *Hall Boy*, p. 28.

45. Adams, *The Complete Servant*, pp. 97–8.

46. King, *Green Baize Door*, p. 62.

47. James, *House Steward*, p. 58.

48. Lewis, *Private Life*, pp. 134–7.

49. Thomas, *Wait and See*, p. 69.

50. King, *Green Baize Door*, p. 10.

51. Russell, *Butler Royal*, p. 53.

52. Anon., *The Footman's Directory*, pp. 70–1.

53. Baize – a light wool with a nap, similar to flannel, much of it made in Essex, usually dyed green or red.

54. Lanceley, *Hall Boy*, p. 162

55. Notes from Mary Hunter, kindly supplied by Cragside.

56. Horne, *What the Butler Winked At*, pp. 93, 104.

57. King, *Green Baize Door*, p. 17

58. Lewis, *Private Life*, p. 138.

59. Russell, *Butler Royal*, pp. 50, 53.

60. King, *Green Baize Door*, p. 37.

61. Colza oil – pressed from a plant of the rape family, widely grown in nineteenth-century France.

62. Robert Kerr, *The Gentleman's House: or How to Plan English Residences from the Parsonage to the Palace*, (John Murray, 1864), p. 259.

63. Hartcup, *Below Stairs*, pp. 61–2.

64. Lanceley, *Hall Boy*, pp. 180–2.

65. Eileen Balderson and Douglas Goodlad, *Backstairs Life in a Country House* (Newton Abbot and London, David & Charles, first edn 1982, second edn 1986), pp. 66, 63.

66. Holland – a stout, plain-woven linen cloth, when used for household purposes often unbleached and sometimes stiffened with size; brown holland – unbleached, of a beige colour and fairly coarse woven, with a smooth finish, much used for household covers and blinds.

67. Lanceley, *Hall Boy*, p. 25.

68. King, *Green Baize Door*, p. 19.

69. Mullins and Griffiths, *Cap and Apron*, p. 36.

70. Viola Bankes, *A Kingston Lacy Childhood: Reminiscences of Viola Bankes*, (Wimborne, Dorset, Dovecote Press, 1986), p. 17.

71. Horne, *What the Butler Winked At*, pp. 148, 150.

72. King, *Green Baize Door*, p. 12.

73. Ibid., p. 18.

74. Contrary to popular belief, sedan chairs were used in the streets of London and the more fashionable cities well into the nineteenth century. Instructions on how to manage them are included in *The Footman's Directory*, 1825 and there are references to them in the diary of Thomas, the Sutherlands' footman, in 1838.

75. Anon., *The Duties of Servants: A Practical Guide to the Routine of Domestic Service*, (first published 1894), p. 60.

76. Dawes, *Not in Front of the Servants*, pp. 16–17.

77. Horne, *What the Butler Winked At*, pp. 48–9.

78. King, *Green Baize Door*, p. 43.

79. Horne, *What the Butler Winked At*, p. 78.

80. Mullins and Griffiths, *Cap and Apron*, p. 38.

81. Lanceley, *Hall Boy*, p. 33.

82. Horne, *What the Butler Winked At*, p. 64.

83. Lanceley, *Hall Boy*, p. 47.

84. Mullins and Griffiths, *Cap and Apron*, pp. 35–6.

85. Lanceley, *Hall Boy*, pp. 13–14. Notice the difference between the fashionable family meals (breakfast, luncheon at midday and dinner) and the older traditions of the servants' hall (brea-fast, dinner at midday, and supper).

86. King, *Green Baize Door*, p. 10.

87. Notes from Mary Hunter, kindly supplied by Cragside.

Chapter 3

1. Hartcup, *Below Stairs*, p. 112.

2. Ibid., p. 200.

3. Phillis Cunnington, *Costume of Household Servants from the Middle Ages to 1900* (Black, 1974).

4. Hartcup, *Below Stairs*, p. 148.

5. Dawes, *Not in Front of the Servants*, p. 108.

6. King, *Green Baize Door*, p. 44.

7. SRO, Anson MS, D615/E(H)14.

8. Booth, *Life and Labour*, p. 228.

9. Russell, *Butler Royal*, p. 58. According to Russell, this could reveal a lot about the household – if there was a number of sets it meant the staff turnover was rapid and possibly not a happy workplace.

10. Cunnington, *Costume of Household Servants*.
11. Horne, *What the Butler Winked At*, p. 108; see also Dawes, *Not in Front of the Servants*, p. 108.
12. Hartcup, *Below Stairs*, p. 37.
13. James, *House Steward*, p. 97.
14. Hair powder was taxed from 1786 to 1869. See Horn, *Victorian Servants*, p. 9.
15. SRO Sutherland MS, D593/R/7/2, voucher bundles.
16. Mullins and Griffiths, *Cap and Apron*, p. 35.
17. King, *Green Baize Door*, p. 20.
18. Fustian – a strong mixed cloth of a linen warp and cotton weft with a soft nap and usually coloured beige or grey.
19. Anon., *The Footman's Directory*, pp. 168–9.
20. Lanceley, *Hall Boy*, p. 169.
21. Dawes, *Not in Front of the Servants*, p. 75.
22. Ibid., p. 142.
23. Horne, *What the Butler Winked At*, p. 236.
24. Ernest King recalled the same problem in a household in Paris in the 1920s. Even though busy, one footman rarely returned to his bed before it was time to serve breakfast at 7.30: King, *Green Baize Door*, p. 44.
25. Booth, *Life and Labour*, p. 228.
26. Dawes, *Not in Front of the Servants*, pp. 76–7.
27. SRO, D615/E(H)10 and D593/R/7/10b; 'Attingham Park inventory', 1913, kindly lent by Attingham Hall.
28. 'Inventory and Valuation of furniture . . . at Kelmarsh Hall, Northampton, December 1905' (Kelmarsh Hall).
29. Burnett, *Useful Toil*, p. 183.
30. For a discussion of servants' social lives in the eighteenth century, including theatres, dances and visiting see Hecht, *Domestic Servant Class*, pp. 130–9.
31. Burnett, *Useful Toil*, p. 178.
32. See, for example, housemaids at St Fagan's Castle, Cardiff, singing as they worked: Christine Stevens, 'In Service at St Fagan's Castle', *Medel*, No. 3 (1986), 26–9.
33. Horne, *What the Butler Winked At*, pp. 98–9.
34. Lanceley, *Hall Boy*, p. 161.
35. Dawes, *Not in Front of the Servants*, p. 147. At Welbeck at Christmas, the senior footmen were given a crisp £5 note each, in an envelope with a wax seal bearing the family crest.
36. Dawes, *Not in Front of the Servants*, pp. 142–3.
37. Lanceley, *Hall Boy*, p. 23.
38. John Macdonald, *Memoirs of an Eighteenth Century Footman*, 1745–79 (Routledge, 1927).
39. King, *Green Baize Door*, p. 22.
40. Girouard, *Country House Companion*, p. 139.
41. Gladys Scott Thomson, *Life in a Noble Household, 1641–1700* (Cape, 1937), p. 120.
42. Burnett, *Useful Toil*, pp. 184–5.
43. Pamela Sambrook, *Country House Brewing in England, 1500–1900* (Hambledon, 1996).
44. King, *Green Baize Door*, pp. 13, 41, 96.
45. Lanceley, *Hall Boy*, pp. 166–7.
46. Thomas, *Wait and See*, p. 100.
47. John Robinson, 'A Butler's View of Man-Service' in *The Nineteenth Century*, vol. XXXI (January–June 1892), reprinted in Burnett, *Useful Toil*, pp. 202–9.
48. James, *House Steward*, p. 16; Thomas, *Wait and See*, p. 29; according to Balderson, *Backstairs Life*, p. 67, the first footman was usually called 'James', the second was 'John' and the third was 'Charles'.

49. 'English servants, whether employed by great lords or gentlemen of moderate means, have practically nothing to do. They are the laziest set of people it is possible to meet. All they have to do is to wait at table and at tea, sometimes to dress their master's hair': François de la Rochefoucauld, *A Frenchman in England* (1784) (Cambridge, Cambridge University Press, 1933), p. 26.
50. King, *Green Baize Door*, p. 43.
51. Scott Thomson, *Noble Household*, p. 118.
52. Horne, *What the Butler Winked At*, pp. 279–80.
53. King, *Green Baize Door*, p. 119.
54. Hecht, *Domestic Servant Class*, p. 55.
55. Booth, *Life and Labour*, p. 228.
56. SRO, Sutherland MS, D593/R/11/12.
57. Hartcup, *Below Stairs*, p. 166.
58. Hecht, *Domestic Servant Class*, pp. 157–76.
59. King, *Green Baize Door*, p. 42.
60. The position of servants' wages in relation to other workers and to changing times is a complex one and has been a point of some discussion; Burnett, *Useful Toil*, pp. 158–64; and Mark Ebery and Brian Preston, *Domestic Service in late Victorian and Edwardian England, 1871–1914* (Department of Geography, University of Reading, 1976).
61. NTTL, 158 EA, Claude Grimes, Anglesey Abbey.
62. Burnett, *Useful Toil*, p. 185.
63. Horne, *What the Butler Winked At*, p. 280.
64. Hecht, *Domestic Servant Class*, pp. 24–5; Macdonald, *Memoirs*, pp. xiv–xviii.
65. SRO, Sutherland MS, D593/R/11/12.
66. Booth, *Life and Labour*, p. 227.
67. MWL Tape 6070, Memories of Alfred Taylor, 1979; King, *Green Baize Door*, pp. 19, 158–60.
68. For a discussion of servants imitating the fashions of their employers see Hecht, *Domestic Servant Class*, pp. 200–19.

Chapter 4

1. Bond, *Tyneham*, p. 25.
2. Kerr, *Gentleman's House*, pp. 425–7.
3. SRO, Anson MS, D615/E(H)44, the Viscount Anson's establishment at Shugborough, 1828.
4. SAMS. R73/44, transcript of tape of Mrs Courtenay.
5. Mertes, *Noble Household*; Lionel M. Munby (ed.), *Early Stuart Household Accounts* (Hertfordshire Record Publications, No. 2, Hertfordshire Record Society, 1986), p. xvii.
6. SRO, Sutherland MS, D593/R/11/12 List of servants and wages, 1840.
7. SAMS, FR2/1/79.
8. For another example see Dawes, *Not in Front of the Servants*, p. 91.
9. Burnett, *Useful Toil*, p. 222.
10. SAMS, R73/44.
11. Mullins and Griffiths, *Cap and Apron*, p. 39.
12. SAMS, R73/44.
13. Lanceley, *Hall Boy*, p. 184; over a period wood ashes 'consumed themselves'.
14. Black lead – graphite, a mixture of charcoal and iron. Originally dug from mines, it was sold first as a powder and then as a paste.

15. A summary of W.E. and Mrs Buck, *The Little Housewife*, Leicester, 1880, as quoted in Mullins and Griffiths, *Cap and Apron*, p. 55.

16. Bath brick – a fine abrasive sand especially useful for bright metal. Originally it was dug from river beds in Devon and made into small bricks. Emery – a natural form of carborundum from Greece, milled and sorted, in the nineteenth century sold as powder or stuck on paper.

17. Jenny Rose, 'An investigation into the Domestic Care of Paintings in English Country Houses in the Eighteenth and Nineteenth Centuries' in Christine Sitwell and Sarah Staniforth (eds) *Studies in the History of Painting Restoration* (Archetype in association withe the National Trust, 1998), p. 147; this contains a very useful compendium of extracts from domestic manuals on picture care.

18. Christopher Gilbert, Janet Lomax and Anthony Wells-Cole, *Country House Floors, 1660–1850*, Temple Newsam Country House Studies no. 3 (Leeds City Art Galleries, 1987), pp. 101–9.

19. Mullins and Griffiths, *Cap and Apron*, p. 41.

20. Hurden – a coarse, strong, sacking-like cloth used for rough aprons, made from 'tow' – the coarser fibres discorded during hemp and flax processing.

21. Hippolyte Taine, *Notes on England*, quoted in Asa Briggs, *Victorian Things* (first published 1988, Penguin 1990), p. 251.

22. Glasse, Hannah, *The Servant's Directory or Housekeeper's Companion* (1760) , p. 29 advises leaving a little water in 'your chamber Chairpans, it prevents any offensive smell'.

23. Mullins and Griffiths, *Cap and Apron*, p. 43.

24. Ibid., p. 40.

25. Calico – a plain, cotton cloth used widely for underclothes.

26. Horne, *What the Butler Winked At*, p. 79.

27. Lewis, *Private Life*, p. 175.

28. Anon., *A Catechism for Servants, pointing out the Duties of the Housemaid and the Servant of all Work* (n.d., but mid-nineteenth century), p. 6.

29. *The Housemaid*, Houlston's Industrial Library, quoted in Turner, *What the Butler Saw*, p. 151. Housemaids were instructed how to check whether a bed was damp: put a warming pan into it and leave for the usual time; take it out and put between the sheets a clear glass tumbler, upside down; leave for a few minutes and if it has only a little steam the bed is dry enough; if it has actual drops of water on it, the bed is damp. Anon., *The Servants' Guide and Family Manual*, (London, 1830), p. 128.

30. Lanceley, *Hall Boy*, p. 181.

31. Ibid., p. 177.

32. Girouard, *Country House Companion*, p. 139.

33. Mullins and Griffiths, *Cap and Apron*, p. 42.

34. Christina Hardyment, (ed.), *The Housekeeping Book of Susanna Whatman*, (Century in association with the National Trust, 1987), pp. 38–41, 51–2.

35. Lewis, *Private Life*, p. 175; King, *Green Baize Door*, p. 21.

36. Lanceley, *Hall Boy*, p. 16.

37. 'An Old Servant', *Domestic Service* (Constable, 1917), p. 102.

38. In the 1830s the Trentham household paid a local locksmith, George Smith, 3s 4d twice a year for cleaning and oiling the door locks: SRO. Sutherland MS, D593/R/1/14/4, House Steward's Accounts

39. Lewis, *Private Life*, p. 176.

40. Calendering – smoothing by rollers, in this case probably put through the box mangle.

41. Sand – the most widely used abrasive for domestic purposes, usually a sharp, silver, sea sand; also powdered pumice stone.

42. Fuller's earth – a fine, absorbent, grey-brown clay used in de-greasing textiles.

43. Hardyment, *Susanna Whatman*, pp. 21, 37, 57.

44. SRO, D685/6/1, Minute Book of the Inspecting Committee of Stafford Infirmary, 1833.

45. Glasse, *Servant's Directory*, p. 31.

46. Gilbert et al., *Country House Floors*, p. 110.

47. A modern metal pot scourer is a good substitute.

48. Pamela Clabburn, *The National Trust Book of Furnishing Textiles*, (Viking in association with the National Trust, 1988), p. 197.

49. 'An Old Servant' *Domestic Service*, p. 94.

50. Rose, 'Domestic Care of Paintings', pp. 150–3, quoting M. Holyoake, *The Conservation of Pictures* (1870). One of the contemporary manuals giving such advice was a manuscript book written by a housekeeper at Felbrigg Hall.

51. Lewis, *Private Life*, pp. 176–7.

52. A.A. Strange Butson, *The Art of Washing* (Griffith and Farran, 1880), p. 68.

53. Ibid., p. 78. This was probably not far from the truth. In 1892 Shugborough commissioned an inspection of its drains and one of the recommendations was to stop servants putting salmon tins down the drains: SRO Anson MS, D615E(H)3, report on the sanitary arrangements and drainage system at Shugborough.

54. Clabburn, *Furnishing Textiles*, p. 172.

55. Christopher Morris, (ed.), *The Illustrated Journeys of Celia Fiennes, 1685–c. 1712),* (Macdonald, 1982), p. 232.

56. Rose, 'Domestic Care of Paintings' p. 147.

57. Lanceley, *Hall Boy*, p. 20; it is not totally clear from Lanceley's text whether the boy actually climbed inside the chimneys; if he did it was in contravention of the law of 1855 making the use of climbing boys illegal.

58. Frank Tyrer (tr.) and J.J. Bagley (ed.), *The Great Diurnal of Nicholas Blundell*, 1702–11 (Record Society of Lancashire and Cheshire, 1968, vol. 1, Appendix J, 3 March, 1710).

59. SRO. Anson MS, D613/E(H)22, blacksmith's bill.

60. SRO, D3125, key and plan of chimneys at Shugborough, May 1855, as inspected by Peter Hall, inspector of the Pottery Humane Chimney Sweeping Association. The chimney sweeping 'machine' consisted of a series of brushes attached to a framework of jointed copper tubes.

61. J.C. Loudon, *Encyclopedia of Cottage, Farm and Villa Architecture and Furniture* (Longman, 1842), p. 598.

62. Munby, *Household Accounts*, p. 68.

63. Whitening – a natural, fine, white, non-abrasive pipeclay.

64. Hearthstone – a mixture of white clay and 'rottenstone', a natural limestone that breaks down easily into powder. This was compressed with water into a block, white or grey, and used for scouring stone floors.

65. Munby, *Household Accounts*, pp. 178–94.

66. All of these are a little ambiguous; the rubbing brush we would probably recognise as a scrubbing brush, but the hair broom could be either for brushing hair or made of hair; similarly the flag brush (though brushes made from flags or rushes were usually home-made).

67. Lamp black – early name for black lead.

8. Hartshorn – a soapy liniment used for many cleaning purposes and made by mixing ammonia and oil. Made from horn shavings, a good source of ammonia.

9. Neatsfoot oil – made from cattle bones and used for dressing leather.

0. For scouring floors, tables, pots and pans and for putting down on floors to keep them clean. Photographs of country house kitchens sometimes show loose sand sprinkled on the floor and left to soak up spills. But from the mid-eighteenth century manuals advised that table and dresser tops be scoured with soap and water rather than sand because it did not leave grittiness.

1. The distinction was that brooms were properly made brushes, besoms were bundles of twigs, often birch, tied onto a handle and bought in large quantities.

2. Probably pigs' bladders; carefully blown up, lubricated with grease and cut into shape, they made airtight and waterproof lids for pickled onions – the eighteenth-century version of cling film.

3. Salts of lemon – a highly poisonous form of oxalic acid.

4. SRO, Anson MS, D615 E(H), household accounts.

5. SRO, Sutherland MS, D593/R/10/10/1, Mrs Ingram's vouchers.

6. Greaves – cakes of compressed fat used as dog food. SRO, Sutherland MS, D593/R/3/2/6/2, account book with R. Nicholson, 1864.

7. Sambrook and Brears (eds), *The Country House Kitchen*, pp. 201–2.

8. Hartcup, *Below Stairs*, p. 96.

9. SAMS, R73/44.

0. Anon., *Catechism*, p. 1.

1. Mullins and Griffiths, *Cap and Apron*, p. 43.

2. Turner, *What the Butler Saw*, pp. 263–4.

3. Ibid.

4. Some researchers dispute the frequency of recruitment of girls in their early teens. Whenever possible, housemaids were recruited in their late teens, when they were more experienced in housework; Seymour, 'Servants under the Age of Fifteen', p. 39; also Gerard, *Country House Life*, p. 184.

5. Hannah Cullwick moved down the servant ladder rather than up it; once she started to accept positions advertised in newspapers she moved from upper-class households such as Aqualate to middle-class homes where she was either the only servant or one of two or three: Liz Stanley (ed.), *The Diaries of Hannah Cullwick, Victorian Maidservant* (Virago Press, 1984); Davidoff, *Worlds Between*, pp. 114–50.

6. Dawes, *Not in Front of the Servants*, pp. 22–3.

7. Louise Jermy, *The Memories of a Working Woman* (Goose & Son, Norwich, 1934), p. 83.

8. Elizabeth Roberts, *A Woman's Place: an Oral History of Working-Class Women, 1890–1940*, (Oxford, Blackwells, first published 1984, reprinted 1995), pp. 58–9.

9. Mullins and Griffiths, *Cap and Apron*, p. 42.

0. Waterson, *Servants' Hall*, p. 116.

1. A poem left in the Berwick Hall laundry gives an interesting view of servant–child relationship. The child is taught to appreciate the hard work of Sally the laundress by doing her own dolls' wash: 'The Dolls Wash' by Juliana Horatia Ewing, 1841–85.

2. Bankes, *Kingston Lacy Childhood*, p. 69.

3. Anon., *Catechism*, p. 13.

94. Mrs Pickersgill working at East Norton Hall, in Mullins and Griffiths, *Cap and Apron*, p. 43.

95. Davidoff, *Worlds Between*, p. 85–6.

Chapter 5

1. Gervase Markham, *The English Housewife* (first published 1568–1637, paperback edition with introduction by Michael Best, Canada, McGill-Queen's University Press, 1994).

2. Davidoff, *Worlds Between*, p. 26.

3. Recollection by a visitor to Shugborough, of a young housemaid at Kingston Lacy being put to 'menial' work in the laundry as punishment for some misdemeanour. As it turned out the maid in question died of TB (in the 1930s) which was felt to be 'a very poor reflection on the Kingston Lacy household and its management of servants'; SAMS, Laundry Book.

4. Mark Girouard, *Life in the English Country House: a Social and Architectural History* (New Haven and London, Yale University Press, 1978), p. 283.

5. Paula Bartley, 'Sinking and Saving: the Reform of Prostitutes and the Prevention of Prostitution' (unpublished Ph.D. thesis, University of Wolverhampton, 1995); Patricia E. Malcolmson, *English Laundresses: a social history, 1850–1930* (University of Illinois Press), 1986.

6. Henry Algernon Percy, *The Regulations and Establishment of the Household of Algernon Percy, the Fifth Earl of Northumberland, at his Castles of Wresill and Lekinfield in Yorkshire in 1515* (London, 1770, reprinted 1827 and 1905), p. 16; in 1515 the Percy family would not have been sleeping without sheets. Robert Kerr related the use of feather beds and linen sheets to the increasing numbers of private bed chambers for the members of the household throughout the fourteenth and fifteenth centuries; likewise the provision of washing closets or 'eweries', and cupboards rather than chests; Kerr, *Gentleman's House*, pp. 39–40.

7. Santina M. Levey, *An Elizabethan Inheritance: the Hardwick Hall Textiles*, (National Trust, 1998), p. 33.

8. Ibid., pp. 44, 102, 104.

9. Ibid., p. 11.

10. Margaret Spufford, *The Great Reclothing of Rural England: Petty Chapmen and their Wares in the Seventeenth Century*, (Hambledon, 1984); and Barrie Trinder and Jeff Cox, (eds), *Yeomen and Colliers in Telford* (Phillimore, 1980), pp. 20–38.

11. 1.4 pairs of sheets to each bed in 1660–9 to 4.8 pairs in 1740–9.

12. The timescale seems to be that before the 1670s most imported textile goods were for household use. The 1670s and later saw an increase in imported textiles for fashionable clothing. This resulted in protectionist legislation in 1700 which levied duties on imported silks and printed calicos: John E. Wills, 'European Consumption and Asian Production in the seventeenth and eighteenth centuries', in Brewer and Porter, *Consumption*, pp. 133–47.

13. Damask – silk or linen fabric with a woven pattern reversed on the back. Huckaback – linen, later cotton cloth with tiny, raised, seed-like geometric shapes, very absorbent and traditionally used for towels and kitchen tablecloths. Diaper – like huckaback but better quality, a linen or cotton cloth

woven with a raised lozenge pattern in diagonal lines, used for tablecloths and towels.

14. Clabburn, *Furnishing Textiles*, p. 118.
15. SRO, Sutherland MS, D593/R/1/3/3, general household disbursements, 1645–6.
16. SRO, Sutherland MS, D593/R/1/64, disbursement book. Cotton candle wicks cost 3s a dozen and linen 4s 6d a dozen. Linen wicks burnt more readily than cotton.
17. SRO, Sutherland MS, D593/7/2, bills for bedlinen, 1799–1802.
18. David Ramsey, *The Weaver and Housewife's Pocket-Book; containing Rules for the Right Making of Linen cloth* (1750), p. vi.
19. Trinder and Cox, *Yeoman and Colliers*, p. 61. William Pitt, *Account of the Agriculture of the County of Stafford* (1796), p. 237; 'There is no considerable public management of linen, but a good deal of hurden, hempen and flaxen cloth got up in private families: a great many people resident in the country being now and having long been in the habit of growing a patch of hemp and flax.'
20. Levey, *Elizabethan Inheritance*, pp. 102, 104.
21. SRO, Sutherland MS, D593/7/2; for example, prices paid for blankets were from 10s 6d, 22s 6d, 32s 6d and 50s a pair; huckaback varied from 1s 6d to 4s 6d a yard and sheeting from 1s 6d a yard to 2s 8d a yard.
22. *Staffordshire Advertiser*, (26 April 1800), p. 1, col. 2.
23. J.F., *The Merchant's Whare-house laid open: or the Plain Dealing Linnen Draper* (printed for John Sprint at the Bell and Geo Conyers at the Golden Ring, 1696), p. 2.
24. Hempen – linen-like fabric made from the fibres of the cannabis plant. Ramie – Chinese and Indian plant of the nettle family, whose fibres were strong, durable and amazingly fine. In India it was used widely for everything from fishing to tapestries.
25. Waterson, *Servants' Hall*, pp. 76–7.
26. SRO, Sutherland Mss., D593/R/7/2.
27. Hartcup, *Below Stairs*, p. 67. Horn cloths were for cleaning servants' horn cups used for beer allowance.
28. Anon., *The Workwoman's Guide*, pp. 178–90.
29. Anon., *The Footman's Directory*, p. 60.
30. Note that well into the nineteenth century, a 'dressing table' was for preparing food, especially cutting up and stringing meat.
31. Malcolmson, *English Laundresses*, p. 31.
32. Bolster cases were considered old-fashioned at that time: *Cassell's Book of the Household*, vol. 2 (1890), p. 346.
33. Clabburn, *Furnishing Textiles*, pp. 117–21.
34. Ibid., p. 121.
35. Blanket material was woven in lengths weighing a 100 lb; see Ibid., p. 122.
36. Ibid., pp. 166–71.
37. Elizabeth Stuart, *English Fauteuil a la Reine* (typescript monograph on the suite of furniture in the Red Drawing Room at Shugborough, 1975, in William Salt Library, Stafford).
38. Clabburn, *Furnishing Textiles*, p. 175.
39. DRO, Bankes MS, D/BKL, inventories of linen, 1844 and 1851.
40. Levey, *Elizabethan Inheritance*, p. 104.
41. For the use and reuse of textiles within a middle-class context in the eighteenth century, see Vickery, 'Women and the World of Goods', p. 282.

42. SRO, Sutherland MS, D593/R/7/2, vouchers, 1780–1804.
43. Pat Baines, *Linen: hand spinning and weaving* (Batsford, 1989), p. 165.
44. Hardyment, *Susanna Whatman*, p. 47.
45. Kerr, *Gentleman's House*, p. 264.
46. Until well into the nineteenth century all women wore linen or cotton caps indoors all the time.
47. Blanche St Clair, 'Practical Washing Petticoats' and 'Intimate Underwear' in Mrs Stuart Macrae, ed., *Cassell's Household Guide*, vol. v (Waverley Book Co., 1911), pp. 1166–70, 1202–4.
48. The word 'linings' is still used today in parts of northern England to denote underpants.
49. For dress cleaning and storage see Christina Walkley and Vanda Foster, *Crinolines and Crimping Irons: Victorian Clothes, how they were Cleaned and Cared for*, (London, Peter Owen, 1978).
50. Pearlash – a form of potassium carbonate made by re-calcining crystallising potash, a soluble salt formed from crystallised plant lye, mostly imported from America and Russia. Borax – sodium borate, used as a milder bleach for clothes than washing soda (sodium carbonate).
51. Davidoff, *Worlds Between*, p. 85.
52. Percy, *Regulations*, p. 23.
53. Munby, *Household Accounts*, pp. 178–94.
54. Ibid., p. 69. For references on the cost and frequency of washing at Hardwick Hall, see Levey, *Elizabethan Inheritance*, p. 81.
55. SRO, Sutherland MS, D593/R/1/3/3, disbursement book.
56. SRO, Sutherland MS, D593/R/1/64, disbursement book.
57. SRO D593/R/1
58. Scott Thomson, *Noble Household*, pp. 213–15.
59. Sir Mathew Nathan, *The Annals of West Coker* (Cambridge, Cambridge University Press, 1957), pp. 350, 361–2.
60. Anon., *Workwoman's Guide*, p. 188. See also J.H. Walsh, A Manual of Domestic Economy (Routledge, 1857), p. 338, for calculations of payment by the year.
61. Glasse, *Servant's Directory*, pp. 46, 48–9.
62. Davidson, *Woman's Work*, p. 150.
63. Ibid.
64. Anon., *Domestic Economy adapted to the Code of 1881* (Chambers Educational Course, 1881), p. 19.
65. SAMS, R73/44.
66. David Freeman, *Tredegar House Below Stairs* (leaflet published by Tredegar House).

Chapter 6

1. Davidson, *Woman's Work*, pp. 138–48.
2. Glasse, *Servant's Directory*, pp. 45–6.
3. Davidson, *Woman's Work*, p. 142.
4. Donald Woodward, 'Straw, Bracken and the Wicklow Whale: the Exploitation of Natural Resources in England since 1500', in *Past and Present*, 159 (May 1998), pp. 70–1.
5. John Hatcher, *The History of the British Coal Industry, 1, Before 1700* (Oxford, Clarendon, 1993), pp. 1–55.
6. Norman Penney (ed.) *The Household Account Book of Sarah Fell of Swarthmoor Hall* (Cambridge, Cambridge University Press, 1920), p. 485.
7. Shugborough bought ashballs from a hawker at the back door.

8. Robert Plot, *The Natural History of Staffordshire* (1686), pp. 334–5; Morris, *Celia Fiennes*, pp. 112, 147.
9. Davidson, *Woman's Work*, p. 143.
10. Jane Ashelford, *The Care of Clothes* (National Trust, 1997), p. 8; for other references see Woodward, 'Straw, Bracken', p. 70.
11. Davidson, *Woman's Work*, p. 142.
12. Anon., *The Laundrymaid*, p. 69.
13. R. Lucock Wilson, *Soap through the Ages* (Unilever, seventh edition, 1959), pp. 4–6, 8; Davidson, *Woman's Work*, p. 145.
14. Davidson, *Woman's Work*, p. 145, citing Henri de Valbourg Misson, *M. Misson's Memoirs and observations in his travels over England* (Browne, 1719), p. 303.
15. In 1612 scented soap was bought at Gawthorpe Hall at a price of 2s 2d for 6lb; Ashelford, *Care of Clothes*, p. 8.
16. Dorothy Hartley, *Water in England*, (Macdonald, second edition, 1978), p. 248.
17. Davidson, *Woman's Work*, p. 145, citing John Houghton, *Husbandry and Trade Improv'd*, vol. 1, (Woodman and Lyon, 1728), pp. 348–54.
18. Ibid., p. 145 citing *The Lady's Advocate: or, An Apology for Matrimony. In answer to the Bachelor's Monitor*, (1741). But see chapter 8.
19. Malcolmson, *English Laundresses*, p. 132–3.
20. Hartley, *Water in England*, p. 238.
21. Davidson, *Woman's Work*, p. 145.
22. Margaret Cuthbert Rankin, *The Art and Practice of Laundry Work for Students and Teachers* (Blackie, n.d.), p. 174.
23. SAMS, Shugborough Laundry Book.
24. SRO, D593/R/10/10/1, Mrs Ingram's vouchers.
25. Wilson, *Soap* pp. 11, 13.
26. Ibid., pp. 14–15.
27. In 1833, for example, the inspecting committee running Stafford Infirmary authorised the purchase of a new stove for sterilising bedlinen and mattresses; SRO, D685/6/1 Minute Book of the Inspecting Committee of Stafford Infirmary, 3 August 1833, which records agreement: 'That a Baking Stove for disinfecting Clothes and Beds be erected in the Fever Wards on account of its immediate necessity, in consequence of the prevalence of Erysipelas in the House, cases having occurred from the circumstances of Patients having taken the disorder from sleeping in Beds that have not undergone such a process.'
28. K.F. Purdon, *The Laundry at Home* (Wells Gardner, 1902), p. 24; according to F.B. Jack, *The Art of Laundry Work*, (Edinburgh, Jacks, 1913), p. 10, boiling linen with paraffin in the water was introduced by a Mrs Gordon Cumming. Two table-spoonfuls of paraffin were added to 6 gallons of boiling water and a quarter pound of soap jelly. The clothes were boiled in this for half an hour.
29. *Victorian Shopping: Harrods Catalogue, 1895* (Newton Abbot, David & Charles Reprints, 1972); *Yesterday's Shopping: Army & Navy Stores Catalogue, 1907* (Newton Abbot, David & Charles Reprints, 1969).
30. 'This kind of washing with lye would not do at all for cotton articles, but, if carefully done, answers very well for strong linen clothes, making them remarkably clean, sweet and wholesome; nor does batting, if judiciously done, wear or injure the linen as it might be supposed to do. Bucking suits best with home-made linen': Anon., *The Laundrymaid*, pp. 54–6; Baines, *Linen*, p. 74.
31. G. Eland, (ed.), *Purefoy Letters* (2 vols, Sidgwick & Jackson, 1931).
32. Anon., *The Laundrymaid*, p 53.
33. Hannah Glasse did not like bucking; in 1760, she recommended steeping and soap-wash rather than bucking with lye even for great clothes; lye was suitable only for the very coarsest linen; Glasse, *Servant's Directory*, pp. 48–50.
34. Davidson, *Woman's Work*, pp. 144, 226, citing James H. Bloom, *Folk lore, old customs and superstitions in Shakespeare land* (Mitchell), p. 32; Allan Jobson, *An hour-glass on the run*, (Hale), p. 54; and Marcus Woodward, *The Mistress of Stantons Farm*, (Heath Cranton, 1938), p. 153.
35. Anon., *The Laundrymaid*, pp. 54–6. This is an instance where a retrospective account is given in a prescriptive manual.
36. Ibid., pp. 38–44.
37. Examples of these were Twelvetrees' 'Liquid Preparation', Manby's 'Crystal Washing Powders', Hudson's 'Extract of Soap' and 'Sapoline'.
38. Anon., *The Laundrymaid*, p. 52.
39. Françoise de Bonneville, *The Book of Fine Linen*, (Paris, Flammarion, 1994), p. 52.
40. Susanna Whatman gave orders: 'Any linen that is become yellow by laying by should be used once in the spring or summer when the cloaths can be dried out of doors. If the weather proves unfavorable rough dry them, and keep them to another wash, then dip them in water and hang them out again.' Hardyment, *Susanna Whatman*, pp. 53–4.
41. Bleaching newly woven linen was a separate part of the linen-making trade. The best bleachers were in Switzerland and Holland; linen weavers from as far afield as Scotland or Silesia sent their linen to Haarlem to be whitened on grass over a period of several months; Baines, *Linen*, p. 157.
42. Purdon, *Laundry at Home*, p. 18.
43. MOHP, Coalville, tape of 'Molly', laundrymaid at Coleorton Hall, Leicestershire.
44. Glasse, *Servant's Directory*, p. 49.
45. De Bonneville, *Fine Linen*, p. 52.
46. Hardyment, *Susanna Whatman*, p. 59.
47. Beverly Lemire, 'The theft of Clothes and Popular Consumerism in Early Modern England' in *Journal of Social History*, vol. 24, no. 2, (1990), p. 263.
48. Pitt also condemned the wasteful practice of using wheat flour for making hair powder; William Pitt, *Account of the Agriculture of the County of Stafford* (1796).
49. Anon, *Domestic Economy*, p. 21; Butson, *Art of Washing*, p. 57; also recollected by a retired laundrymaid visiting Shugborough in 1990.
50. Purdon, *Laundry at Home*, p. 28.
51. French chalk – a very fine, absorbent, grey chalk.

Chapter 7

1. Trinder and Cox, *Yeomen and Colliers*; Francis Steer (ed.), *Farm and Cottage Inventories of mid-Essex, 1635–1749* (Phillimore, 1950 and 1969); D.G. Vaisey 'Probate Inventories of Lichfield and District, 1568–1680' in *Historical Collections for Staffordshire*, fourth series, vol. v (1969).
2. The use of brewhouses as laundries survived well into the twentieth century, at least in name if not in practice; in Birmingham and the Black Country backyard wash-houses behind industrial terraced housing are still sometimes called 'the brewhouse', though most have never been used for anything except washing.

3. Kerr, *Gentleman's House*, pp. 257, 262.

4. Mark Girouard, *Robert Smythson and the Elizabethan Country House* (New Haven and London, Yale University Press, 1983), p. 178; this was a design which was never carried out.

5. Kerr, *Gentleman's House*, p. 45.

6. Information kindly given by Barrie Trinder.

7. John C. Loudon, *An Encyclopedia of Cottage Farm and Villa Architecture and Furniture* (London, 1842 edn), p. 358.

8. Robert Kerr's plan of Oxburgh Hall in Norfolk (*c.* 1774) shows a laundry and wash-house separated by a fuel store and more strangely a dairy; this was probably the result of needing two good-sized windows in both wash-house and laundry but not in the dairy. Kerr, *Gentleman's House*, p. 41 and plate 7.

9. 'Attingham Park inventory', 1913, supplied by Attingham Hall.

10. 'A Catalogue of Furniture etc.', Attingham Hall (1827), p. 193.

11. Kerr, *Gentleman's House,* plates 12, 13.

12. Ibid., p. 235.

13. Loudon, *Cottage, Farm and Villa Architecture*, p. 358.

14. Kerr, *Gentleman's House*, p. 236.

15. The advantage of using a brewing copper for boiling clothes was that it had a convex bottom which enabled all the water to be drawn off by the tap. A laundry boiler had a concave bottom and usually no tap, so it had to be emptied by bucket and dipper. For the difference between brewing and laundry boilers see Sambrook, *Country House Brewing*, pp. 32–3.

16. MOHP, 'Molly'.

17. NTTL, 219.EA, Lady Phyllis Macrae recalled her childhood at Ickworth when she and her sister had to go to the lavatory at the same time so that one flush would do for both.

18. John Dunbar, 'Kinross House, Kinross-shire' in Howard Colvin and John Harris (eds), *The Country Seat: studies in the History of the British Country House* (Penguin, 1970), p. 66.

19. Newby seems to have been well appointed with domestic arrangements for the garden and offices which were served by piped water and a cistern, and the stables, coachhouse and all the offices Celia Fiennes described as 'very good' and 'very convenient': Morris, *Celia Fiennes*, p. 97.

20. Rankin, *Art and Practice*, p. 44.

21. Kerr, *Gentleman's House*, p. 237; Ashelford, *Care of Clothes*, p. 14.

22. NTTL, Coleshill, Michael Wickham.

23. Rankin, *Art and Practice*, p. 53.

24. Tyrer and Bagley, *Great Diurnal*, vol. 3 (1720–8 Appendix F, 26 May 1723).

25. MOHP, 'Molly'.

26. Jack, *Laundry Work*, p. 21.

27. As late as 1723 Nicholas Blundell of Crosby Hall was sending this type of work out: 'Starching and making up Heads and Ruffles, making new ones and altering some – £1 0s 7 d ha'penny'; Tyrer and Bagley, *Great Diurnal*, vol. 3, 1720–8 Appendix F, 26 May 1723).

28. Oliver St John, *A Gallimaufry of Goffering*, (privately reproduced, n.d.), p. 4.

29. St John, *Goffering*, p. 7 cites William Harrison, *A Historical Description of the Islande of Britayne*, (1587 edn), for the date of the introduction of poking sticks; and Fanny Bury

30. St John, *Goffering*, citing Thomas Nash, *Pierce Pennilesse, his Supplication to the Devil* (1592).

31. For a discussion on the origins and use of the name 'Italian' iron, see St John, *Goffering*, pp. 21–3; its use was common but restricted to nineteenth-century England.

32. Rankin, *Art and Practice*, p. 59.

33. St John, *Goffering*, pp. 24–38.

34. Lewis, *Private Life*, p. 175.

35. Clabburn, *Furnishing Textiles*, p. 130.

36. De Bonneville, *Fine Linen*, p. 60.

37. Anne, Duchess of Hamilton ordered a box mangle from Edinburgh in 1696 at a cost of £53 (Scottish), arranging for the maker to fix it up in the house and train her staff to use it: Davidson, *Woman's Work*, p. 156.

38. Most of the memories mentioned in this account derive from interviewing visitors to the reconstructed laundry at Shugborough, Staffordshire and are recorded in the Laundry Book kept there.

39. As recorded at Attingham Hall in 1818; Hartcup, *Below Stairs*, p. 181.

40. Catalogue of *An Exhibition of Back-Stairs Furniture from Country Houses* (Leeds, Temple Newsam House, 1977), p. 28.

41. Patent Office, class 138 specifications and abridgements.

42. John Holland, *A Treatise on the Progressive Improvement and Present State of the Manufactures in Metal*, vol. 2 (Longman, 1831–4), pp. 255–9.

43. Loudon, *Cottage, Farm and Villa Architecture*, pp. 658–9.

44. Advertisement appearing in Shalder's *Directory, 1854*, quoted in Colin Giles, 'John Pickin, Box Mangle, Birmingham' (privately published, n.d.).

45. 'A Catalogue of Furniture . . .', 1827, supplied by Attingham Hall.

46. Picksley, Sims and Co.'s Price List, no. 15 (n.d.), p. 43.

47. JRL, Tabley MS, accounts, 'Abstract of one week's washing done at Laundry, October 25th, 1823'.

48. Trade catalogue of *Laundry Goods* by T. and C. Clark & Co., (1892), p. 91.

49. Advertisement for Baker's mangle in Ariss *Birmingham Gazette*, (1863), quoted in Giles, 'Pickin'.

50. Giles, 'Pickin'.

51. The laundry at Killerton, Devon, has an oral record of a fairly recent use of the box mangle, kept in the wash-house, as a wringer.

52. Even cotton stockings could be mangled successfully if done with the right side out, the opposite if they were ironed. This description of loading the mangle was recorded at Shugborough from a laundrymaid, Mrs Peggy Hollinshead.

53. Purdon, *Laundry at Home*, p. 21.

54. A common misconception about box mangles is that the linen was somehow laid flat on the bed of the mangle and the rollers moved over the top. Dorothy Hartley clearly describes this, but it must have been surmise on her part. In practice, loading the linen in this way is virtually impossible and no first-hand account has been found to corroborate it; Hartley, *Water in England*, p. 272–3.

55. Hardyment, *Susanna Whatman*, p. 48.

56. The wheels referred to here are tiny guide wheels attached to the inside of the frame to ease the box movement.

57. Rankin, *Art and Practice*, p. 39.

58. E. Henney and J.D. Brett, *Modern Home Laundrywork* (1934).

59. The built-in bread oven is another example of the timeless quality of simple but effective technology.

60. Anonymous description of contract laundering for Peterhouse College, Cambridge. There are records of very young children operating a box mangle at home – so young, indeed, that they could not reach the handle when it was at the top of its rotation and had to use a scarf to pull it down; Malcolmson, *English Laundresses*, p. 21.

61. A poignant account of a girl mangler working in the family business is in Jermy, *Working Woman*, pp. 28–34.

62. 'Outline of Work for Odd Man' at Berrington Hall.

63. Hardyment, *Susanna Whatman*, p. 48.

64. Walsh, *Domestic Economy*, p. 413.

65. Ibid., p. 413.

66. Rankin, *Art and Practice*, p. 38–9: 'In the case of a two-rollered mangle being used, the clothes should be passed two or three times between the rollers until the desired gloss is obtained.'

67. Jack, *Laundry Work*, p. 20.

68. Beeton, *Household Management*, p. 1011.

69. Hartley, *Water in England*, p. 209.

70. Correspondence of Ashley Montagu, M.F., *Isis*, vol. xxxiv, (1942).

71. See, for example, *Cooks and their Books: household recipes from York Manuscripts* (York Branch of the Workers' Education Association, 1997), p. 62, thanks to Ann Rycraft.

72. Butson, *Art of Washing*, p. 51.

73. *Catalogue of Thomas Bradford and Company*, 1867, p. 48.

74. *Victress Vowel Catalogue* (1862).

75. *Catalogue of the Royal Jubilee Exhibition, Manchester*, (1887).

76. Susan Strasser, *Never Done: a History of American Housework* (New York, Pantheon, 1982), p. 120.

77. SRO, Anson MS, D615 E(H)7 report on the electrical installation at Shugborough, 1927. For the introduction of electric power plant into country houses see Clive Aslet, *The Last Country Houses*, (New Haven and London, Yale University Press, 1982), pp. 100–17.

78. Ibid., pp. 105–6.

79. The extent to which the British washing machine industry lagged behind foreign counterparts and the extent to which housewives were reluctant to buy electrical white goods has been well documented. See Celia Mary Rhodes, 'The Domestic Domestic Washing Machine Industry', (unpublished thesis for HND, Faculty of Business and Professional Studies, Bristol Polytechnic, 1970); Malcolmson, *English Laundresses*, p. 135; C. Zmrocek, 'Dirty Linen: women, class and washing machines, 1920–1960', *Womens Studies International Forum* (1992), 15.

80. Transcript of oral recording in author's collection. The machine in question was taken out of a large steam laundry in Harrogate, where it was considered old-fashioned.

81. The Thor advertisement apart, the machine which was usually recognised as the first electric washer was made by A.J. Fisher in 1908. Like the early Thor this was driven by a motor attached to the frame under the washtub. It had an exposed belt drive and dripping water caused frequent electric shocks to the operator; Rhodes, 'Washing Machine Industry', p. 3.

Chapter 8

1. Sambrook, *Country House Brewing*, pp. 200–14.

2. The weekly wash was part of the monastic rule; Eileen White, 'The Measure of the Meat; Monastic Diet in Medieval England' in C. Anne Wilson (ed.), *Food for the Community: Special Diets for Special Groups*, Food and Society Series no. 6 (Edinburgh, Edinburgh University Press, 1993), pp. 40–1.

3. Servant list kindly supplied by Knole, Kent. Printed in Mark Girouard, *Country House Companion*, pp. 126–7.

4. Munby, *Stuart Household Accounts*.

5. Girouard, *Country House Companion*, p. 132.

6. Natalie Rothstein, (ed.), *Barbara Johnson's Album of Fashions and Fabrics* (Victoria & Albert Museum in association with Thames & Hudson, 1987), p. 158 *passim*. George Thomson's accounts survived solely because for some unknown reason the pages they were written on were used later by Barbara Johnson to compile a scrapbook of fabric samples and cuttings.

7. A conclusion directly contradicting Weatherill's findings from Richard Latham's accounts for a similar period – Weatherill, *Consumer Behaviour*, chapter 6.

8. SRO, Sutherland MS, D593/R/1/92, Accounts, 1693–4.

9. Sue McAlpine and Caroline Wiggins, *Soapsud Island: the Acton Laundries, a resource pack for teachers* (Ealing Education Services, 1994).

10. Lewis, *Private Life*, p. 39.

11. Information from Faith Hines.

12. Shelley Tobin, 'Wringing Fact from Fiction', *The Royal Pavilion and Museums Review*, 1, (Brighton, 1992), 11–12.

13. JRL, Tabley MS, abstract of washing done at the laundry.

14. Hardyment, *Behind the Scenes*, p. 235, quoting J.J. Stevenson, *Small Country Houses of Today, 1873 – House Architecture* (Macmillan, 1880).

15. Hartcup, *Below Stairs*, p. 134.

16. Pamela Sambrook, 'Aristocratic Indebtedness: the Anson Estates in Staffordshire, 1818–1880' (unpublished Ph.D. thesis, Keele University, 1990), p. 30.

17. Hartcup, *Below Stairs*, pp. 115, 159.

18. SRO, Sutherland MS, D593/R/1/25/8.

19. Similarly in the 1920s and '30s Mrs de Wichfield, rich American wife of Count Axel de Wichfield, had six women servants in constant attendance – two maids, (one French, one Belgian), a personal laundress (French) and three secretaries; King, *Green Baize Door*, p. 36.

20. Mme Rousseau was the servant who helped Thomas the footman with his accent. Traditionally, Denmark and France were considered to provide the most skilled laundresses; so much so that it is said that Henry VIII used to send his linen to France to be washed.

21. SRO, Sutherland MS, D593/R/10/3, correspondence between George Loch and Mrs Ingram.

22. Gerard, *Invisible Servants*, p. 186.

23. Mrs P. was following in a long-established tradition; in 1847 a servant used her bustle to take home 12 yards of best French velvet, 42 yards Valenciennes lace, 12 cambric pocket handkerchiefs, 3 dozen white gloves, 9 pairs of silk stockings, a pair of stays and a wig; recorded by Henry Mayhew, *London Labour and the London Poor* (1851).

24. DRO, Bankes MS, D/BKL, washing book, 1848–50. The recipient of the laundry payments for most of the period

was a Mrs Troke. For a time perhaps she was ill, for payments were made to other women for short periods. Mrs Troke then returned to do the quality linen only. Although it survived with the main Kingston Lacy papers, the washing book does not actually state that it refers to Kingston Lacy rather than, for example, George Bankes's house in East Cheam. But the names of two of the laundresses were Blanchard and Whareham, both local Dorset names, so it seems highly probable that the book does refer to Kingston Lacy.

25. DRO, Bankes MS, D/BKL, leaves from Mrs Bankes's housekeeper's book, 1822.

26. SRO, Anson MS, D615 E(H)40, maids, washing and beer money vouchers, 1885–9.

27. Hartcup, *Below Stairs*, p. 167.

28. Hardyment, *Susanna Whatman*, p. 38.

29. King, *Green Baize Door*, p. 36.

30. Malcolmson, *English Laundresses*, p. 25.

31. Hardyment, *Susanna Whatman*, p. 59.

32. K.F. Prochaska, 'Female philanthopy and domestic service in Victorian England', *Bulletin of the Institute of Historical Research*, LIV (1981), 79–85.

33. SRO, Anson MS, D615/E(H)44 the Viscount Anson's establishment at Shugborough, 1828.

34. Hardyment, *Behind the Scenes*, p. 61.

35. By 1974 this laundry had long since disappeared but was recalled through the matron's account book which came into the ownership of Amoret and Christopher Scott, writers on domestic bygones; Ann Cripps (ed.), *The Countryman Rescuing the Past* (Newton Abbot, David & Charles, 1974), pp. 166–8.

36. SAMS, R72/35,37,38.

37. SAMS, R89/4/1.

38. Author's private collection.

39. Ibid.

40. MOHP, 'Molly'.

41. As with the laundry at Alnwick noted above, Nesta's parents were quoted £100 a year when they enquired about the cost of an apprenticeship at a commercial laundry handling quality work from the aristocracy.

42. Other examples of bothy-type laundries have been recorded from Nidd Hall, near Harrogate (personal information from Arthur Richard Inch) and Ardtornish in Morvern, Scotland.

43. NTTL, 158EA, Claude Grimes.

44. NTTL, Clockhouse, Coleshill, Michael Wickham.

45. RHC, Reading University.

46. This is reminiscent of Susanna Whatman's instruction to her household at Turkey Court in 1799 that 'the laundrymaid is to keep her own ironing flannel for her own use, and the other maids iron on a different dresser'; Hardyment, *Susanna Whatman*, p. 49.

47. SAMS, Shugborough Laundry Book.

48. Ibid.

49. For the importance of linen and its accounting in the domestic sphere, see Vickery, 'Lancashire Consumer', p. 282.

50. Cassells, *Book of the Household*, vol. 2, p. 344.

51. De Bonneville, *Fine Linen*, p. 53.

52. Ibid., p. 53.

53. Baines, *Linen*, p. 169.

54. Ibid. pp. 157–61.

55. Joanna Bourke, 'Housewifery in Working-class England, 1860–1914', *Past and Present*, 143, (May 1994), p. 196,
quoting from *Commission on the Employment of Children, Young Persons, and Women in Agriculture* (1867): *First Report of the Commissioners*, Part 1, Appendix, p. 17.

56. Emma Smith, *A Cornish Waif's Story: an autobiography* (Odhams Press, 1954), p. 113.

57. See SRO, Sutherland MS, D593/R/10/3, letter from Mrs Ingram.

58. SAMS, Shugborough Laundry Book.

59. Davidoff, *Worlds Between*, p. 83.

60. Sambrook, *Country House Brewing*.

61. Both instances quoted by Gerard, *Country House Life*, p. 232.

62. Girouard, *Life in the English Country House*, p. 284.

63. SRO, D593/N/2/8/1, regulations for the lodge-keeper and lodge-keeper's book, 1810.

Chapter 9

1. Davidoff, *Worlds Between*, p. 78.

2. Julia McNair Wright, *The Complete Home* (1879) quoted in Asa Briggs, *Victorian Things*, (first published 1988, Penguin edn 1990,) p. 219.

3. As early as 1698 Celia Fiennes described the common rooms at Chippenham Park as being 'all new convenient and neate with double doores lined to prevent noises'; Morris, *Celia Fiennes*, p. 141.

4. Sambrook, *Country House Brewing*, p. 209.

5. NTTL, 158 EA, Claude Grimes.

6. Ibid.

7. Lanceley, *Hall Boy*, p. 19.

8. Notes from Mary Hunter, kindly supplied by Cragside.

9. Dawes, *Not in Front of the Servants*, p. 69.

10. At Shugborough, housemaids wore a lilac stripe, laundrymaids blue and kitchenmaids red; SAMS, R73/44.

11. Davidoff, *Worlds Between*, p. 25.

12. NTTL, 219. EA Ickworth, Lady Phyllis Macrae commenting on seeing laundrymaids walk into the house: 'Well, that just didn't look right.'

13. Glasse, *Servant's Directory*, p. 23.

14. Purdon, *Laundry at Home*, p. 49.

15. 'An Old Servant', *Domestic Service*, p. 53 .

16. For example, see Turner, *What the Butler Saw*, p. 263; Davidoff, *Worlds Between*, p. 77.

17. Davidoff, *Worlds Between*, p. 31.

18. Blundell was perhaps an exceptional case even for the 1720s. He was an active Catholic, and therefore to some extent excluded from the social life of his peers, thrown back on the comforts and occupations of his own domestic life. Yet even so he was more concerned with outdoor than indoor domesticity; Alan Crosby, 'The Squire and the Poacher: some thoughts on self-sufficiency', *Regional Bulletin of the Centre for North-West Regional Studies*, Lancaster University, New Series, No. 10 (Summer 1996), 59.

19. A good example at Kingston Lacy.

20. Davidoff, *Worlds Between*, pp. 78–9.

21. Keith Thomas, 'Cleanliness and godliness in early modern England', in Anthony Fletcher and Peter Roberts (eds), *Religion, culture and society in early modern Britain* (Cambridge, Cambridge University Press, 1994), p. 70.

22. Johnson, *Fashions and Fabrics*, p. 152.

23. Randle Holme, *An Academy of Armory* book II, (1688), p. 29.

4. Thomas, 'Cleanliness and godliness', pp. 70–1.
5. Quoted in Thomas, 'Cleanliness and godliness', p. 80.
6. Ibid., p. 73.
7. De la Rochefoucauld, *Frenchman in England*, p. 25.
8. Hermione Sandwith and Sheila Stainton, *The National Trust Manual of Housekeeping* (Penguin in association with the National Trust, revised edn, 1993), p. 91.
9. Thomas, 'Cleanliness and godliness', p. 71.
10. Mary Douglas, *Purity and Danger: an Analysis of Concepts of Pollution and Taboo* (Ark, 1966), p. 12.
11. Davidson, *Womans' Work*; Davidson gives an interesting discussion of standards of cleanliness and methods of cleaning (pp. 115–35) and time spent on housework (pp. 183–92).
12. For example, Vickery, *Lancashire Consumer*, pp. 274–8; Weatherill, *Consumer Behaviour*, pp. 194–6.
13. Levey, *Elizabethan Inheritance*, p. 90.
14. For laundry work used as punishment and cleansing of sin see Bartley, 'Seeking and Saving'.
15. That the Victorian value-system saw a connection, albeit a complex one, between dirt, abasement and sexual obsession, is well illustrated by the diaries of Hannah Cullwick which relate the very strange relationship between herself as a housemaid and Arthur Munby: Stanley, *Diaries of Hannah Cullwick*; and Leonore Davidoff, 'Class and Gender in Victorian England: the case of Hannah Cullwick and A.J. Munby' in *Worlds Between*, pp. 101–50.
16. Anon., *Duties of Servants*, p. 62.
17. Rose, 'Domestic Care of Paintings', p. 149.
18. Davidoff, *Worlds Between*, p. 27.
19. Vickery, 'Lancashire Consumer', p. 283.
20. Horne, *What the Butler Winked At*, p. 78.
21. Ibid., p. 82.
22. For reference to menservants' 'loss of masculinity' and suicide see Gerard, *Country House Life*, p. 269.
23. Turner, *What the Butler Saw*, p. 214.
24. Davidson, *Woman's Work*, p. 127.
25. Sandwith and Stainton, *Housekeeping*, p. 15.
26. Davidoff, *Worlds Between*, p. 97, quoting J.K. Galbraith, *Economics and the Public Purpose*, (Boston, 1973).
27. One retired laundrymaid confided to the author that although she was grateful to her daughter who did her washing and ironing for her, in the privacy of her room she would wet it again and re-iron it to her own standards. It seems a common experience for servants to be teased by their families in later life about their 'finickiness'.
28. Current work in hand by the author.
29. In the medieval noble household the groom of the chambers looked after the family's private accommodation while the usher of the hall supervised the public dining areas. At Trentham in the 1840s the groom of the chambers was responsible for the specialist maintenance of furniture and fittings and had a full-time upholsterer working under him. The nature of the post at this late date is clear from an advertisement placed in the *Morning Chronicle* (2 July 1794), p. 4 and quoted in Hecht, *Domestic Servant Class*, p. 51: 'A young man aged about twenty-five years . . . would be glad to serve any nobleman or gentleman as groom of the chambres having served his apprenticeship in a very capital house in the Upholstery and Paper-hanging branches, and is very well acquainted with the practical part thereof.'
50. Girouard, *Country House Companion*, p. 167.
51. SRO, Anson MS, D615 E(H)2/1–2, bill from J. Bramah and D615 E(H)3, report on the sanitary arrangements and drainage system at Shugborough, 1892.
52. Turner, *What the Butler Saw*, pp. 249–50.
53. Girouard, *Country House Companion*, p. 174.
54. Bond, *Tyneham*, p. 22: Tyneham in Dorset was compulsorily evacuated in 1943; after the war, it was never returned to the family, as had been promised, and both house and village fell into ruin.
55. For example, centralised vacuum cleaners, see Aslet, *Last Country Houses*, pp. 107–9.
56. SRO, Sutherland MS, D593/V/7/87.
57. Bankes, *Kingston Lacy Childhood*, p. 61.
58. Cassell's, *The Household*, vol. 3, pp. 90–1.
59. Anthony Heasel, *The Servants Book of Knowledge* (1773), p. 62; also Glasse, *Servant's Directory*, p. 45.
60. 'An Old Servant', *Domestic Service*, p. 38.
61. Jack, *Laundry Work*, p. 29.
62. Bourke, 'Housewifery', pp. 167–97.
63. King, *Green Baize Door*, p. 10.
64. Mullins and Griffiths, *Cap and Apron*, p. 35.
65. Horne, *What the Butler Winked At*, p. 42.
66. MWL, Tape 6070.
67. James, *House Steward*, p. 15.
68. SRO, Sutherland MS, D593/R/1/26/15, correspondence, 1836–40.
69. Russell, *Butler Royal*, pp. 57–8.
70. Horne, *What the Butler Winked At*, p. 11.
71. Davidoff, *Worlds Between*, p. 26.
72. Thomas, *Wait and See*, p. 1.
73. James, *House Steward*, p. 96.
74. Burnett, *Useful Toil*, p. 185.
75. James, *House Steward*, p. 13.
76. Burnett, *Useful Toil*, p. 185.
77. Notes on the Crozier family, kindly supplied by Cragside.
78. Hartcup, *Below Stairs*, p. 163.
79. Thomas, *Wait and See*, p. 67.
80. Jill Barber, '"Stolen Goods": The Sexual Harrassment of Female Servants in West Wales during the Nineteenth Century', *Rural History*, vol. 4, 2 (October 1993), 123–36.
81. P.R.A. Hinde, 'Household structure, marriage and the institution of service in nineteenth century rural England', in Dennis Mills and Kevin Schurer (eds), *Local Communities in the Victorian Census Enumerators' Books*, (Oxford, Local Population Studies Supplement, 1996), pp. 317–25.
82. Lewis, *Private Life*, p. 134.
83. Davidoff, *Worlds Between*, p. 97.

Bibliography

Place of publication is London unless otherwise stated

Archival collections, tapes and transcripts.

DRO – Dorset Record Office, Bankes MS, D\BKL
JRL – John Rylands Library, Manchester, Tabley MS
MOHP – Mantle Oral History Project, Coalville, Leicestershire, 'Molly'
MWL – Museum of Welsh Life, St Fagan's, Cardiff, Tape 6070, Alfred Taylor, 1979
NTTL – National Trust Tape Library, Anglesey Abbey, Coleshill, Ickworth
Patent Office, class 138 specifications and abridgements
SAMS – Staffordshire Arts and Museums Service, R72/35,37,38; R89/4; R 73/44; R79/2; Shugborough Laundry Book
SRO – Staffordshire Record Office, Anson MS, D615 and Sutherland MS, D593

Autobiographies and Diaries

'An Old Servant', *Domestic Service*, Constable, 1917
Balderson, Eileen and Goodlad, Douglas, *Backstairs Life in a Country House*, Newton Abbot, David & Charles, 1982 and 1986
Bankes, Viola, *A Kingston Lacy Childhood: Reminiscences of Viola Bankes*, Wimborne, Dorset, Dovecote Press, 1986
Bond, Lilian, *Tyneham: a lost heritage*, Wimborne, Dorset, Dovecote Press, 1956 and 1984
Burnett, John, *Useful Toil: Autobiographies of Working People from the 1820s to the 1920s*, Allen Lane, 1974
Horne, Eric, *What the Butler Winked At*, Werner Laurie, 1923
'Thomas', 'A Daily Journal or Memorandum Book, 1838–9', unpublished manuscript in SRO, D4177/1–2
James, John, *The Memoirs of a House Steward*, Bury Holt, 1949
Jermy, Louise, *The Memories of a Working Woman*, Norwich, Goose & Co., 1934
King, Ernest, *The Green Baize Door*, William Kimber, 1963
Lanceley, William, *From Hall Boy to House Steward*, Edward Arnold, 1925
Lewis, Lesley, *The Private Life of a Country House*, Newton Abbot, David & Charles, 1980
Morris, Christopher, (ed.), *The Illustrated Journeys of Celia Fiennes, 1685–1712*, Macdonald, 1982
Mullins, Samuel and Griffiths, Gareth, *Cap and Apron: an Oral History of Domestic Service in the Shires, 1880–1950*, Harborough Series no. 2, Leicestershire Museums, Art Galleries and Records Service, 1986
Macdonald, John, *Memoirs of an Eighteenth-Century Footman, 1745–1779*, Routledge, 1927
Russell, Peter, *Butler Royal*, Hutchinson, 1982
Smith, Emma, *A Cornish Waif's Story: an autobiography*, Odhams, 1954
Stanley, Liz, ed., *Diaries of Hannah Cullwick, Victorian Maidservant*, Virago Press, 1983
Thomas, Albert, *Wait and See*, Michael Joseph, 1944

Edited collections of inventories, accounts etc.

Eland, G., ed., *Purefoy Letters* 2 vols, Sidgwick & Jackson, 1931

Hardyment, Christina, ed., *The Housekeeping Book of Susanna Whatman*, National Trust, 1987

Munby, Lionel M., ed., *Early Stuart Household Accounts*, Hertfordshire Record Publications, no. 2, Hertfordshire Record Society, 1986

Penney, Norman, ed., *The Household Account Book of Sarah Fell of Swarthmoor Hall*, Cambridge, Cambridge University Press, 1920

Percy, Henry Algernon, *The Regulations and Establishment of the Household of Algernon Percy, the Fifth Earl of Northumberland, at his Castles of Wresill and Lekinfield in Yorkshire in 1515*, 1770, reprinted 1827 and 1905

Rothstein, Natalie, ed., *Barbara Johnson's Album of Fashions and Fabrics*, Victoria & Albert Museum in association with Thames & Hudson, 1987

Steer, Francis, ed., *Farm and Cottage Inventories of mid-Essex, 1635–1749*, Chelmsford, Essex Record Office Publications, 1950 and 1969

Trinder, Barrie and Cox, Jeff, eds., *Yeomen and Colliers in Telford*, Phillimore, 1980, pp. 20–38

Tyrer, Frank (tr.) and Bagley, J.J., (ed.), *The Great Diurnal of Nicholas Blundell, 1702–28*, Record Society of Lancashire and Cheshire, 1968, 3 vols

Vaisey, D.G. 'Probate Inventories of Lichfield and District, 1568–1680', *Historical Collections for Staffordshire* 4th series, vol. V, 1969

Trade catalogues

Bradford, Thomas, and Co., *Catalogue*, 1867

——, *Victress Vowel Catalogue*, 1862

Clark, T. and C. & Co., *Laundry Goods*, 1892

Picksley, Sims and Co., *Price List*, No. 15, n.d.

Catalogue of the Royal Jubilee Exhibition, Manchester, 1887

Other contemporary sources

Booth, Charles, *Life and Labour of the People in London*, vol. VIII 'Population Classified by Trades' Macmillan, 1896

De la Rochefoucauld, François, *A Frenchman in England, 1784*, Cambridge, Cambridge University Press, 1933

Greville, Lady Violet, 'Men-Servants in England', *National Review*, vol. XVIII, Sept–Feb 1892, 812–20

Holland, John, *A Treatise on the Progressive Improvement and Present State of the Manufactures in Metal*, Longman, 1831–4

J.F., *The Merchant's Whare-house laid open: or the Plain Dealing Linnen Draper*, printed for John Sprint at the Bell and Geo. Conyers at the Golden Ring, 1696

Kerr, Robert, *The Gentleman's House: or How to Plan English Residences from the Parsonage to the Palace*, John Murray, 1864

Loudon, John C., *An Encyclopedia of Cottage Farm and Villa Architecture and Furniture*, Longman, 1836 edition

Pitt, William, *Account of the Agriculture of the County of Stafford*, 1796

Ramsey, David, *The Weaver and Housewife's Pocket-Book; containing Rules for the Right Making of Linen cloth*, 1750

Robinson, John, 'A Butler's View of Man-Service', *The Nineteenth Century*, vol. XXXI, Jan–June 1892

Manuals

Adams, Samuel and Sarah, *The Complete Servant* first published 1830, facsimile by Southover Press, 1989

Anon, *The Laundrymaid, her Duties and How to Perform them*, Houlston's Industrial Library, no. 23, 1877

Anon, *The Footman's Directory and Butler's Remembrancer*, fourth edition, 1825

Anon, *A Catechism for Servants, pointing out the Duties of the Housemaid and the Servant of all Work*, n.d, mid-nineteenth century

Anon, *The Duties of Servants: a Practical Guide to the Routine of Domestic Service*, first published 1894, republished Copper Beech Publishing, n.d.

Anon, *Domestic Economy adapted to the Code of 1881*, Chambers Educational Course, London, 1881

Anon, *The Servants' Guide and Family Manual*, 1830

Beeton, Isabella, *Beeton's Book of Household Management*, 1859–61, reprinted Chancellor Press, 1989

Black, Mrs, *Household Cookery and Laundrywork*, Collins & Son, *c*. 1882

Calder, F.L. and Mann, E.E., *A Teacher's Manual of Elementary Laundry Work*, 1891

Cassell's, *Book of the Household*, vol. 2, 1890

Cassells, *Household Guide*, 4 vols, *c*. 1900

Cassells, *The Household Guide*, vol. 5, 1911

Glasse, Hannah, *The Servant's Directory or Housekeeper's Companion*, 1760

Henney, E. and Brett, J.D., *Modern Home Laundrywork*, 1934

Jack, Florence B., *The Art of Laundry Work*, Edinburgh, Jack's, 1913

Markham, Gervase, *The English Housewife*, first published 1568–1637, paperback edition with introduction by Michael Best, Canada, McGill-Queen's University Press, 1994

Purdon, K.F., *The Laundry at Home London*, 1902

Rankin, Margaret Cuthbert, *The Art and Practice of Laundry Work for Students and Teachers*, Blackie, n.d., early twentieth century.

Strange Butson, A.A., *The Art of Washing*, Griffith & Farran, 1880

Walsh, J.H., *A Manual of Domestic Economy: suited to families spending from £100 to £1000 a year*, Routledge, 1857

Secondary Sources

Ashelford, Jane, *The Care of Clothes*, National Trust, 1997

Aslet, Clive, *The Last Country Houses*, New Haven and London, Yale University Press, 1982

Baines, Patricia, *Linen: Hand Spinning and Weaving*, Batsford, 1989

Barber, Jill, '"Stolen Goods": The Sexual Harrassment of Female Servants in West Wales during the Nineteenth Century', *Rural History*, vol. 4, no. 2, October 1993, 123–36

Bourke, Joanna, 'Housewifery in Working-class England, 1860–1914', *Past and Present*, no. 143, May 1994,167–97

Boynton, L.O.J., 'Bedbugs', *Furniture History Society*, vol.1, 1965, 15–31

Brewer, John and Porter, Roy, eds, *Consumption and the World of Goods*, Routledge, 1993

Briggs, Asa, *Victorian Things*, published 1988, Penguin edition, 1990

Catalogue of *An Exhibition of Back-Stairs Furniture from Country Houses*, Temple Newsam, Leeds, 1977

Clabburn, Pamela, *The National Trust Book of Furnishing Textiles*, Viking in association with the National Trust, 1988

Colvin, Howard and Harris, John, eds, *The Country Seat: studies in the History of the British Country House*, Penguin, 1970

Cripps, Ann, ed., *The Countryman Rescuing the Past*, Newton Abbot, David & Charles, 1974

Crosby, Alan, 'The Squire and the Poacher: some thoughts on self-sufficiency', *Regional Bulletin of the Centre for North-West Regional Studies*, Lancaster University, New series, no. 10, summer 1996, 54–63

Davidoff, Leonore, *Worlds Between: Historical Perspectives on Gender and Class*, Oxford, Polity Press, 1995

—— 'Mastered for Life: Servant and Wife in Victorian and Edwardian England', *Journal of Social History*, vol. VIII, 4, 1974, 406–28, reprinted in Davidoff, *Worlds Between*, pp. 18–40

Davidson, Caroline, *A Woman's Work is Never Done: a history of Housework in the British Isles, 1650–1950*, Chatto & Windus, 1982 and 1986

Dawes, Frank Victor, *Not in Front of the Servants: a True Portrait of Upstairs, Downstairs Life*, first published in 1973, Century 1989

de Bonneville, Françoise, *The Book of Fine Linen*, Paris, Flammarion, 1994

de Groot, Gertjan and Schrover, Marlou, eds., *Women Workers and Techological Change in Europe in the Nineteenth and Twentieth Centuries*, Taylor & Francis, 1995

Drury, Elizabeth, *Victorian Household Hints*, Oxford, Past Times, revised edition, 1994

Ebery, Mark and Preston, Brian, *Domestic Service in late Victorian and Edwardian England, 1871–1914*, Department of Geography, University of Reading, 1976

Gerard, Jessica, *Country House Life: Family and Servants, 1815–1914*, Blackwells, 1994

—— 'Invisible Servants': the Country House and the Local Community', *Bulletin of the Institute of Historical Research*, vol. LV11, No. 136, November 1984, 178–88

Gilbert, Christopher, Lomax, Janet and Wells-Cole, Anthony, *Country House Floors, 1660–1850*, Temple Newsam Country House Studies no. 3, Leeds City Art Galleries, 1987

Giles, Colin, 'John Pickin, Box Mangle, Birmingham', privately published, n.d.

Girouard, Mark, *Life in the English Country House: a Social and Architectural History*, New Haven and London, Yale University Press, 1978

—— *Robert Smythson and the Elizabethan Country House*, New Haven and London, Yale University Press, 1983

—— *A Country House Companion*, Century, 1987

Hardyment, Christina, *Mangle to Microwave*, Oxford, Polity Press, 1989

—— *Behind the Scenes: Domestic Arrangements in Historic Houses*, National Trust, 1997, previously published as *Home Comforts: a History of Domestic Arrangements*, Viking in association with the National Trust, 1992

Hartcup, Adeline, *Below Stairs in the Great Country Houses*, Sidgwick & Jackson, 1980

Hartley, Dorothy, *Water in England*, Macdonald, second edition, 1978

Hecht, J. Jean, *The Domestic Servant Class in Eighteenth-century England*, Routledge & Kegan Paul, 1956

Higgs, Edward, 'Domestic Servants and Households in Victorian England', *Social History*, vol. 8, no. 2, May 1993

Hinde, P.R.A., 'Household structure, marriage and the institution of service in nineteenth century rural England' in Dennis Mills and Kevin Schurer, eds, *Local Communities in the Victorian Census Enumerators' Books*, Local Population Studies Supplement, Oxford, 1996, pp. 317–25

Horn, Pamela, *The Rise and Fall of the Victorian Servant*, first published 1975; Stroud, Alan Sutton Publishing, 1986

Lemire, Beverly, 'The Theft of Clothes and Popular Consumerism in Early Modern England', *Journal of Social History*, vol. 24, no. 2, 1990

Malcolmson, Patricia E., *English Laundresses: a social history, 1850–1930*, Illinois, University of Illinois Press, 1986

Marshall, Dorothy, 'The Domestic Servants of the Eighteenth Century', *Economica*, vol. IX, nos. 25–7, 1929

McAlpine, Sue and Wiggins, Caroline, *Soapsud Island: the Acton Laundries, a resource pack for teachers*, Ealing Education Services, 1994

McBride, Theresa, *The Domestic Revolution: the Modernisation of Household Service in England and France, 1820–1920*, Croom Helm, 1976

Mertes, Kate, *The English Noble Household, 1250–1600; Good Governance and Political Rule*, Oxford, Basil Blackwell, 1988

Prochaska, F.K., 'Female philanthropy and domestic service in Victorian England', *Bulletin of the Institute of Historical Research*, LIV (1981), 79–85

Rhodes, Celia Mary, 'The Domestic Domestic Washing Machine Industry', unpublished thesis for HND, Faculty of Business and Professional Studies, Bristol Polytechnic, 1970

Roberts, Michael, '"To bridle the falsehood of unconscionable workmen, and for her own satisfaction": what the Jacobean housewife needed to know about men's work, and why', *Labour History Review*, vol. 63, part 1, 4–30, 1998

Robertson, Una, *The Illustrated History of the Housewife, 1650–1950*, Stroud, Sutton Publishing, 1997

Rose, Jenny, 'An investigation into the Domestic Care of Paintings in English Country Houses in the Eighteenth and Nineteenth Centuries' in Christine Sitwell and Sarah Staniforth eds, *Studies in the History of Painting Restoration*, Archetype, 1998

Sambrook, Pamela A., *Country House Brewing in England, 1500–1900*, Hambledon, 1996

Sandwith, Hermione and Stainton, Sheila, *The National Trust Manual of Housekeeping*, Penguin in association with the National Trust, revised edition, 1993

Schwartz Cowan, Ruth, *More Work for Mother: the Ironies of household Technology from the Open Hearth to the Microwave*, New York, Basic Books, 1983

Scott Thomson, Gladys, *Life in a Noble Household, 1641–1700*, Cape, 1937

Seymour, Claire, 'Indoor Domestic Servants under the Age of Fifteen in England and Wales, 1850–1914', unpublished PhD thesis, University of Keele, 1991

Spufford, Margaret, *The Great Reclothing of Rural England: Petty Chapmen and their Wares in the Seventeenth Century*, Hambledon, 1984

St John, Oliver, *A Gallimaufry of Goffering*, privately published, n.d.

Strasser, Susan, *Never Done: a history of American Housework*, New York, Pantheon, 1982

Sykes, Christopher Simon, *Private Places: Life in the Great London Houses*, New York, Viking, 1986

Thomas, Keith, 'Cleanliness and godliness in early modern England' in Anthony Fletcher and Peter Roberts, eds, *Religion, culture and society in early modern Britain*, Cambridge, Cambridge University Press, 1994

Turner, E.S., *What the Butler Saw: two hundred and fifty years of the Servant Problem*, Michael Joseph, 1962

Vickery, Amanda, 'Women and the World of Goods: a Lancashire consumer and her possessions, 1751–81' in Brewer and Porter, *Consumption*, pp. 274–301

Vincent, David, *Bread, Knowledge and Freedom: a study of nineteenth-century working-class autobiography*, Europa Publications, 1981

Wajcman, Judy, *Feminism Confronts Technology*, Oxford, Polity Press, 1991

Walkley, Christina and Foster, Vanda, *Crinolines and Crimping Irons: Victorian Clothes, how they were Cleaned and Cared for*, Peter Owen, 1978

Waterson, Merlin, *The Servants' Hall: a Domestic History of Erddig*, Routledge & Kegan Paul, 1980; new edition published by National Trust, 1990

Weatherill, Lorna, *Consumer Behaviour and Material Culture in Britain, 1660–1760*, Routledge, 1988

—— 'The Meaning of Consumer Behaviour in late seventeenth- and early eighteenth-century England' in Brewer and Porter, *Consumption*, pp. 206–27

Wilson, C. Anne, ed., *Luncheon, Nuncheon and Other Meals: Eating with the Victorians*, Stroud, Alan Sutton Publishing, 1994

Wilson, R. Lucock, *Soap through the Ages*, Unilever, seventh edition, 1959

Woodward, Donald, 'Straw, Bracken and the Wicklow Whale: the Exploitation of Natural Resources in England since 1500', *Past and Present*, no. 159, May 1998, 70–1

Zmrocek, C., 'Dirty Linen: women, class and washing machines, 1920–1960' *Womens Studies International Forum*, 1992, 15

Page references in bold indicate illustrations

Index

Page references in bold indicate illustrations